STOP THE PRESSES, I WANT TO GET OFF!

STOP THE PRESSES, I WANT TO GET OFF!

Inside Stories of the News Business from the Pages of [MORE]

EDITED AND WITH AN INTRODUCTION

BY Richard Pollak

RANDOM HOUSE / NEW YORK

Library of Congress Cataloging in Publication Data

Pollak, Richard, comp.
    Stop the presses, I want to get off.

    CONTENTS: Cockburn, A. Death rampant! Readers re-
joice.—Cockburn, A. How to earn your trench coat.—
Hendrix, K. Remember the neediest. [etc.]
    1. Journalism—Addresses, essays, lectures.
I. More. II. Title.
PN4733.P58   070.4'12   74-29601
ISBN: 0-394-49742-2

Manufactured in the United States of America
9 8 7 6 5 4 3 2
First Edition

Contents

BETWEEN THE LINES

PROFILES

INSTITUTIONS

Traditionally, a new publication is launched with a Ringing Declaration of Purpose. The trouble with such noble manifestoes, however, is that you then have to live up to them. This often proves exceedingly difficult. Despite your best intentions, little old ladies from Dubuque do pick up your magazine. Or some newspaper editor (or even publisher) momentarily forgets the marble admonition in the lobby and gives the news partially with both fear *and* favor. Not surprisingly, this causes a certain embarrassment. But worse, it turns out to be quite costly as well. For, having fallen short of your R.D.P., you are forced to keep up appearances by noting your achievements in large, expensive advertisements on the back page of the *Times* or *The Wall Street Journal*. With luck, these advertisements will persuade your readers that at least you are doing something worthwhile. But then there's your staff. They're a pretty savvy bunch and they really know how far you are from the old R.D.P. So to bolster their morale, you have to give them air travel cards and thousands of pencils reminding them that they work for the world's most quoted newsweekly. Obviously, our budget will never be able to support such extravagances, so we have reluctantly put aside our own Ringing Declaration of Purpose (and a clarion call it was, too) in favor of a sentence or two on what we *hope* to accomplish. Our goal is to cover the . . . press—by which we mean newspapers, magazines, radio and television—with the kind of tough-mindedness we think the press should but seldom does apply to its coverage of the world. We hope to do this seriously, but not without wit, fairly but not "objectively". . . .

—*From the pilot issue of* [MORE], *June 1971*

Introduction

Like most journalists my age (forty) or older, I grew up with the notion that cynicism was a fundamental credential for the skillful practice of my profession. (If it is a profession: I graduated from college on Friday, declared myself a journalist over the weekend and began work on Monday.) Long before I ever entered a city room myself, I was persuaded by the rumpled *demi-literati* who passed through my home on the South Side of Chicago that the world was populated largely with thieving city councilmen, war-mongering congressmen, venal businessmen and rascality in general. The newspaper game, as it was then called, was every bit a part of this bleak scene, the chief villain in my bailiwick being a presence named Colonel McCormick, who, I gathered quite early on, spent his afternoons high up in the Tribune Tower eating babies.

Secure in this dark vision of the universe, I set out on my career determined to enlarge my byline at every step and convinced that the know-nothings or the petrified would always be in charge. Such cynicism (*healthy* cynicism, it is sometimes called) must have an outlet, though. So I bitched. At the Worcester (Massachusetts) *Telegram,* where I broke in, I bitched. At the *Evening Sun* in Baltimore, where I covered politics, I bitched. At *Newsweek,* where I tried to write about the press, I bitched. So did almost all of my colleagues along the way. We did it at our desks, in the cafeteria, in bars, at parties, to our wives and husbands, to anyone who would listen. It is safe to say, I think, that in no occupation is bitching quite so endemic as in journalism. Some of this bellyaching stems from the inevitable inequities and ego clashes of any enterprise, large or small. But most of it is triggered by the nagging realization that right now, today, in the newsroom in which one is sitting, the talent and energy are available to make a journalism that might not drive one to the nearest saloon at the end of the day.

Anyone who doubted that the talent and energy were roiling need only have dropped in on the first A. J. Liebling Counter-Convention in 1972. When we sat down to plan this gathering of working journalists "counter" to the annual April meeting of the American Newspaper Publishers Association at the Waldorf Astoria, none of us at [MORE] even faintly anticipated the turnout. For two days and two nights, crowds jammed the Martin Luther King Labor Center on Manhattan's West Side—as many as 1,500 at a time—to listen and debate as nearly a hundred panelists catalogued the shortcomings of American journalism, both print and electronic. True, occasional grandstanding and panel envy turned more than one session into a Happening, and some of the talk could charitably be described only as bullshit. Yet the sense of enthusiasm and questing was altogether contagious.

Around midnight of the second day, after I. F. Stone had spoken both sentimentally and eloquently upon receiving the magazine's first A. J. Liebling Award, and after the final panel had ended, my old friend Philip Evans grabbed me by the arm. Phil and I had groused together for five years on the *Evening Sun* in Baltimore, and he has spent the better part of two decades trying to get newspapers to make sense. "I've been to almost all the discussions over the last two days and I've heard almost nothing new," he told me, as I sagged wearily in my chair. "But never have I felt such a sense of excitement, such a sense of hope in the profession. It's incredibly encouraging."

There was, of course, very little new to say. What mattered, what was so different, was that for the first time the legitimate grievances of the working journalist were being aired not in private gripe sessions but openly, and with an increasing insistence on confrontation. There, at a panel on sexism, racism and elitism in journalism, was Roger Wilkins, just become the first black editorial writer on the Washington *Post.* He warned that the paper had to do a much better job in hiring, promoting and understanding the problems of blacks, while his publisher, Katharine Graham, who had come over from the Waldorf, stood in the back of the room. There was Tom Wicker, speaking at the convention lunch only a block away from the *Times,* urging his young audience to abandon so much of what has been for decades fundamental at the *Times* and in journalism generally: the heavy reliance on official sources, the front-page mentality that "imposes such a deadly sameness on our newspapers," the "spurious objectivity" so many editors demand. "We must insist," he said, "that somehow we have got to be set free to do our best work."

For a long time I believed that the kind of emancipation Wicker called for could only be achieved in any meaningful way through fundamental reform in how news organizations are controlled. And in theory I still do. "Freedom of the press," as Liebling said, is, indeed, "guaranteed only to those who own one." For every benevolent dictatorship run by a Sulzberger, Graham or Chandler, hundreds of publications and broadcast stations continue to operate on the same principle as ball-bearing factories. This is unlikely to change, I think, and journalists will not be freed to do their best work unless they gain some substantial say in how their organizations are run. And in the wake of that first, heady counterconvention, I hoped [MORE] could galvanize the working press into seeking a greater "voice in the product"—much as journalists have (with admittedly mixed results) in Europe in recent years.

Neither Bill Woodward nor Tony Lukas, with whom I co-founded [MORE] in 1971, shared my enthusiasm for *la participation,* as it is called at *Le Monde.* In the months before we started the magazine, both had tried a little of it and quickly discovered how easily management could deliver *le coup de grâce.* At the New York *Post,* where Bill was a reporter, he and some colleagues met several times with publisher Dorothy Schiff, who listened politely to their criticisms of the paper and then went about business pretty much as usual. At the *Times,* a similar group in which Tony was involved (known in some circles as "the cabal"), made equally far-reaching gains. But beyond their personal experience, Tony and Bill argued that whatever the case for redistribution of power in American journalism, hardly anyone was interested. I think that is too bad, but it is undeniably true—in part because the odds against it are so great, in part because journalists are not basically activists, in part because it may simply be an idea whose time has not yet come in the United States.

But if [MORE] has failed to ignite a movement, it has, I think, created an increasingly effective check on owners and their more autocratic apparatchiks. When CBS killed a five-minute radio broadcast in which Roger Mudd criticized the network for ending "instant analysis" of presidential television addresses, we published the broadcast and the story of the censoring. When the publisher of the Baltimore *Sun,* after a phone call from Spiro Agnew, killed a piece about the government improvements in the ex-vice president's Maryland home, we printed the spiked article and told the story behind it. These and other tales like them that have appeared frequently in [MORE] are not in this book, but they are at the heart of the magazine's mission: to embarrass the nation's media managers whenever they deserve it—and thus (with luck) to nudge change.

Yet much more fundamental change than that is needed. Reminding a servile television news director or a heavy-handed publisher that someone is watching and recording his actions may improve the atmosphere in a given newsroom for a while, but it hardly touches on the larger failings of American journalism. In the pages that follow, we have tried to tackle just such issues, among them the simple-minded world view that misinforms so much U.S. foreign correspondence, the middle-class mind-set that skews so much reporting on all subjects, and perhaps most serious of all, the almost total failure of the media to cover the private sector in anything but the most superficial fashion. As A. Kent MacDougall writes in his protrait of the *Wall Street Journal,* the paper may do a reasonable job of finding rotten apples in the barrel, but it never questions the shape of the barrel itself.

Though the title of this book belies it, we *have said a few* good things about American journalism (with considerable justification, I think). And in the spirit of Liebling's advice that journalists should take the story, not themselves, seriously, we have also tried to have some fun. But enough. Like Ringing Declarations of Purpose, Introductions run the danger of cranking up expectations.

I would only add, especially in the wake of all the first persons singular above, that [MORE] began as and still is very much a community project. We wouldn't be around today were it not for Bill Woodward's generosity and editorial fair-mindedness. Nor could we have gone very far without Tony Lukas's many articles and his incessant prodding to do better. In addition, there is the largesse of our investors, the loyalty of our subscribers, and not least, the incredibly spirited performance of an underpaid and overworked staff. But our real debt is to the community of journalists that has eagerly contributed to the magazine. From the start, their enthusiasm has been contagious. So if anyone deserves credit for this book, it's our contributors—those who made it into these pages and those who didn't.

January 1975
New York, N.Y.

THE BIG PICTURE

Alexander Cockburn

Death Rampant!
Readers Rejoice

It is, I think, becoming more and more evident that the American press is ceasing to carry out one of its prime functions: namely, the proper reporting of disasters. Part of this dereliction can be ascribed to the termination of *Life* and part to Watergate, which has led to a collapse of all standards. Journalists now feel they have to go out and uncover facts, find unnamed sources and confuse people about mortgages in Key Biscayne. This may be fine for those who like to boast about the press being the watchdog of our freedoms, etc., but is very vexing for the general reader who wants what he has always wanted in a free press: dramatic descriptions of other people being killed.

A word of warning: newspaper readers do not want to hear about *all* the people who are killed or die in the world every day. Apart from the evident impracticality of the idea, a large number of deaths are simply uninteresting to the casual reader. For example, about 55,000 people are killed on American roads every year. Indeed, about a million American citizens have perished on the highways since 1950. Such news may be of interest to insurance companies, auto companies, Ralph Nader or morticians, but the newspaper reader is more discriminating. Each case must be judged on its merits. Was it a multiple crash? Was there fog? Was grandad on a Christmas visit after fifty years? Was there a priest on hand to give extreme unction to the dying?

In the old days, news editors had their priorities straight. They knew what disasters were, and the rules to be followed. There was, if you like, a simple Richter scale of human (and, indeed, animal) calamity. When forest fires raged, it was essential that the undergrowth be alive with creatures fleeing to safety; a couple of fire fighters had to be cut off and incinerated in the blaze; one of these fire fighters had to have been recalled from his wedding leave. In particularly fortunate cases the bride would be tearfully on hand. Weary fighters of the blaze which menaced thousands would pause to sip steaming mugs of coffee, their faces blackened with wood ash. Spokesmen would say that the blaze was under control, and would announce they feared arson. But it took a fire which consumed half the trees in the west of the United States, early in 1973, even to get the event on the front pages.

American editors seem to feel that people don't want to read about catastrophe and death, in the way that the bulk of the population doesn't want to watch *King Lear* or *Oedipus Rex.* In my opinion such editors are making a grave mistake, stemming from liberal illusions about what the duties of a free press really are. A newspaper is not a telephone directory of facts, but a series of dramas, which it is hoped will excite readers and cause them to come back for more, thus satisfying advertisers. Of what interest is a tedious plod through Kissinger's latest pronouncement or some DA's bid for headlines when stories like this are thrown away in *The New York Times:*

CASA GRANDE, Ariz. Oct. 22 (AP) Linda Wright, who was married last month after a parachute jump with her husband-to-be, plunged to her death yesterday while attempting a solo sky dive. The eighteen-year-old Phoenix woman's main parachute and back-up parachute did not open as she fell 35,000 feet. Her husband. Rod, was watching from the ground.

Where's the interview with the husband; with the shocked bystanders; with the pilot of the light aircraft who exchanged the last words with her? Where's the photograph?

But that's not a disaster, you say. That story only involved the death of Linda Wright. And of course if you start talking in absolute terms you will be right. What of Linda, when thousands are dying in famine-plagued Ethiopia or cholera-stricken Benares. Perhaps if *five* people had jumped out of the plane in Arizona and all had been killed, then that would have constituted an accredited disaster. Such absolutes may be all very well for statisticians, but they have nothing to do with journalism. The only working definition of disaster, so far as the media are concerned, is that a dramatic intimation of death or of catastrophe is presented to the reader. Numbers are irrelevant.

Indeed, death itself need not occur. Mark this story in the London *Daily Express,* which still takes disasters seriously. First of all, a double banner headline: "RACE THROUGH THE HELL FIRE. Train passengers run oil blaze gauntlet." There is then a splendid eight-column photograph of an oil blaze. Then the story:

> A crowded express raced past a wall of flame last night as fire swept through an oil tanker train only feet away. Paint of the front of the diesel engine was scorched. And a passenger said, "It was hell. We were lucky to get through." The express—the 2:45 p.m. from Plymouth to Paddington—went past minutes after the tanker train exploded into flames at the Total oil depot . . . Mrs. Clare Hicks, a passenger on the express, the last train to get through, said: "The train was moving quite slowly as we approached the fire. Then the driver put his foot down and we raced past. The flames were very close. We could feel the heat inside the train" . . . *Houses in*

Meadowfield Road and Mead Road came within feet of total destruction. For just 30 ft. from the blazing train were six giant storage tanks filled with fuel. Said a senior fire officer, "If that lot had gone up the explosion would have destroyed the whole village . . . Three firemen were rushed to hospital suffering from smoke and heat exhaustion." Said a colleague, "Amazingly no one else was hurt, even though an area a hundred yards long was engulfed in flames in seconds."

The story runs over from the front page to page 5, where more details follow along with a ten-inch-square picture of a goat in a back yard. The goat seems calm amid the blaze of the night sky. The caption: "The village of Langley is engulfed by giant flames after last night's explosion. But for a goat tethered in a nearby field the illuminated night seems to pass unnoticed." This was the *Express*'s main story on October 6, 1973. As is evident, nothing actually happened—in the strict sense that no one was killed, not even the goat. But the *Express*' two and a half million readers were given an agreeable intimation of what might have been *if.* In a suitably chastened spirit, they could then turn their eyes to a smaller story, also on the front page, headed DEATH CRASH:

> MARL, Friday.—At least five people were killed and another 49 injured when two trains collided near the railway station in Marl, West Germany, tonight.

The European press still likes disasters and is not ashamed of them. Teams of journalists stand ready, alert to speed to the scene of catastrophe, and poke a notebook or a microphone in the faces of the bereaved. A curious sense of modesty seems now to prevail in the United States. Even accessible stories lack adequate record. Look at this one, from a recent *New York Times* headline, in a mean-spirited 14-point type at the bottom of the page: 54 HORSES DIE IN FIRE IN NEW JERSEY.

Fifty-four horses perished when a fire raced through the Hilltop Stables in the New Jersey community of Harding Township . . . The animals, including show horses, jumpers and hunters were valued at $2,000 to $15,000 each by the owner of the stable, Clarence Nagro. . . .

Only *ten lines* (in the original) for the whole episode. What of the panic-stricken neighing of the stampeding beasts? The groans of the owner who has lost all? The negligent stable lad, who doesn't even appear in the story, but who must have been there? We read, sure enough, that Clarence "dashed into the barn and freed 15 horses before flames enveloped the barn," but what's a reader to make of that? Was he half suffocated? Did his wife scream for him to desist? Did he save his champion horse? Or faithful old Dobbin, the companion of his youth? Where's the picture of Clarence amid the ashes of his dreams? *Times* reporters these days just don't seem to care.

Admittedly, the New York *Daily News* can rise to the occasion, and the newsweeklies make a good showing from time to time. But it seems to me that the American media are losing their grip a little. The old zest just is not there. Air crashes get fudged; fires are often so cursorily treated that it takes a strike by the firemen of New York and thus the virtual certainty of some tragic incineration to get the hounds out. So before the great disaster tradition passes into the pages of journalistic history, let me try and record the old rules and priorities. First, disasters that are more or less God's fault:

FLOODS

Pictures crucial. Always have people perched on rooftops, cows with noses above water. Also pictures and stories of people who have lost all and survey the wreckage of their homes. Floods are *always* rising and therefore stress frantic urgency of hold-off operations. Families sandbagging their homes, engineers manfully building dikes. Quote people berating the weathermen, who gave no warning of catastrophe. Stress indifference of federal authorities and the sparsity of relief funding. Photograph local politicians aiding the rescuers. Promising scandal here that can stretch over months. Good chance for stylists to brood on "swollen, sullen flood" which is usually "silt-brown" and invariably has some dead cows and horses in it.

AVALANCHES

Emphasize "frantic rescuers clawing at the snow." Also get accounts of survivors and remember to have one of them say, "There was a crack like a pistol shot and then a terrifying roar. Then it was on us." Stress risk of further avalanches in the area which can be set off by the slightest sound. Once again imply negligence of local authorities in not heeding warnings of sage old mountain folk. Stick around till the bodies are dug out. It is a virtual certainty that one of the doomed skiers took a photograph of the avalanche seconds before it engulfed him. Thus: last snaps of a doomed man. NB: stay on the scene for at least forty-eight hours, in case someone is dug out alive.

TIDAL WAVES

Generally these occur in out-of-the-way places, like Micronesia or the Philippines. Therefore, merely have TIDAL WAVE RACES ACROSS PACIFIC, KILLS HUNDREDS, MAKES THOUSANDS HOMELESS. "Two hundred thousand people are believed to be homeless following the onslaught of the tidal wave which . . ." If you have a newsman in the area, get him to do a follow-up on "The Empty World of Koturana." A fisherman stands amid the wreckage of his home. Stress possibility of plague. Also strong action of local military authorities against looters.

TORNADOES

Get a good photograph if you can. Stress malign fury and awesome strength of the twister, "hurling cars hundreds of yards, tearing up houses." There are usually about three deaths per town per tornado. Emphasize miraculous escape of child in pram. Ask where it will strike next. Advise people what to do.

HURRICANES

Remember that a hurricane is always *nearing* a major population center. Get a pilot to fly through it if possible. With any luck you will have a terrific devastation story to follow through with. Remember to have "winds of up to 150 miles an hour" and also don't forget the quiet center of the hurricane's eye. Remember that this may be the chance for a record. Is it the worst hurricane in living memory?

EARTHQUAKES

This is a big one. First of all, what force was it on the Richter scale? Quick comparisons with other earthquakes. Secondly, where is it? Usually in "remote eastern Turkey" or in "the arid center of Iran." But with luck it will have occurred in marginally more accessible Latin or Central America. Good chance for colorful description. Most of the buildings destroyed; others leaning at crazy angles. Constant flood of refugees. People clawing at rubble. Survivors crawling, blinking into the light of day. Babies miraculously unhurt amid piles of bricks. Preliminary tremors, then "for six seconds the earth shook." Make sure to get picture of one building still standing (usually a church in Roman Catholic countries or a mosque in Muslim ones). Get interviews from American survivors. Animadvert on general danger of earthquakes, particularly in San Francisco area. Most important of all: get casualty figures and escalate them each day. Remind people that 200,000 people died in the Lisbon earthquake.

VOLCANOES

Usually inaccessible, except by plane. Best for network news, with aerial shots. Emphasize inexorable onrush of lava. Have an expert talk about "dormant" and "active" volcanoes. Quote primitive local tribesmen on the wrath of the fire god. Remind people about Krakatoa and the tidal wave which that eruption sent round the world.

FAMINE

Properly speaking, this phenomenon should be in the man-induced list of disasters which follows, but recently it has made the transition to the God-induced category of inevitable horrors beyond human intervention. The blunt fact is that famine is not a good disaster story to cover. There's usually too much of it. Reporters have to make costly journeys across whole continents to assess it. It turns out that millions are dying. Readers no longer feel comfortable with pictures of children with distended bellies, or peasants backed by the whited bones of their oxen. Furthermore, it turns out that people are going to go on dying—that famine threatens MILLIONS, and that millions may already be dead. Then the details about relief shipments of grain tend to blur on people, who grow impatient with these Indians and Africans and their interminable famines. So best on the whole to keep clear of actual famines in progress and dwell on famines to come. Talk of famines that will sweep across Asia, decimate Africa. Quote experts who feel only despair. Speak on the encroachment of the Sahara over hitherto fertile land. Attribute the catastrophe to the sacred cow of India which eats food which otherwise . . . or blame the African goat which munches vital vegetation. Above all, speak of the

World Food Problem, and then start quoting United Nations surveys. In this way you will hurry the reader on to pleasanter subjects.

There are two further additions to the list of disasters for which humans cannot be called responsible by a vigilant press—namely comets and planetary collisions. But let us go on to disasters for which humans can be made directly responsible.

HOUSING COLLAPSES

Very good story. Rescuers clawing again at the rubble Note the seconds of warning. Emphasize incredible good fortune of those who went shopping moments before the tragedy. Rapidly produce evidence that the building had been declared unsafe. Animadvert on culpability and venality of landlords, laxity of urban officials. Stress grave condition of the poor. Report kindliness of local religious missions in taking in homeless. The miracle of Towser, the dog that survived. If possible, have grim-faced mayor on the scene. If need be, have him "personally take charge." Always a bad sign.

TRAIN CRASHES

Always good, particularly if the crash occurs in a tunnel. Speak of the quiet heroism of ordinary people and lack of panic. Or speak of panic and hysteria. Have people cheerfully chatting with rescuers as they lie trapped beneath the wreckage. In almost all cases the engine driver has been killed; if so, produce reports that the train was speeding dangerously. If he is still alive, hold back such comment. Speak of shocking state of the tracks and unsafe condition of the cars. Have a few priests on hand. Normally one or two deaths and many injured.

AIRPLANE CRASHES

Waning in favor. There now has to be some extra ingredient, apart from the mere fact of mass death. Is it the first jumbo jet to go down? Was there a famous person on board? Did some famous person almost go on board? Did the crash take place near a mountaintop, in which case snow and rain always impedes the rescuers? Did it appear to try and land? Did the pilot try to broadcast a last message, or was radio contact abruptly lost? Has the black box been recovered? Is sabotage feared? Is wreckage scattered over a large area? Did it almost crash on top of a city? How likely is it that a plane will crash on Manhattan? Speak of inevitability of crashes as traffic increases. But not to excess, since too many people now fly by plane and the airlines are good advertisers.

FIRES

Essential to cover them, but are people trapped? Is arson suspected? Particularly good when people have to jump from high windows. Have backgrounder on menace of fire in high-rise buildings. The *Daily News* is strong on fires. TEN FEARED DEAD IN HOBOKEN BLAZE read one headline in the fall of 1973. Beneath it:

> The fire flared at 1:10 A.M. and within minutes engulfed all four buildings . . . Jose Lopez, 18, said people on the first floor ran into the hallway to help those trapped above, but the stairs were already burning. Jose says he saw Juana Requeno jump. "She had to jump, she was burning up," he said.

The *News* added that the fire was "of suspicious origin." Suggestions of arson always pep up such stories.

SHIPWRECKS

These can be superb. Stress insufficiency of lifeboats. Terrible seas, hindering rescue; incapacity of captain/heroism of captain. Ugly riots in the steerage. The flames and smoke from the engine room that gradually consume the ship. Stress insurance value and possible claims. Have at least ten ships steaming to the scene. Ferryboats are particularly dramatic if they sink. For example, this account of a Greek ferryboat disaster in the *Sunday Times* of London:

> Several of the dazed survivors whose voyage back from a Greek holiday turned into a nightmare bitterly attacked some of the officers and crew. They alleged lack of directions and failure of the lifeboat system . . . Giuseppe Gentile, a 59-year-old fisherman from Monopoli, picked up five bodies and twenty survivors. He said, "There were so many people in the sea that it was impossible to get near them because they were all trying to scramble aboard. I saw at least one lifeboat that had been smashed."

Two familiar themes here: charges against the officers (which they will later deny) and panic among the passengers over the lifeboats. Judging by such reports, it seems best to avoid lifeboats altogether and "cling to a piece of driftwood."

ASSASSINATION

Counts as a disaster. Follow established procedures, such as eyewitnesses, actual murder on television. Do not forget the security guard or close friend hammering on the ground or wall with his fist shouting, "No, no, no!" Have vigil in hospital if health permits. Explain that Critical is worse than Dangerously Ill. Make sure that doctors have stethoscopes.

Picture wife in waiting room. Speak of effects on nation. Run articles on gun control (if assassination takes place in United States), otherwise speak of tradition of violence in whatever country you happen to be in. Always have someone saying, "My God, what is happening to our country."

PLAGUE

Generally only happens in the East. Usually "hushed up." Fact of life in India due to insanitary habits of the population and dead bodies in the Ganges. Stress acts of selfless heroism by Catholic missionaries. Occasionally warn that plague may sweep the earth. Also learnedly refer to Spanish flu epidemic of 1919.

GENOCIDE

Perpetrated these days by African tribes. Have reports "trickling through" of senseless slaughter by the Hutus or the Tutsis. Watch for Ruanda or the Congo. Always a good chance for a reporter to come back with an exclusive genocide story. Discount appeals for UN intervention, pointing out that it is an internal matter for the country concerned.

NUCLEAR HOLOCAUST

Discounted these days, but just to keep readers on their toes, quote an expert every six months or so as saying that the dangers of nuclear holocaust have never been greater. Then turn off tap by talking about SALT.

No doubt many readers will have their own favorite disasters, to which they may feel I have not done justice. What about the stock market, or of the eco-catastrophe that threatens mankind? Just add them to the list, but in the meantime a cautionary word about numbers.

News editors should remember that there are large parts

of the world in which people simply do not exist in groups of less than 50,000. Before getting to these hordes, let us start at the top. The death of one famous American can always be recorded, however tedious the circumstances of his or her demise. If the American is not famous or noted in some way, at least two or three have to die (or one in very odd circumstances) to be worth attention. In the case of blacks the numbers escalate at once.

In the next category come northern Europeans. Count about ten of them for every one American. Then we have southern Europeans (Italians, Spaniards, Portuguese, Greeks). Count about thirty of these for every one American. Then Turks, Persians, and Latin Americano. Count about a hundred of these for every one American. Some perfectionists would include north Africans in this category.

Next, southeast Asians. Two to three hundred for every one American. Some would include Indonesians here. I fancy, since eight hundred thousand were slaughtered in the coup without undue fuss, that the count here is about a thousand to one. Indeed, we have reached the limits of number, because in the next category we have *hordes without number.*

Indians, Africans and Chinese. No sense of number is involved at all. People only start to focus if we speak of fifty to a hundred thousand. Indeed, experts have calculated that roughly fifty thousand Indians are equal in terms of news value (relative to their terminal experiences) to ten Americans. And certain groups are excluded altogether: Canadians, Australians and Scandinavians, since they are never visited by disasters; also Soviet bloc countries, because their disasters are covered up. Obviously the sense of number that people have about the Soviet Union is that millions were killed in the purges, and millions were killed in the war. Little else counts. The Japanese now occupy equivocal status. At the moment they are both numberless and also singular, representing the rapid fluctuations in their country's financial fortunes.

The fact is—within the basic rules outlined above—that number counts for nothing in the theory and practice of disasters, so far as the media are concerned. Drama is all, and distance the great anesthetist. Late in the 1930s the London *Times* reported in a terse paragraph that "more than five million people are believed to have lost their lives in the Yellow River floods." How could the fate of those indiscriminate millions rank against those who perished in the crash of the *Hindenberg,* one of the century's famous disasters where thirty-six people died and sixty-two survived?

At first sight there seems to be a kind of haphazard and immoral frivolity in the media's approach to disaster. Why should an earthquake in Managua receive more attention than the Christmas bombing of Hanoi? Evidently part of the reason is that the media, conservative in outlook and performance, always tend to confuse the inevitable with the intolerable: avoidable famine—or devastation by high explosive—comes to appear as ineluctable as an earthquake; tragedy supersedes evil. In political idiom, disasters, so far as the media are concerned, serve a reactionary function in the sense that they represent catastrophe reduced to tolerable proportions.

On the one hand, disasters represent the opaque workings of providence; on the other, they symbolize the folly and wickedness of man. Voltaire could not countenance a God that permitted the Lisbon earthquake to occur—but most people cannot endure an impersonally malign universe. People cannot, at some sympathetic level distinct from mere indifference, confront squarely a world in which millions can and do die of hunger or disease. By deploying the ancient rituals and idioms of disaster coverage the media blunt and control such basic horrors.

Disasters are what is wrong with the world. What the media do, in carefully forged language, is to immunize people against horror by devaluing it. So in the end the soothing distress of misfortune befalling other people is something that readers and viewers begin to crave, starting at the simple level of relief that it is happening somewhere else to someone else.

The distress is soothing, since most people, even in advanced industrial countries, expect disaster to befall them. On the superstitious level, as a symbol of such neurotic apprehension, such fears emerge in the disaster coverage of truly popular papers such as the *National Enquirer* or the *National Star,* which deal in the idiom of planetary collision, or the menacing onrush of meteorites; on a more respectable level it emerges in such mechanism of disaster coverage as the Dow Jones index, a kind of cardiogram of national apprehension, a *memento mori* of when disaster can finally come home.

December 1973

How to Earn
Your Trench Coat

We may as well face it. Foreign correspondence is not quite the trade it once was. Given a good war or two, the situation might reverse itself. But for the moment it is neither necessary—if it ever was—to speak a foreign tongue, nor to hold a passport to get ahead in journalism. In this lull we may as well try and come to a few conclusions about the nature and practice of foreign news gathering.

I originally had it in mind to center attention on C. L. Sulzberger, famed overseas columnist for *The New York Times.* Following his intrepid, unending voyage through the capitals of Europe, one had the feeling that in the end one would have a lexicon of clichés—an immense word hoard of all the banalities any man could ever set down about foreign affairs. It seemed to me that C.L. had become the *Mariner 10* of journalism, a typewriter rushing through the vastness of space, pulsing back its twice-weekly message. Perhaps one day the typewriter will fall silent—perhaps it already has— but through a time lag across the light-years one feels the messages will still come, datelined Vienna or Paris or Rome —and one will sense that although the man himself has departed, his column will adorn *The New York Times* Op Ed page forever.

I began to clip his articles, to leaf through old copies of the *Times*. In my imagination I traveled with him. Here he is in Amsterdam. Is he staying at the Amstel, peering out across the river with a glass of champagne at his elbow, pondering the day's interview with some appropriate big wig? Perhaps he is fussing about the plane reservations for Rome the next day? Will he stop over in Florence? Who is the right man to interview in the Italian government? Is there an Italian government? After all these years does his stomach still tighten at the thought of having to put something over the wires to New York? And then there is his morning patrol through the London *Times, Le Monde, Corriere della Sera,* the *Allgemeine Zeitung,* the *Cumuriyet* . . . where will he travel next? Does he occasionally feel despair, like Hamlet's father "doomed for a certain time to roam the earth"?

The ground he covers is tremendous. The old files bear witness to his prodigious energies. Here he is in Israel speaking to "a most authoritative Israeli official" ("I found some interest in both Cairo and Tel Aviv when I proposed the Rafa-Port Suez line, which was the actual frontier between Egypt and Ottoman Turkey at the start of World War I . . ."); now in Italy ("Italy might be heading towards a Chilean solution . . . opening to the left . . . nor does much time remain"); then briefly back to London ("Democracy need not always abide by what seems to be old-fashioned majority rule") before setting off for Athens and Istanbul ("There is a widespread fear that anarchy and a massive disaster are looming").

Late in 1971, we find him briefly in Vienna, pondering the hundredth anniversary of Stanley's discovery of Livingstone. He emits a cry from the heart: "During Stanley's leisurely era, a taste for lonely adventure and for uninhibited literary composition were essential . . . In those nostalgic days the roving reporter was a kind of verbal aristocrat. Boldness of spirit, elegance of style and frequently astonishing knowledge were the assets he combined to prepare literary reports for an audience that depended on newspapers for immediate understanding of the spacious world about it." It is a poignant cry.

Throughout my perusal of these old clips I found myself softening towards Sulzberger. Very often both he and James Reston would appear on the same page together. Somehow there is consolation in the heavy predictable march of their columns down the page. Reston always sees grounds for hope; Sulzberger reasons for despair. From his vantage point in Washington, Reston can always discern a silver lining, or find someone to tell him that such a phenomenon exists. In his never-ending voyage, Sulzberger, one feels, confronts the world with sadness. After all, he chooses Vienna—a city of ghosts—as a place to compose a threnody to the great days of Stanley and the romantic days now gone. And why mock him, roaming this weary earth, forever pushing 900 words uphill, twice a week, towards a conclusion no one will ever remember?

But I can hear mockery. What has C. L. Sulzberger got to do with the practice of foreign reporting, people ask. "Why, he's an embarrassment at the *Times*," a *New York Times* staffer told me. Far from it. It seems to me that C.L. is the summation, the platonic ideal of what foreign reporting is all about. It's true that we do not find him courageously observing Cambodian soldiers on the outskirts of Phnom Penh, but this is incidental. C.L. has divined the central mystery of his craft, which is to fire volley after volley of cliché into the densely packed prejudices of his readers. There are no surprises in his work. NATO is always in crisis. There is and always has been an opening to the left in Italy. *He never deviates into paradox.* His work is a constant affirmation of received beliefs. So why spurn the work of the old Zen master? Perhaps it is shaming to concede that foreign reporting contains little room for maneuver because the world changes rather slowly. For as long as I have been

foolish enough to read newspapers there has been "an opening to the left in Italy." It would be a savage shock if this
suddenly ceased to be true.

C. L. Sulzberger is much too experienced a hand to avoid
the obvious whenever he has a chance to consort with it. We
find him in Nairobi, face to face with the course of events on
the dark continent, and sure enough, we find that "Africans
are accustomed to dwelling in tribal societies and respect
authority . . . The greatest question for the next generation
of leaders is: Can nation-states in the future be maintained
over the disintegrating thrust of ancient tribalism?" This is
expert stuff, fulfilling the first law of all journalism, which is
to confirm existing prejudice, rather than contradict it. It
requires many thousands of words to prepare a reader for the
new thought that "one thing is clear. The disintegrating
pressures of ancient tribalism have lost their potency. Nation-states are here in Africa to stay." No sensible foreign
editor would admit this kind of thing into his newspaper. It
merely bewilders the reader and denies him that satisfactory
sentiment that, abroad, things are falling apart.

The main problem with Sulzberger is that I fear he is not
taken seriously enough, that somehow he is a relic of the
past, that a new generation of foreign correspondents, neatly
arrayed in khaki drill shirts, are out there in the field, bringing back the *real* word from foreign parts. The truth, of
course, is that foreign correspondence has somewhat lost its
glamour and its career appeal. Are the great reputations now
made on foreign soil or on Capitol Hill? The action seems to
be on the home front, and that is where reputation and
fortune are to be found. Gone are the great days when European correspondents were cocks of the walk, face to face with
Fascism, or watching bombs fall from the roof of the Savoy.

Consider the lot of a resident foreign correspondent in
some Middle Eastern city today. Day after day he files his
dispatches. A conference looms on his beat. Eagerly he culti-
vates his contacts, hones his insights. There is a shattering

roar from the airfield as Kissinger lands and half the Washington press corps leaps from the plane. The crucial conference has already been held, 30,000 feet up in the sky. Bleary-eyed scribes, crazed from jet lag, rush past him to replenish their canteens. Another roar of sound and the caravanserai is off again. Bye-bye, Walter; see you soon, Marvin.

But this change in the foreign correspondent's position should not lead one to suppose that there have been any basic changes in the demands of his craft. Sometimes one hears the superficial view that "the world has become more complex," that a new kind of sophistication is required of the foreign correspondent, submerged as he is in OPEC, détente, MBFR rapprochement, SALT, etc. Not so. If anything his task has become easier. In the old days there were certain generalized ideological demands required of the writer: he had to be on the right side of the cold war, properly apprehensive of the Communist threat, constantly fearful of Communist advances in whatever theater he was situated. Vigilant to the prejudices of his owner or editor, he had to trim accordingly. Nowadays many of these harsh demands on the brainpan have gone. Most of the time ideological orientation becomes a matter of not falling asleep from exhaustion as Kissinger discloses his latest flight plan and tactics.

We should not take this line of argument too far. So-called détente has made things a little more relaxed, but no one is going to make himself popular by repeated calls for a Communist takeover in Southeast Asia. It's somehow more fun coming from Henry Kissinger rather than John Foster Dulles, but the foreign correspondent's task is to get the general line of march from official sources and then get down to business. And as I have said, that business is essentially a matter of talking about the world the way his readers want to hear it talked about.

So, armed with Sulzberger's Maxim, "Never shun the obvious," let us see how the foreign correspondent should address himself to the world.

There are certain blank areas one should simply keep clear

of. Australia and New Zealand, for example: vast territories covered with sheep. Nothing of any interest has ever been written about New Zealand, and indeed very little is known about it. In Australia, if it becomes absolutely necessary to go there, one can touch on (a) convict heritage of the inhabitants, (b) tendency of prime ministers to drown themselves, (c) philistine nature of Australians—see (a) above—and (d) erosion of the Great Barrier Reef.

Moving north a little we find ourselves nearing New Guinea. This is simple stuff: headhunters face to face with the twentieth century. Interview a worried district officer. Speak of the menace of the modern world for these simple, yet unpredictable tribes which are usually coated with white clay. Are oil companies about to exploit assets which some geologists speculate may *equal those of the Middle East?*

Indonesia, first of all, is a *teeming archipelago.* It is still shaking itself free of the confused yet charismatic leadership of Sukarno. There was a massacre, but *the wounds are healing* (or, the schisms still run deep and *much bitterness remains*). There are contrasts. Wealth coexists uneasily with desperate poverty. There are Moslems (a growth subject). The students may be becoming discontented with the rule of the generals. There is much U.S. investment, which so far has done little to adjust the stark contrast between rich and poor.

Now we are in Malaysia, where one of the few successful examples of counter-insurgency occurred. Under the wise leadership of Sir Robert Thompson the Chinese Communists were routed. Relative contentment prevails. Hurry on to Singapore and stay at the Raffles Hotel. Interview Harry Lee. Singapore is *a fast-growing economic center.* It has a powerful class of Chinese businessmen whose sympathies may well lie with Singapore's *powerful neighbor to the north.*

We are now into Southeast Asia proper. Some simple rules for a complex subject: Analyses of Laotian, Thai, Cambodian or Burmese politics are strictly for professionals or addicts. Speak of the timeless rhythms of the countryside wherever possible. Never underestimate the Buddhists. Always *revisit*

places ("For Lon Tho, a simple peasant, life has not changed
. . ."). Great areas of the countryside are under Communist
control. The Communists have so far failed to make serious
inroads in the cities. This is not really a growth area for
journalism any more. Be particularly careful about Burma.
Most people cannot remember whether it was Siam and has
become Thailand, or whether it is now part of Malaysia and
should be called Sri Lanka. To be sure, refer to it as the
homeland of U Thant.

You can go east now, to Hong Kong. This is a *time bomb,*
but also a *listening post,* inhabited by China watchers who
will eye you with disdain. *Hideous* contrasts between rich
and poor. Highest suicide rate in the world. It teems. Avoid
Macao, which is for gamblers only and is *seedy* and *rundown.*
Go straight to China. A few simple rules: *always* get an
interview with Chou En-lai. He is civilized, but a *dedicated
revolutionary.* He has an *uncanny command of detail.* This
interview should take place late at night and go on for several
hours. He speaks of the Russian threat. Note the presence of
wall posters. Stress cleanliness of the streets and *puritanical*
nature of Chinese people. Discard your underwear in the
hotel wastepaper basket and have it returned by an honest
maid. Stress difficulty of knowing what is *really* going on in
China. Is Mao alive or dead? Who are the next generation
of leaders?

Be careful about China. It may have peaked as a growth
subject. But it still is quite safe to be very favorable about it.
Save any general conclusions for your return to Hong Kong
and interviews with experts. What is going on in cities off the
beaten track of Western visitors? If possible, get off the
beaten track yourself, if only for a moment. Avoid Formosa
and its *aging generalissimo,* tacitly conceding the impossibil-
ity of eventual return to the mainland.

Japan. You can be much more racist about the Japanese
than most other people. E.g., they can only copy—albeit
superbly—Western inventions. Fearful pollution. No street
maps. Workers are intensely loyal to their companies. (Ig-

nore labor militancy.) Tanaka is *dynamic* but *beset by problems.* (The proper adjectival adornment for leaders is a vast and complex subject. If he is one of *our* dictators then use words like *dynamic, strong man, able.* He *laughs* a great deal, is always *on the move, in a hurry.* He *brushes impatiently aside* questions about franchise and civil liberties: "My people are not yet ready for these amenities you in the West feel free to enjoy . . ." If, on the other hand, he is one of *their* dictators, then use words like *unstable, brooding, erratic, bloodthirsty, indolent.* He seldom ventures out of his palace unless under *heavy guard.* He is *rumored to be ailing.* Oddly enough he is often *charismatic.* At the moment it is particularly dangerous to use any adjectives about Arab leaders. Stick to general concepts in this case, like *converted to Western ways* or *deeply religious.*) Back to Japan. What about militarism? What about soy sauce? Stress unease about Western intentions.

Let us quicken the pace a little, for there is much ground to be covered and the presses are waiting. Up and away we go, past the Philippines, where Marcos is brushing questions about democracy impatiently aside, ever intent on *dragging his country into the twentieth century* and on *putting an end to corruption;* past Tahiti, where syphilis is *rife* and down into our All-Purpose Latin American country.

It seems to *symbolize* the problems of a *young continent,* still *scarred by its Conquistador heritage.* An *impoverished Indian population* has little say in the fortunes of a republic scarred by *rampant and souring inflation,* presided over by an *aging dictator,* backed by a *junta. Young officers in the air force* are plotting *an ill-fated but bloody coup* that is deplored by *thoughtful and troubled intellectuals,* uneasily aware of their *great neighbor to the north* which they view with *mixed emotions.* The country has *long democratic traditions* which have been *reluctantly abandoned. Armed with a new-found sense of responsibility* the *Catholic hierarchy* is pressing for a return to *cherished democratic norms. Shanty towns* sprawl. Roads cleave the *fast-receding jungle* which itself is squeezed between the *long spine of the Andes* and the superb beaches, playground of a *newly affluent middle class.* The *romantic appeal* of Castro can nowhere be sensed. There is, on the other hand, *abundant evidence* of American investment, though *seasoned businessmen* view the future with trepidation. For though the country *craves strong government,* they *note privately* the growing power of the trade union movement and *seething* discontent among the students. The university is closed.

Away we go again, high over Canada, conscious as always of its language problem and of its *neighbor to the south,* over Iceland covered with *geysers* and surrounded by *fish,* and down towards Europe.

General features are immediately evident. There is a crisis in the *Common Market;* a crisis in *relations with the United States;* a crisis in *NATO;* a huge *immigrant laboring population.* But we relax at once, for we are in London, where the *civilized pace of life* can be observed. *Class distinctions* are as *subtle but as emphatic as ever,* even though *smiling policemen* constantly pause to give us street directions. The city is stuffed with theaters and much invigorated by the *growing power of the Liberals,* even though the pound is ailing. We spend much time watching the BBC, which is *unmarred* by commercials. We are, however, perturbed by the state of British industry, *disrupted by strikes,* prey to the demands of a *powerful trade union movement* which is supported by *indolent workers.* It is clear, as we observe the *tolerant affection* in which the Royal Family is held, that *Britain has lost an Empire but not yet found a role* and that *thoughtful Britons* still believe the United States to be Britain's best friend, and that in the E.E.C. Britain may prove a *valued counterweight* to French designs. However, Roy Jenkins is *puzzled* by *our American cousins' lack of understanding* for the Ulster problem, which we at once hurry off to inspect. Our stay is brief, for Belfast is a *dour,* tense city, and though it is believed that the British army has fought the IRA to a standstill, *eight men have been killed in an ambush.* There seems to be *no immediate solution.*

Spain is afflicted by *the Basque problem.* Who is to succeed Franco is a *constant source of speculation.* He is *believed to be ailing.* Portugal is *war-weary.* On the whole the *Iberian peninsula* seems to be lagging behind the rest of Europe, even though they are still *loyal members of the Western alliance.* In this respect they differ from France, which seems intent on *wrecking any concerted Allied strategy.* With its abundant population of *small farmers* and mutinous workers, France seems still enslaved by the heritage of *Descartes* and *De Gaulle.* There's a lot of *Gallic logic* around. The buildings are very clean, but the small markets of rural France seem to be fast disappearing in the face of American-style enterprises. On the whole we leave with a sense of optimism, for it seems that *Gaullist illusions of grandeur* are a thing of the past, even though fervent belief in the destiny and *civilizing mission of La France* remain. It is *chic* to have a sandwich *pour* brunch and to note that the French language is becoming contaminated by Americanisms.

Belgium has a language problem, too, as Walloons battle it out with Flems. But Brussels is a *soulless city of international institutions,* so we pass on to Germany. At once we are conscious of a dilemma. Has the country finally *exorcised the nightmare of Hitler,* or does the *new interest in Hitler* presage a return to the ugly passions of the thirties? Germans view Brandt's *Ostpolitik* with guarded caution although they can understand the *sense of realism* on which the policy is based. All Germans work extremely hard, leading to *constant trading surpluses* and frequent *revaluations of the mark.*

Italy is a nightmare. *Venice is sinking;* workers are constantly on strike; neo-Fascism is gaining new adherents; corruption is rife and the cabinet is in crisis. The Christian Democrats, in power since 1947, have just closed the door on the opening to the left. The Pope is on holiday (or ill), and the Mafia still retains its grip. Furthermore, there is a pasta strike. The beaches are awash with sewage, particularly at Ostia, and old churches are being constantly stripped of their *priceless treasures.* The country seems in a way to be yearning for a return to the strong government of Mussolini.

Avoid Austria, home of *Bruno Kreisky,* former center of the Austro-Hungarian Empire, birthplace of Hitler, and, indeed, avoid Scandinavia, too; even Finland, uneasily aware of its *giant neighbor to the east.* There is little to detain the zealous newsman here. Even the passions of Eastern Europe have died down. The *old wounds* of '56 in Hungary seem to be healing and *Cardinal Mindzenty* has left. Poland still has its *drunks* and its *Catholics* and its *openness to modern strains in Western art.* No one knows where Dubcek is. Rumania seems still zealous *to steer an independent diplomatic path but shows little signs of any relaxation of the iron grip of the Communist party.* Bulgaria is still *Russia's closest ally* and as befits the homeland of *rose attar* is *always first to toe the Kremlin line.* Yugoslavia is *troubled by Croats* but seemingly gone are *the brave years* when Tito defied its *neighbor to the far north.* We can see only the dim outline of Albania, once the West's *only listening post to the immense enigma of China,* now merely *enigmatic* or merely *a remote backwater.*

The U.S.S.R. is for the specialist, but there are a few tips. Try (a) new cities in Siberia, (b) sturgeon poaching in the Caspian, (c) the old men of Azerbaijan, perennially capable of copulation at advanced ages and reputedly invigorated by a diet of kasha and goats' milk (NB—There are newly emerging rivals to these Azerbaijanis in Ecuador. Follow the situation closely), (d) pollution of Lake Baikal, (e) disappointing harvest in the virgin lands, (f) no bath plugs in the old-fashioned Victorian hotels, (g) foreign factories on the Volga, (h) nostalgia for years of Stalin, (i) abiding fears of German militarism; the legacy of Hitler has not been forgotten, (j) interview a Jewish would-be-émigré; (k) take Samizdat.

A quick swing through Turkey, still *heaving itself* into the twentieth century, conscious of the *heritage of Ataturk,* its sky aglow with the gilded minarets of Byzantium, and on through southern Turkey, despoiled by archaeologists, to Iran. A big growth area: essential to have an interview with the Shah, seated on the *Peacock throne.* Stress his land reforms. Iranians are *sophisticated,* unlike the Syrians and Iraqis, who are *cruel* and merit *harsh treatment.* Both Iraq and Syria are confusingly under the sway of the Ba'athist party. Contrast their leadership with mature Egyptians and with the little ruler of the *Hashemite Kingdom,* always *piloting his own plane, surrounded by loyal Bedouins*—King Hussein. Lebanon is of course *the crossroads of the Middle East.* Mop up the rest of the area with jocular references to per capita income in the sheikdoms. Leave Israel for others.

We are mostly left with India and Africa: *the world's largest democracy* and *a continent in many ways still dark.* There is much to chose from: *sacred cows, religious sects, the Vale of Kashmir, legacy of the Raj, the corrupt Congress party, Jains, Westerners in search of truth, dust, starvation* on an unparalleled scale. In Africa, the *onward march of the Sahara, kwashiorkor, tribalism, President Nyerere, South African labor laws, guerrillas in Mozambique, genocide, famine, still proud Masai, once proud Tuaregs and still small Pygmies.*

We've done it. These are the basic rules. There are many subtleties, of course. The proper treatment of *islands* merits a whole chapter in the novice's manual *(tiny, yet strategically vital; hotly disputed by its giant neighbors;* lying *athwart* what is *possibly* the world's most crucial waterway; *seeking to avoid* the traps and pitfalls of "modern" life; *threatened* by volcanos/tidal waves/nuclear fallout). Then again, the treatment of a deposed leader: is he *unceremoniously bundled into exile, stripped of his duties, long rumored to be ailing* but dominated by an *ambitious wife* whom many believe to hold the true reins of power. What about allegations of torture? Are they *brusquely dismissed* as fabrications, or *widely accepted* as having some basis in fact?

There are problems of timing: When should one leave the

war-torn scene of crisis? After the shooting has stopped; one month after that; six months later? Should one go back ("War still rages in 'peaceful' . . .")?

By and large avoid the *underdeveloped* or *third* or *newly emerging* world. Reporting of famine and mass starvation holds little consistent appeal for Western readers, and unrestrained speculation about the probable number of dead (one million, two million, ten million) merely bewilders and depresses people. Stick to the main highways of Western diplomacy and American policy, and ignore, as Kissinger does, the southern half of the world. *Never* talk about imperialism, unless of course it is *Soviet-style imperialism.* Remember that your cliché hoard is for *consolation* and *affirmation,* and that it requires a true specialist to be consoling about genocide or famine.

Remember that most tricky material, like trade wars, the dominance/decline of the dollar, oil politics and so forth, can be safely handled in Washington. Above all, never be *premature* in any criticism of your nation's policy. Wait for domestic protests and contradictions to escalate a little. Don't be too grudging if your government seems to have gotten away with constant lies. It's too bad that there won't be another Vietnam in the immediate future, where reputations can be made and Americans interrogated as though you were back in Washington. Remember that the world turns slowly and that almost without exception what was true about a country ten years ago is still true today. *Life goes on as usual.* Bear in mind Lord Northcliffe's sage advice to journalists: "Never lose your sense of the superficial." Happy landings.

May 1974

KATHLEEN HENDRIX

Remember the Neediest

Jo lives—that is to say, Jo has not yet died—in a ruinous place known to the like of him by the name of Tom-all-Alone's. It is a black, dilapidated street, avoided by all decent people, where the crazy houses were seized upon, when their decay was far advanced, by some bold vagrants who after establishing their own possession took to letting them out in lodgings. Now, these tumbling tenements contain, by night, a swarm of misery. As on the ruined human wretch, vermin parasites appear, so these ruined shelters have bred a crowd of foul existence that crawls in and out of gaps in walls and boards; and coils itself to sleep in maggot numbers, where the rain drips in; and comes and goes, fetching and carrying fever and sowing more evil in its every footprint than Lord Coodle, and Sir Thomas Doodle and the Duke of Foodle, and all the fine gentlemen in office, down to Zoodle, shall set right in five hundred years—though born expressly to do it.

—Bleak House

In December *The New York Times* turns over the front page of its Sunday entertainment section to its annual reminder that we all should Remember the Neediest! Jo's story, of course, would qualify hands down for this year's appeal, although the *Times* probably would strike out that business about "the fine gentlemen in office." For every year since the pitch began back in 1912, the Neediest Cases have arrived more tightly wrapped than the best of Christmas packages, hermetically sealed, in fact, from a social and economic world of cause and effect. Unlike Dickens, the *Times* does not accuse or criticize. The *Times* takes up a collection.

True, the cases do focus on a part of society few *Times* readers personally experience. But in each year's compendium of heartrending tales there is seldom even a hint of "haves" interacting with "have-nots." In 1912, rather than demand decent wages and working conditions from employers, the *Times* praised the courage of those who worked a twenty-hour day, assuring readers these Neediest were not paupers but worthy. In 1971, rather than ask why a deserted mother had no alternative but to quit her job and live in a rat-infested building with her children, the *Times* praised her strength and drew comfort from the fact that a counselor was helping her to cope until things got better. This patronizing attitude is very much part of the *Times*'s public face (the Sunday paper features the cases, the daily paper reports the contributions, the editorial page supports the drive); and although poverty and the poor are dealt with elsewhere in the paper, the Annual Neediest Cases Appeal reflects a mind-set that, as we shall see, has no small effect on that coverage. It is a charity mentality, still not too far removed from Dickens, that permeates the society and its journalism—a placebo of noblesse oblige, righteousness and institutionalism.

The goal of the *Times*'s appeal, first announced in an editorial on December 17, 1912, and repeated every year since, is "not giving, but elevating to self support and self respect." Its other purpose, also reiterated through the years, is educational. On Sunday morning, December 15, 1912, a banner headline across the magazine section read: "Santa Claus Please Take Notice: Here Are New York's 100 Neediest Cases." One hundred paragraphs presented "the uttermost dregs of the city's poor," as guaranteed by three charitable organizations. Although no direct requests for funds had been made, within forty-eight hours contributions of cash, gifts, used clothing and toys, offers of adoption and requests to visit the Neediest were pouring into the *Times.* An institution had been created. By Christmas Day, over $3,600 had directly relieved all one hundred cases. By the end of the 1971–72 Christmas season, $1,010,764 had been collected for the eight private welfare organizations participating in the Sixtieth Annual Appeal.*

Over the years, the appeal has gone through several transformations. For a while, the amounts of money needed to rehabilitate each case were specified; daily articles charted funds, listed donors, excerpted their letters. Earmarking of contributions became popular and donors often wrote that it took hours to select which case was the most deserving. One 1932 contribution arrived "in memory of my dear old cat, Cassius," and was earmarked for "some old person who clings to a pet cat or dog." Large contributions were welcomed, but small donors were encouraged to send in their "mites."

It was never too early to acquire the habit of noblesse oblige. A 1922 editorial told parents: "Most instructive and useful it would be for children to read, or have read aloud to them, specimen cases. It is not simply a question of how the other half lives, but of acquiring knowledge of the bitter need which sometimes overwhelms individuals and families and which inclines every heart to melting charity." Little Nelson and David Rockefeller's donations were recorded that year, their father fleshing out the family contribution to $900, while older brother John sent his own $50. Acknowledgement was made that same day, December 20, of the $100 gift from the Sunnybank Collies, "faithful quadrupeds."

At times it was positively zany. The Royal Nuts of Mt. Vernon held a party at which everyone was given a royal title and fined if they addressed a fellow Nut without using his title. The fines were sent to the Neediest. Felicia the Cat also

---

*The Community Service Society, the Federation of Jewish Philanthropies, the Catholic Charities of the Archdiocese, the Brooklyn Bureau of Community Service, the Children's Aid Society Foster Care Service, the Catholic Charities of the Diocese of Brooklyn, the Staten Island Family Service, the Federation of Protestant Welfare Agencies.

contributed that year, embarrassed that she lived better than some bipeds.

Follow-up articles would appear throughout the year on rehabilitated cases, such as one 1922 family whose eldest daughter was now employed and turning over every penny of her "small income" to her mother. The mother's health had improved since Christmas and *Times* readers would be happy to know that her Christmas wish "for a 'blanket and a bit of coal' was granted and friends say she has never ceased talking about the joy of sleeping warmly."

Indeed, the general mood of the 1922 appeal was one of optimism. An editorial on December 12 observed that "if need is great, the ability and riches to give are greater." While the steadily rising cost of living was acknowledged as a burden to the poor—bringing high rents and food prices, plus unemployment—there was, nonetheless, a feeling that poverty could be wiped out. For example, tuberculosis, a major cause of destitution, had been cut by half since 1912 and was now preventable. The *Times* conceded that cold, poor nutrition and worry weakened people to the disease. But educating the poor about the illness was most important. As one welfare official explained to appeal readers, the poor have an "incapacity and inability . . . to meet the modern conditions of life. Ignorance and lack of adaptation lead to bareness of living and then to actual suffering and distress."

The Depression meanly intruded around this point. The poor were now often next-door neighbors, and their predicaments hit closer to the donor: yet even then work was regarded as the simple antidote to poverty. It was acknowledged—with respect, of course—that many of these victims of the Depression, newcomers to poverty, almost starved before they would ask for help. One Neediest Case was a prosperous businessman who had lost everything and was dying from overwork as a janitor. Even here, that same patronizing language distinguishes this man from those who could give, thus making him pitiful as he valiantly adjusts his family to their basement apartment by "papering his kitchen a cheerful color." The goal was still "not giving, but elevating into self support and self respect." Meanwhile the *Times* reported the daily progress of hunger marchers. Washington police stood guard as 3,000 of them made their way to the capital from Albany, N. Y.

With the coming of Social Security, welfare and the W.P.A., some concepts about poverty began to change. Supposedly, the government now provided for health and material needs of the poor. Private agencies were redefining their purpose, and in 1942 the *Times* found it necessary to explain why the appeal was still needed. There would still be some material relief, but the emphasis now would be on supportive services—housekeeping, vocational training, counseling. In 1942, for the first time, some of the funds would go towards social workers' salaries. Readers had always been told funds went directly to the needy. It was stressed that social workers were not administrators, but acted as a direct service to the needy. Increasingly, too, the *Times* began to face the fact that America was not going to get rid of poverty. It was not simply a matter of new immigrant groups catching up, and of transitory economic setbacks. Public welfare was an institution of the state. There was an awareness in the appeal that the poor would always be with us.

The *Times,* however, was not about to blame the American social or economic system. Reaching back into a mythology older than this country, the *Times* blamed fate. Fate had been spotted lurking around the poor ever since 1912, but never had it been attacked with the vehemence of 1942. The language broke down under the burden. "It's no use to snarl at fate, but when fate is caught cogging the dice she ought to be exposed," decreed the editorial page in an uncharacteristic burst of passion. The poor were those on whom "time and chance have played an evil trick." For a newspaper that eschewed crusades, the *Times* pulled no punches with fate. The Neediest were the "prisoners of misfortune . . . the cards were stacked against them . . . these innocents have had more than their proportionate share of the cuffs and kicks of fortune." There was a way out, however, because not everyone had been cuffed and kicked around. The *Times* appealed, as always, to the nobler instincts of these lucky ones: "Let us redress the balance a little, set them on their feet again, put them on their way to health and employment, try to give them—and to some for the first time—a little happiness."

In the fifties people with emotional problems and marginal income families began to dominate the appeal. Deserted wives began showing up in increasing numbers and the *Times* was merciless with their husbands, calling them "weaklings, cowards, or mere scoundrels." But, then, some Neediest have been beyond the pale right from the start in 1912: runaway husbands, families with incest problems, ex-convicts futilely job-hunting, welfare cheats, etc. Such unsavory types, when shown at all, are brought on stage as troublemakers affecting the True Neediest. "The *Times* does interpret the needs of the poor, but it leaves a segment out —those who are not appealing, people who haven't done for themselves," says Richard Hackman, who oversees the appeal for the Community Service Society. Hackman thinks the *Times* is accurate in gauging what the public wants, and suggests that, as an ideal case, "a woman with five children whose husband gets hit over the head at work and is now a vegetable would be nice."

The poor, of course, represent society's failure, and part of that failure is that so many of the poor end up in prisons that fail. Yet as recently as 1971, a *Times* editorial compared the Neediest to the prisoners at Attica, concluding once again that the poor received their sentence by a judgment of fate. "The pleasure of the season," concluded another editorial last year, "can only be enhanced for those who divert some of their spending from the purchase of holiday goods for those who have much to the spreading of holiday cheer to those who have nothing." It is all so, as the editorial put it, "poignant."

John B. Oakes, editor of the editorial page, concedes that

the notion of direct charity is dated. "It's not the starving Armenian, clothe the naked kind of thing any longer, but the Appeal does remain a genuine effort to involve people in the lives of another part of the community," he told me in an interview recently. How, I asked, could this effort be genuine when it makes no connection between the poor and the rich in the community? Oakes said making those connections about the Cases was where the editorial department came in. Then, hearing the Attica editorial blame only fate for poverty, he winced. "The message you're throwing at me does put me back on my heels. I thought we had been stressing the societal aspects. What I've been saying sounds a little lame when I hear that." As for the suggestion about spreading holiday cheer to those less fortunate, he commented, "Aside from the fact that that is a horribly written sentence, is there really anything so terribly wrong with that? Acknowledging the societal aspects doesn't negate that at Christmastime we should get across the idea that you should share. It doesn't mean you can't endorse the old-fashioned Christian and Judaic ideals, does it?"

The Neediest Cases appear each December in the Arts and Leisure section of the Sunday *Times*. Daniel Schwarz, Sunday editor, says there's no particular reason for that location. He reveals with some amusement that David Merrick complains about its placement every year at the stockholders meeting. "But where else would you put it?" Schwarz asks. "Sports? It doesn't belong anywhere. Business and Finance?" He half smiles, waiting for the absurdity of that to sink in. From time to time the men at the *Times* do ask themselves if they are going to have the Neediest forever, but, Schwarz comments, "I don't see how we can ever stop. The momentum is so great. The money from bequests alone brings in a few hundred thousand dollars a year. Short of the day when there is no more private charity, it will continue. It ought to be an anachronism, but it isn't." Schwarz feels there is a responsibility to help the person in need, something the government, with all its welfare functions, can't always do. "It's not always that simple for a bum to go on welfare." Schwarz dismisses the idea that one should look beyond the individual cases to an examination of the nature of poverty with impatience. They do that elsewhere in the *Times,* he points out, adding that by now people should know about poverty.

Indeed they should. But when they read the *Times* to find out, their knowledge, and subsequently their consciousness, is skewed in favor of the System pretty much as it is. *Times* editors care about the poor, but not enough to ask the really hard questions and base their news policies on the even harder answers that might result from such open-mindedness. One can argue, of course, that like the nation's other news organizations, the *Times* is irrevocably trapped in a system that sustains it and that it is unreasonable to expect any radical departures. One can argue, too, that *unlike* most of the nation's other news organizations, the *Times* at least makes a serious attempt to cover poverty. Whatever their merits, though, neither argument helps much to focus poverty coverage in a way that might provide some meaningful impact on the problem.

For the most part, poverty and the poor are covered in the *Times* from an institutional point of view that is almost synonymous with welfare. The tangle of governmental legislation and bureaucracies, and their interactions, are reported extensively and often well. Still, there were whole weeks last summer when poverty appeared as a problem residing in Jule Sugarman and the city's Human Resources Administration, which he heads. Most articles resulted from announcements made by the HRA—estimating the effect of welfare cuts on the poor, reporting stricter identification procedures, indictments of welfare cheaters, reactions to mandatory work programs, predictions that all these get-tough policies (not labeled as such) would result in a drop in the numbers on relief. Internal difficulties at HRA surfaced—the firing of consistently tardy workers, and, most extensively, the financial controversy surrounding the resignation of Ted Gross as director of HRA's Youth Services Agency.

A few attempts were made to interpret welfare problems in human terms. Michael Kaufman described the fear and theft that accompany the twice-monthly welfare checks—a horror for welfare workers, the post office and the recipients (August 17). David Shipler wrote that the Social Security raises were backfiring on the elderly, making some ineligible for welfare and Medicaid benefits (October 3).

Lately, some of the best insights into the welfare side of poverty have been provided by outside writers in the *Times* Sunday magazine. On October 22, Sol Stern took a long look not only at Jule Sugarman's office, but at the local offices where desperation and frustration have been reaching the point of physical violence. The enormity of the mess came through, and improved plans were seen as possible solutions, though partial and fragile. On November 5, an article on unemployment and underemployment (by William Spring, Bennett Harrison and Thomas Vietorisz) exposed "work ethic" for the insidious code term it is. There aren't enough jobs, and most of the jobs available to the inner city population are so low-paying that even when several members of the family work, the combined income doesn't meet official "head-above-water" figures.

Times reporters sometimes provide such insights. But the paper's editorial direction seems stuck with two bad habits: reflexively taking its cues from government and adhering to bankrupt journalistic attitudes about what is newsworthy. As Jule Sugarman points out, "One public official accusing another of doing something wrong, or something happening which offends the public sensibility, such as a welfare family staying at the Waldorf—that's page one. But our efforts at job creation are significant and we're lucky to find that on page eighty-four."

This may sound like bureaucratic sour grapes, but it is not. On November 16, 1972, a headline on page one read: WIDE COMMUNITY CRIME TRACED/TO 'SINGLES' IN WELFARE HOTELS. The story, by Max Seigel, jumped inside to page 52 and ran a total of 65 column-inches, not including a picture that showed us the Manhattan Towers Hotel on Broadway, where 186 single welfare recipients live and where, according to Sgt. Joseph A. Burns of the 20th Precinct, 15 percent of the precinct's robberies occur. In his story, Seigel is all over town interviewing cops, politicians and "community leaders." Not one hotel resident, never mind a welfare recipient, makes it into the article. Seigel quotes one of the community leaders as saying "most solutions are too simplistic." That does not deter Seigel. In the next paragraphs he approvingly describes a "solution" put to him by Sgt. Thomas J. Conrad of the 24th Precinct. The Bonjay Hotel, at Broadway and 103rd Street, has managed to cut crime within its walls, says the sergeant, by inviting the police to patrol the hotel and by requiring every applicant for a room to supply his employer's name and address if he has a job, his social security number and references. Sergeant Conrad, writes Seigel, "pointed to the Bonjay's clean lobby and to a neat, courteous clerk behind a counter. 'My flesh used to crawl when I came into the lobby here,' he said. 'and look at it now'."

This kind of playing up to public sensibility is almost routine at the *Times*. And when the poor are up to something *really* violent, watch out! When Dr. Wolfgang Friedmann, the distinguished Columbia University law professor, was mugged and murdered in broad daylight not far from the campus last September, the *Times*'s news columns bristled with indignation for days—helped along by a stabbing/mugging of another prominent white man, Dr. Selwyn Brody, a psychiatrist who was walking to the Penn Central Station on 125th Street, also during the day. For five days, detailed accounts of the assaults stretched through the *Times* along with Friedmann's obituary, a profile of the neighborhood, and reactions from the academic community and politicians. In short, Outrage—the same kind the *Times* reserves for the periodic crime waves around its skirts in Times Square. Implied, of course, is a double standard on the value of human life, exactly the double standard in our Vietnam policy that the *Times* editorial page so rightly condemns. Black and brown people die by violence every week in New York City, but unlike those yellow people thousands of miles away, their stories seldom make page one or any other page.

In an editorial on September 25, the *Times* noted the coverage the events had been receiving from the media and hoped that an understanding of causes might prevent recurrences. It recognized that "the flurry of interest which springs largely from the prominence of the victims may create the impression of an extraordinary event—something to be countered with a little extra policing and personal caution. In fact these highly visible crimes merely prove that nobody is safe from an epidemic that has claimed so many victims." The visible-invisible nature of murders in New York, of course, owes at least something to what the *Times* chooses to report. The editorial went onto say, "The link between slum-bred poverty and violent street crime is easy to establish," but that understanding that doesn't mean we have to accept violence until "urban inequities have been eradicated." Calling for a quick and visible response to violence from the police and courts, it concluded, "Above all, of course, there remains a desperate need to step up the fight against the causes of the urban sickness. Far from being in conflict with each other, the battles against crime and against social injustice are part of the same strategy to save the city."

Of course, many individual reporters and editors on the *Times*—but by no means most—recognize how simple-minded much of the institution's reaction to poverty is. When David Shipler was covering housing, for example, he was hardly unaware of the fact that every day during the winter people were freezing in apartments. "It's a continuing catastrophe," he says. "Maybe it should be on page one every day, but the news business isn't like that." Yet it can be, as Shipler himself dramatically demonstrated four winters ago. He decided to do a portrait of one tenement, to present the catastrophe and explain it. On January 18, 1969, his piece appeared on the front page of the second section. It was strong: elderly whites, black and Puerto Rican welfare families, junkies who mugged other tenants, a super who pushed drugs—all existing in a crumbling building on West 104th Street without heat or running water. What distinguished the article was its well-documented charge that owning a rent-controlled building, letting it rot and then abandoning it is a calculated exercise in profit. Moreover, Shipler reported, it could all be accomplished with impunity. When the owner appeared in court for his fourth failure to provide heat, the judge, who could have given him one year in prison and fined him $1,000, fined him $5.

Several years later, the *Times* gives its readers this kind of journalism very rarely. Instead, the news department prefers features on the poor. It would be unfair to characterize these stories as merely patronizing exercises. They are not. But collectively these pieces do little more than the annual Neediest Cases Appeal. They evoke our sympathies for the down-and-out poor who are powerless and no threat to us. OLD AND ALONE IN NEW YORK CITY, THE CITY'S ITALIAN AMERICAN NEEDY: TOO PROUD TO TAKE THE AID THEY EARNED, Bowery derelicts in rehabilitation programs, the elderly being forced out of the Nevada Hotel on Broadway. Most of these tugs at our conscience are one-dimensional, good for buttressing a central story which makes an effort to understand the problem, but which is not there. And the play of these stories may be the most telling comment of all. Like Shipler's piece, most appear on the front page of the second section. Features, you understand, not *news*.

In the end, maybe the best thing the *Times* could do is quantify poverty for its readers. Americans love lists and statistics and the *Times* is expert at this kind of thing. Television and radio listings, four columns; weather, two-and-a-half columns; shipping news, eight column-inches; stock quotations, acres—plus basketball scores, football scores, hockey scores, tennis scores, soccer scores, *cricket* scores and, of course, race results by the furlong. If it is page-one news when Dow-Jones pushes over 1,000, if the *Times* can find room each day to tell us that "Father of the Bride" is on Channel 7 at. 4:30 P.M., that it drizzled yesterday in Buenos Aires, that Stenerud of the Kansas City Chiefs has made 16 of 23 field goals attempted this season, and that Filbert Creme Brulee requires seven egg yolks lightly beaten, then somewhere in the paper there must be room for a daily catalogue of housing violations, evictions, ratbites, muggings, school drop-outs, unemployment statistics, rapes, buildings without heat, prison population, recividism, etc. And maybe next year, just for a change of pace, the *Times* could skip the Neediest and instead do profiles of the Greediest, those Coodles, Doodles, Foodles and Zoodles in the city who do so much to make poverty possible.

December 1972

How to Become a Reliable Source

In May of 1960, the day after his surprise defeat at the hands of John F. Kennedy in the West Virginia Democratic Presidential primary, Senator Hubert Humphrey was considering mounting evidence that the Kennedy organization had stolen that election in a way that can only be done in West Virginia. Humphrey lieutenants in the field were reporting that Kennedy operatives had made handsome payments to popular local candidates to list Kennedy on their slates, assuring him the votes of their supporters. Recognizing that Kennedy's West Virginia victory, by supposedly burying the Catholic issue, had clinched the nomination, Humphrey felt that his only hope was to have the results declared a fraud. In a series of discussions with his advisers, Humphrey had about decided to get affidavits from the field and make formal charges in federal court. The move might have succeeded—and just possibly another man might have ultimately occupied the White House—had one of Humphrey's trusted counselors not leaked the slating story to reporters, who wrote it up as a defeated candidate's sour grapes. I was that trusted counselor.

For the past twenty years, I have spilled secrets in Washington on a scale that would qualify me for the firing squad in Spain, South Vietnam and much of what President Nixon calls the "free world." I have had a hand in the resignation of Sherman Adams, the downfall of Bobby Baker, and the embarrassment of countless politicians whose greed for power was matched only by their respect for money. If a Washington reporter is looking for a scandal or a hot political tip, the word has gotten around to call me, and I will do my best to oblige.

Why do I do this? Because I like reporters better than any other kind of people. I like to be seen in their company in swank restaurants, to eat their food and drink their liquor as they ply me for leads. I love to exchange bits of political gossip, to join in the reporters' cynical assessment of politicians and their jealous criticism of the columnists, who make so much more money than they for what seems to be easier work. My biggest high comes when in the middle of a formal dinner party I let drop a particularly juicy item, and a reporter takes his pad out of his dinner jacket and starts making notes. I will give reporters almost anything they want to keep them interested in me.

I wanted to become a reporter myself, but my father insisted I become an accountant. That was in the days when young men did what their fathers told them. You can't imagine how dull my profession is, or how it narrows the interests of the people who work in it. If it weren't for the fact that because of the new disclosure rules on campaign contributions and expenditures, a good accountant is indispensable to politicians, I would be frittering away my life helping large corporations lie to the Internal Revenue Service and to their stockholders. As it is, I am a confidant of senators and governors. They tell me things because they trust me and need my expertise. They even listen to my suggestions on political matters, because they need my knowledge of financial matters to keep them out of trouble. So I sit in on their meetings with their top political advisers. By relaying just a small part of what I learn, I can be part of the exciting life of a journalist without ever having to chase around after stories or meet a deadline.

How did I get my reputation as a reliable source? I'm the guy that got Harold Talbot. You may not remember the name, but Harold Talbot was Secretary of the Air Force in the Eisenhower administration. That is, until he was caught writing letters to defense contractors on official Air Force stationery—to drum up customers for his old engineering firm. It was the first major scandal for old Ike, who had promised an administration that was "clean as a hound's tooth."

I was working in the comptroller's office of the Air Force at the time. A representative of a defense contractor showed me one of the letters and said it looked a little strange. I thermofaxed the letter (the Xerox machine had not yet been invented) and sent it to a friend of mine who worked for the Senate Committee on Government Operations. I told him he could use my name, since I was about to leave the government anyway. The chief counsel to the committee happened to be Robert F. Kennedy. He passed the letter to his friend Charles Bartlett of the Chattanooga *Times,* who broke the story. Talbot resigned. Bartlett won a Pulitzer Prize. I started getting phone calls from reporters asking if I "had anything else." I was on my way.

On a normal news day I get four or five calls from reporters looking for information. In the usual week I assist in the development of two political stories and as many columns. The columns are easier because they simply involve analysis and speculation, which I can do in my sleep. I once gave Stewart Alsop the same column, about the same political figure, that I had given him six years before—and then sent him copies of both his columns, just to make him mad. As a Democrat, I find it easier to operate with my party out of power. It gives me more freedom, as well as the means to try to stop administration proposals I consider wicked. Actually, since I had little use for Lyndon Johnson (or him for me), I consider that I have been out of power—and free to leak what I please—for the last ten years.

This hobby of mine involves risks, of course. If the word ever gets around that I talk, politicians will stop talking to me. And reporters will erase my phone number from their books. That's why I make it a rule never to reveal a confidence unless I know it has been told to at least three other people besides me. And rather than give out a story directly, I prefer to tell a reporter where he can find it. That way, the story can never be traced back to me. In fact, some of the most fun I have is talking to reporters about how to find a bit of scandal I know is there. We go through a list of contributors to the Committee to Re-elect the President. This money man sounds suspiciously like the owner of a Miami television station. Why not check to see if his license is up for renewal, I suggest. (I know damn well it is—my firm's Miami branch does the accounting for the station.) Or check into why a certain Republican state chairman has been telling people he now prefers Rockefeller to Connally for 1976. Could it be that the Chase Manhattan Bank has just made a large deposit in the bank in which the state chairman has stock? (We audit the bank.)

After almost two decades of this, I know all the techniques reporters use: the way they play one source against another; the way they "confront" a politician or government official with uncorroborated details of a story, hoping to get additional information and corroboration from him; and especially the way they make up quotes themselves and attribute them to "friends of Senator X" or "sources close to the investigation." This last is often harmless. A reporter wants to cap his story with a quote that summarizes a situation. So he rephrases something a real source has said, using more colorful or cogent language. Sometimes, though, the practice can be pretty funny. Like the time Nixon visited the Philippines in 1955 and rode through the streets of Manila. "Said one Filipino," reported *Time,* "There goes the symbol of American friendship and resistance to Communist aggression.' "

Some people play the source game to enhance their own reputation. Just before the 1970 congressional elections, Senator Edmund Muskie was preparing a speech on behalf of the Democrats to be delivered on television election eve. The Muskie camp got word that the Associated Press had learned the speech had been drafted by Richard Goodwin, the former Kennedy and Johnson speechwriter. This happened to be true. But it upset Muskie and his staff, who were not eager to share the credit. Goodwin said he would personally check out the source of the rumor. He then called several national columnists and political reporters and said something like the following: "This is Dick Goodwin. I'm in Portland . . . Yes, I've been talking to Senator Muskie . . . I think the speech is very good, but how did you learn who was writing it?" These calls completed, Goodwin reported back to Muskie, saying, "Senator, I have investigated these rumors thoroughly and there is absolutely no basis to think they are coming from here."

As a source for Washington reporters, I am not exactly typical. I guess reporters get most of their information from people who have a vested interest in getting certain facts into the papers. Most Congressional assistants, for example, feed the press information that makes their bosses look good. Then there are the civil servants who feel their special programs are being undermined by stupid policies, or warped by politics. They leak information out of loyalty to their agency, in the hope that the publicity will change policies they think are mistaken. Sometimes they team up to nail their boss. That's what happened to L. Patrick Gray, the acting head of the FBI. As I understand it, a group of FBI officials who were loyal to J. Edgar Hoover's way of doing things were appalled by Gray's mediocrity and his subservience to the White House. For the "good of the bureau" to which they had devoted their lives, they arranged to leak documents to a former FBI official, who in turn fed them to the press. How else do you think reporters learned that Gray had refused to let the FBI interview Martha Mitchell, or had paid out

$100,000 for private airplane transportation because he was afraid if he took a commercial flight he might be hijacked? Such bureaucratic sources are much more reliable than the congressional flacks, but they still have a vested interest—in protecting an ideal or a program, or in simply screwing somebody. But me—I'm the most reliable kind of source there is, because I just do it for fun.

My hobby has become riskier in recent years, and I have to take precautions. Every month, I have my telephone checked and my office swept for eavesdropping devices. When a reporter calls me whom I don't know, I insist on talking to him face to face. I meet him in a bar, checking the olive in his martini to make sure it has no microphone. Or I take him into the bathroom to talk. A source has to protect himself these days. Telephone taps and bugging devices are everywhere. A whole industry has grown up in Washington that does nothing but search out news leaks. "Security experts" like Howard Hunt are hired to make sure secrets don't leak. That's called "defensive security." They end up bugging the opposition. That's called "offensive security."

For anybody who thinks, as I do, that the kicks are worth the risks, and wants to become a reliable source, I offer this advice:

• Tell the truth. If you trim it or twist it, or worse yet send a reporter up a blind alley, you're dead.

• Know to whom you're speaking. Beware the reporter who calls you out of the blue. He may be from the Committee to Re-elect the President. During the 1970 election campaign I got a call at two in the morning from "Bob Morse, the night man at the AP." He asked what I knew about a deal between a senator up for reelection and a member of the Mafia. Fortunately, I keep two telephones in my bedroom. On the pretext of looking up a document, I called the AP newsroom on the other phone and asked for Morse. Of course he didn't exist. So I told "Morse" to give me his number and I would call him back. He said he was having a sudden attack of the runs, got off the phone in a hurry and never called back.

• Don't blow your cover. It's all right if reporters know you are a leak. They know how to protect their sources. But don't let your fellow insiders find out. My most frequent nightmare goes like this: I am sitting in the hotel suite of a leading candidate for the presidental nomination, having breakfast with him and his top staff. That morning *The New York Times* has run a damaging article on his prospects, guaranteed to drive off all the big contributors. It has quotes like this: "Said one senior staff adviser: 'This campaign is in deep trouble. If we don't come in second in the Florida primary, we're finished—and as of today, we're fifth.' " The candidate tries to control his rage. "Okay," he says slowly, "who's the son of a bitch?" All eyes turn toward me.

At the risk of talking myself out of my favorite position, I would venture that the whole idea of reliable sources has been debased—not by the sources, but by the journalists. Until forty years ago, a President would not allow himself to be quoted, directly or indirectly. Reporters had to say "we have learned on the highest authority that . . ." That's how it started, but today hosts of sources spread interesting but inconsequential gossip, and the device is used to lend authenticity to ideas created by the reporter himself.

There are only two types of stories where masking the source produces significant news. The first is the corruption story. The source, because he is dealing with another person's reputation and often his freedom, runs a real risk in exposing himself. He must be protected. The second is the story about an important development in military security or high diplomacy such as the report of the Bay of Pigs invasion the *Times* had and suppressed in 1961; or the proposed increase in the Vietnam troop ceiling to 700,000 at the time of Tet in 1968. Here, premature publicity is the only weapon available to those inside the government who feel the policies are wrong, and they should not have to risk their jobs to use it.

But for the vast majority of government appointments and policy decisions, the opposition can mobilize just as effec-

tively after the official announcement is made. What difference does it make if the public learns a few weeks early that
Nixon intends to name some incompetent segregationist to
the Supreme Court, or phase out the federal free milk program for starving babies? Bad appointments must still get
through the Senate. Good programs can always be recon-
stituted by the Congress. And there is plenty of time to do
these things after an administration has made its move. If
source identification were required in such stories, "scoops"
might get fewer and newsstand sales might slump a little. But
an administration could formulate its recommendations in
an orderly way, safe from premature leaks; and the public
would not be disserved.

When a source is used simply to verify or interpret a story,
there is no need for even anonymous attribution. Reporters
tell me they like to "triangulate" a lead—bounce it off an
expert in the field, or an agency with a different point of view,
to deepen its significance or check its accuracy. This is fine,
but they can use the knowledge they get this way without
sourcing it. It's time reporters were willing to let their inter-
pretations stand on their own two feet.

In political-campaign journalism there are, in my judgment, only two legitimate stories: (1) who wins the nomination and (2) who wins the election. The voters write these
stories. The role of the press is to help them by telling them
what the candidates are like, what they stand for, who owns
them and what the real issues are between them. In almost
all campaigns, these stories are buried under an avalanche of
trivia. Like the candidate's fund-raising problems, or how his
organization is screwing up, or how he plans to woo some
political leader (who couldn't deliver the votes of his own
family). All this garbage, carefully sourced, comes down on
us because of the insatiable desire on the part of political
journalists, months before an election, to report who is
ahead. So you have the candidate scooped in the timing of
his announcement, plagued by leaks, unable to meet with his
supporters, his campaign disrupted and distorted by report-

ers playing the sources game. The poor man gets so he is afraid to pick up the paper in the morning, and he ends up trusting no one.

For example, during his campaign Senator Muskie was engaged in the "endorsement strategy"—the carefully timed dropping of big-name endorsements by political leaders: Governor John Gilligan and Senators John Tunney, Harold Hughes, and so forth, in this instance. Part of Muskie's deal with these pols was that news of their support would be held until each could individually drape his arm around Muskie at a news conference. Yet leaks of each of these endorsements appeared in *The New York Times,* sometimes within hours after the deals were made. Furious, Muskie's campaign manager, Berl Bernard, called a meeting of the senator's top staff and chewed them out for the leaks. One by one, he made them stand up and swear they would stop talking to reporters. Two days after this so-called Silence Meeting, the *Times* broke the story that Governor Schapp of Pennsylvania had decided to endorse Muskie.

Well, you may say, politicians asked for it by going into public life. But I'm not just thinking of them. I'm thinking of the reader, who has to put up with all this political garbage for months and months until his eyes are sore. Just as all judges ought to spend some time in jail to see what it's like, every political reporter and columnist should be forced at gunpoint to read his clips for the past year, to see what farina he turned out in the form of predictions and reliably sourced gossip. If it weren't for the fact that readers quickly forget, most political reporters would be fired.

Reporters should stick to writing the news instead of trying to be fortunetellers and gossipmongers. Editors should demand that all sources be identified, except where it is critical that they not be. People like me would clam up immediately. Much of the trivializing would end. Candidates would be spared ulcers, and the public would still get all the news it needs (more, probably) to cast an intelligent vote.

May 1973

JOHN MCCORMALLY

Who Cares About the Pulitzer Prize?

When I offered the *Columbia Journalism Review* this assessment of the Pulitzer Prizes, its editor, Al Balk, brushed off what he described as "Mr. McCormally's personal problem of not being able to do what every good judge of every award contest must do (and I know this from several years of award experience)—screen out the obvious chaff by skimming and then concentrate on the worthy survivors that remain." I was not offended but delighted by Balk's gratuitous dismissal. It beautifully summarized what I'd been groping for: that at Columbia the Pulitzer is just another prize—like those in Balk's several years of award experience.

Balk's reaction confirmed what I discovered in 1971 as a Pulitzer juror. It solidified suspicions I first felt in 1965 as a Pulitzer winner. And if the Mother House on Morningside Heights has a ho-hum attitude about what is supposed to be journalism's most prestigious award, is it surprising that the working press is little impressed, the general public couldn't care less, and many young would-be journalists don't even know what we're talking about?

I helped select the 1971 Pulitzer winner for local investigative reporting—the category that involves the great tradi-

tional image of the crusading reporter. I don't know whether
the best job of investigative reporting done in America that
year was even considered. I don't know whether, of those
considered, the best one won. I don't know because in nine
hours, five fellow judges and I were expected to consider a
million words, in 134 separate entries, and come up with five
finalists. Later, a board of advisers picked the winner from
the five, without knowing what we, in our haste, had dis-
carded. The system allows for some pretty good journalism
to get lost in the "chaff."

The judges' haste is only one reason to question whether
the Pulitzers are a true measure of journalistic worth in this
time of journalistic sorrow. The Pulitzer process also suffers
because the advisory board is a self-perpetuating aristocracy;
women and the young have been excluded from the judging,
and so has everyone else outside newspaper executive ranks.
Editors of papers with entries under consideration sit on the
juries. Little initiative is taken to solicit candidates for the
prizes, thus a premium is put on orthodoxy. No special effort
is made to go out beyond traditional, established commercial
newspapers to seek daring, or even innovative, work.

When I came in out of the cold in March of 1971, I found
a cardboard sign, taped to a first-floor wall of Columbia's
Journalism building, directing me to the scene of my labors
—the World Room (after Joseph Pulitzer's *World*). The
universality, the omniscience of the name is borne out by its
appearance. It is a church kind of place: comfortably carpeted, with a dais at one end and even a stained-glass window. It seemed an ideal setting for deliberations such as ours.
There was a table of coffee and sweet rolls at one side for
those who had come hungry and chilled out of the March
blizzard.

Forty-eight of us had been chosen as Pulitzer jurors by
John Hohenberg, who submits the names for approval to the
Pulitzer advisory board, of which he has been secretary for
eighteen years. The same unexplained preference which
picked us in the first place had already subdivided us into

juries of four to six and assigned each jury to one of the ten categories for which journalism prizes are awarded. The chairman of each jury had also been designated by Hohenberg, a sixty-six-year-old professor of journalism who has been at Columbia since 1948.

Having accepted Hohenberg's invitation to serve and having paid my way to New York, I was never consulted about my choice of assignment, nor given any voice in selection of my group's chairman. But I didn't mind. They were all perfectly congenial fellows and obviously competent, as their titles attested. John Leard, executive editor of the Richmond *Times-Dispatch* and *News Leader* was chairman of our "Category 3: Local Special and Investigative Reporting." The others were. Robert C. Achorn, editor of the Worcester (Massachusetts) *Telegram* and *Gazette,* Eric W. Allen, Jr., editor of the Medford (Oregon) *Mail Tribune;* Harold E. Martin, editor and publisher of the Montgomery *Advertiser* and *Alabama Journal,* and John McClelland, Jr., editor and publisher of the Longview (Washington) *Daily News.*

My uneasiness began with Hohenberg's announcements. It was going on ten o'clock this Friday morning, and we would break for a two-hour lunch. We weren't to worry if we did not finish by five o'clock. The room would be locked overnight and all the material safe. Another lunch was scheduled for those who might still be here Saturday noon. It was not expected to take longer than that. The chore would not cut too deeply into anyone's weekend. I was stunned. I had come prepared for some long days and perhaps nights of work. I had learned the trade on the only two newspapers in Kansas with Pulitzer Prizes—William Allen White's Emporia *Gazette* and Jack Harris's Hutchinson *News.* I'd grown up in awe of the prizes. I was, as Al Balk later perceived, terribly naïve—a country boy come to the big city.

My unease grew when a hurried count showed 134 nominations in our category. If each submitted the allowed 10 clippings, that would be 1,340 pieces. They might average

1,000 words each. There must have been a million words in that pile. Whole careers were at stake, and my colleagues were talking of perhaps eight—certainly no more than twelve —hours for the job! (We actually spent nine.)

Nor was that the only disturbing discovery. Columbia, a giant of universities in the giant of all cities, was short of space. We couldn't have a separate, quiet room for our deliberations, such as the most minor misdemeanor jury gets in the courthouse back home in Iowa. Some of the groups did merit solitude, but we shared the World Room with three other juries—those judging public service, general local reporting and national reporting. The deliberations of the four separate groups intruded on one another, making concentration difficult. The crowded World Room seemed to suggest that what we were doing wasn't all that important that it required total concentration. It was also a little bit unnerving to try coldly to judge a reporter's work, aware that his editor was sitting across the room.

Our 134 entries were in notebooks and scrapbooks of such varied shapes and sizes as to defy easy stacking. What we needed were long rows of tables on which to spread them for contemplative comparison; but what we had was one medium-sized horseshoe table shoved into one corner of the room. We scattered scrapbooks on the floor, stacked them on the window sill and the piano bench, and tussled with them on our laps.

Our jury's procedure was to divide the stack of entries into subpiles, roughly categorized according to subject area, and each of us waded into a pile. The objective was for each, by the end of the day, to have identified his list of favorites, which would be pared to a list of finalists the following day. Our instruction from Hohenberg stated that "the advisory board does like three to six recommendations from each jury, with strong reasons for each choice in the jury report."

My first, hurried scan of the entries reinforced the first nagging impression of the World Room: stained-glass conformity. Entries were polarized around such well-plowed journalistic terrain as pollution, drugs and welfare abuse. Of course, it is the duty of the press to take notice of these. But it was obvious that, if the press were properly anticipatory, these subjects would have been wrung dry two or three or five years ago. As for crime and corruption in high places—they have been newsroom staples since the penny press! And there they were in profusion. I got through forty-eight scrapbooks by noon.

The commitment to Victorian convention was confirmed beyond doubt when we adjourned at twelve-fifteen for lunch with Columbia President William J. McGill in the Men's Faculty Club. Men's Faculty Club, indeed. But then, why not? There were no women on the Pulitzer juries. Apparently never had been. Never would be. (I was wrong there—but more about that later.) We did include Moses Newsom of the Afro-American Newspapers, so we weren't lily-white, as I'd begun to fear. But here we were, the lesser elite of the American press, come to honor the best among us, and we were totally male—more than a half century after women's suffrage and well into the era of women's liberation.

At the end of the day I had marked sixty-three entries as rejected, not worth further study. The remaining seventy-one I had either not yet looked at or put aside for further study, with a tentative rating on each ranging from "fair" to "very possible." I wanted to spend the night with some of them, but we were shooed out of the room, which was locked behind us. No plans were announced for a night session to try to determine what we were or ought to be looking for. The jurors went their various ways to whatever social engagements called.

I dined with an old friend, a teacher and practitioner of the trade, and poured out my agony. Where, I cried, was the cutting edge? I had looked in vain for the penetrating series on the woman's movement, or on the new definition and new acceptance of homosexuality, for a sensitive study of draft evaders; for something besides the same, prosaic Prohibition-era approach to drugs.

I kept looking for something else, too: for the reporter who had to swim upstream all the way, had to fight state house and city hall and the pulpit and the ad department and maybe his own desk, to get his story into print and give society its rude awakening—and for the paper that would let him. Where was there a real bastard, a Ralph Nader, in the reporting ranks? Most of the investigations, however well done, merely confirmed what the public already knew was wrong. There were crime exposés that had won letters of praise from governor, mayor and police chief; an investigation of the power structure so respectfully done the chamber of commerce sent out reprints.

And I kept looking for good writing. News writing and beautiful writing needn't be mutually exclusive, I insist. Our instructions, set forth in the advisory board's "Plan of Award," were to give "prime consideration to initiative, resourcefulness, research and *high quality of writing.*" It bothered me that in the jury room, as in that preceding sentence, writing came last.

I had found, before the day was over, two entries just enough outside the mold to beguile me: hopeful if imperfect examples of what I'd been searching for. Neither was totally unorthodox or terribly daring. But one was simply exquisite writing. The other was a mildly outrageous assault on community smugness.

The first, by Lawrence C. Hall of the Doylestown (Pennsylvania) *Daily Intelligencer,* caught my eye, I confess, because the nomination had been made by James A. Michener who, I thought, ought to know about good writing. He does. It was the one entry I read for the sheer joy of it. It was another antipollution series, one of ten in the pile, but this one was different. It was a simple, step-by-step chronicle of the death of a little stream: murder by industrial poison, with the blame pinned squarely on corporate and government officials. But it shook no empires, for it was about a small stream, in a small paper in a small town.

The other, by Lucie Lowery and Carter Barber for the

Pasadena *Star-News,* exposed new-style prostitution in massage parlors in Pasadena. An old subject, but handled with refreshing irreverence. What I liked was the way it brought from the pulpits simultaneous praise for public service, and shock at the discovery Pasadena had sex.

While I searched for something better, I kept these two favorites out of the reject pile through most of the following morning, until in the semifinals they fell before more orthodox competition. Our jury's procedure was to go around the table with a final list of twenty or so. We eliminated any against which there was one vote until we got down to five to recommend to the advisory board. In retrospect, here was the time to have argued more forcefully, but institutions can compel conformity not merely by dictum, but also by time and place. One was intimidated by the presence of other, busy juries in the same room. There was no provision for a hung jury, anyway. And besides, it was nearly noon. We would come back from lunch only to write the report, after a total of nine hours' deliberation. I signed the report, not really able to say that the very best available had not been chosen, and nothing rare and brilliant wasted. But I couldn't be sure. Some of those on the reject pile I never got around to reading.

The jury, incidentally, gave first ranking to Gene Hunter of the Honolulu *Advertiser* for a series exposing crime in Hawaii. It was a good journeyman job by a veteran reporter, and reminded me of one of my family's favorite TV shows; the jury noted that Hunter exhibited great personal courage in attacking a serious local problem.

The following month the advisory board overruled the jury and chose our second-place recommendation, an exposé, by William James of the Chicago *Tribune,* of ambulance service abuses that resulted in sixteen indictments in Chicago. The other top reporting investigations in the nation in 1970, we decided, concerned child abuse in New Jersey, police payoffs in New York, and pollution in Florida.

I wrote a couple of columns for the *Hawk-Eye* about my

disillusioning look behind the Pulitzer scene and sent them to Hohenberg. Hohenberg has been described as "crusty and imperious" by Pulitzer critics. He is proud and protective about the Pulitzer process. Writers like Robert J. Bendiner have noted his evasiveness and noncooperation. He politely replied to me that he was sending my columns on to the advisory board. "Coming from the editor of a paper that won the Pulitzer Prize gold medal for public service through this method of judging, I'm sure they'll be impressed," he said. If they were, they kept it to themselves.

No one can argue that the prizes have not been bestowed on outstanding journalists for outstanding work. When obviously superior performance has presented itself (such as Seymour Hersh or David Halberstam on Vietnam), the Pulitzer apparatus does not falter. But neither is it geared to search out the unusual. On the contrary, its make-up almost guarantees it will be stuffy and out of touch. There is a certain anxiety about abiding by the terms of Joseph Pulitzer's will, and maybe that means the Pulitzers are supposed to be guardians of old traditions rather than a breaker of new paths. In any case, no matter what is done to encourage more meaningful nominations or to improve the judging process, the prizes won't mean much unless the Pulitzer board—and the profession as a whole—want them to.

I believe—and I think thousands of lovers of this craft, both in and out of it, would like to believe—that the Pulitzer Prizes can and should mean more. They should be a means of focusing on journalistic greatness—on public service worthy of the First Amendment—to counter the growing criticism of journalism. They should be a tool for luring the brightest, most searching young people into journalism and helping to inspire them once they're in. At this they're a complete flop. At worst, the potential journalists are repelled, at best left in blissful ignorance.

Deans Ed Bassett at Kansas and Malcolm Maclean at Iowa helped me poll students in their journalism schools to test my suspicion that the labors of my fellow jurors and I in 1971 went largely unnoticed by the young people we editors should be most concerned about. The survey, early in 1972, included eighty-six journalism undergraduates at Kansas, forty-two at Iowa. Instructors passed out the three-part questionnaire in class, allowing no opportunity for research. The first question listed the ten categories for which journalism prizes were awarded in May 1971 and asked the students to name as many of the winners as possible. Not a single respondent at either school could name a single winner, except that at Iowa, for "spot news photography" one student wrote—correctly—"the Kent State girl photo." And isn't there something wrong when none of the students at two of the country's top journalism schools could remember that the late Merriman Smith of UPI had won a Pulitzer for his story on President Kennedy's assassination, yet several listed Howard K. Smith and other television lights as winners of a prize reserved for *newspaper* journalists?

Maybe the Pulitzers are hopelessly archaic. But they needn't be, and the best way to rescue them is by reforming the nominating process. Hohenberg is sensitive about what he calls "the principle of unlimited free nominations," and I agree that everyone within the broadest boundaries of whatever is defined as newspaper journalism should be able to enter the competiton. That's just it. While technically anyone can play, nothing is done through the year to search for new talent or unorthodox approaches. Entries come almost automatically from the large papers, some of which even maintain departments dedicated solely to preparing and carrying out this kind of promotion. It is possible that the best work is the last thing the promotion department wants to be reminded of—the story that embarrassed the publisher, lost advertising and got the reporter fired.

As much as women and youth, the Pulitzer juries need also to include some nonpress critics of the press to make the process more representative of and responsive to the most vital forces at work in the society. Somewhere among the jurors or advisers there ought to be room for a Nader, a Jesse

Jackson, a Walter Hickel, a Saul Alinsky, a Gloria Steinem or an F. Lee Bailey; maybe even a Spiro Agnew and a Daniel Berrigan—people able not only to concede what the press is capable of doing, but also recognize what it doesn't do.

One reform definitely needed is to bar completely from judging all representatives of papers with entries in any category. A half-hearted effort is now made to recognize the problem of conflict of interest. In a memorandum distributed to the 1971 jurors, Hohenberg wrote:

> Jury assignments are based on those categories in which individual jurors have no conflict of interest. Occasionally, because an organization submits entries in all categories, a juror may find a possible conflict. If this happens, he may abstain from voting if the entry is not of major importance or withdraw entirely from the judging. But in no event should he participate in discussion of, or voting on an exhibit in which he has an interest and should be marked as either abstaining or not present on such votes.

I suppose that means well. But try concentrating with complete objectivity on the work of a reporter whose editor is across the table or across the room, or chatting at lunch with you. His presence is bound to have an effect, however slight or subliminal. And it is so unnecessary. Let those who want badly enough to be judges refrain from entering anything that year, and vice versa. There will be no shortage of either competent jurors or qualified entries.

Given the times, the changes I have proposed seem altogether modest. Yet if they were made, the Pulitzer Prizes for journalism might stand a chance of becoming a real instrument for improving the quality of writing and reporting in American newspapers. Especially if once the awards were announced some concentrated effort was made to make the public more aware of what good journalists can do. As things stand now, the prizes are simply announced and that's pretty much that. Why not distribute to newspapers, schools, civic organizations and elsewhere packets containing at least excerpts of prize-winning articles and editorials? Of course, that would cost. But no more than the lobbying effort for the "Newspaper Preservation Act" (which now allows newspapers to violate the spirit of antitrust legislation). And this failure of ours to exploit the excellence we're capable of, while perpetuating the pap, may bring us really to the question of our preservation.

None of this matters, of course, if the Pulitzer purpose is professional masturbation—if the prizes are meant only for the self-gratification of a tiny clique of givers and receivers, and if neither the public nor the profession at large is supposed to be bothered. But if that's it, why not just install another stained-glass window in the World Room?

May 1972

BETWEEN
THE LINES

TAYLOR BRANCH

The Scandal That Got Away

It is a safe bet that the secret bombing of Cambodia will fail as a scandal. No one will go to jail. No one will lose his job. No one will cry out about the unanswered questions like what did he know and when did he know it. No general will be summarily drummed out of the Air Force for falsifying records, as was Lavelle. No civilian honcho in the Nixon administration will sneak out of office on some pretext of an honest excuse. No senators will become so famous for protecting the people that the papers will feel obliged to run big features on their eating habits and how they spend a day at home with the folks. And no reporter will make his reputation for dogged pursuit of the facts, or vindicate the honor of the media by showing that the courageous truth can make a President blink.

All this is true, even though Plato or Walter Lippmann could make a pretty good classroom case that the secret bombing is more ominous and deserving of our attention than Watergate. After all, the Watergate break-in was an intelligence operation that occupied perhaps 1 percent of Jeb Magruder's time. It is reasonable to suspect that the bugging plot did not receive the high-level attention that a truly evil, momentous scheme deserves—that no one would have raised the roof if Gordon Liddy had slinked back with his motley strike force to report that it was too risky. In Cambodia, on the other hand, the President himself ordered the chairman of his Joint Chiefs half a dozen times to make sure that no one learned of 3,630 secret B–52 raids that would drop 100,000 tons of bombs on an officially neutral country. Right there in the National Security Council meeting, Nixon scared all the highest officials in his government so bad that they rigged up a system to keep the bombing secret from almost everyone, including the Air Force Vice Chief of Staff. General Earl Wheeler, chairman of the Joint Chiefs, swore to the Senate Armed Services Committee that he would have flatly lied to cover up the bombing if the Secretary of the Air Force had asked him about it casually on the golf course.

The constitutional issues rise quickly out of the Watergate burglary, but in Cambodia you *start* with them. For openers, you have the President conspiring with the military to keep a new war hidden from the Congress, mocking the separation of powers to the extent that Congress was given classified documents showing that the Cambodian bombings took place in South Vietnam. For those who take civil-military relations seriously, you have a whole military phalanx— generals, colonels, pilots, debriefers, radarmen, computer programmers—under strict orders to ignore regular military channels and respond only to secret orders from one immediate superior. Each man has to trust that the secret orders are legitimate, because he is forbidden to question them with anyone, lest he jeopardize the hidden network. The military apparatus for the bombing, in short, had all the ingredients of *Seven Days in May,* with the President in and the Congress definitely out.

Unlike the Watergate team, the operatives for the secret bombing did not bungle away their potential for harm. Thousands of irregular orders were obeyed like clockwork—as people falsified their records and burned their secret orders when they were supposed to so the B–52s could do their work without making any noise back home. When the American war in Cambodia ended in August amidst headlines telling of accidental bombings and civilian massacres, one could only guess whether similar accidents took place in 1969. No one could have known, because the administration didn't talk and the press didn't snoop very hard.

Why was the bombing not discovered when it was going on, and why did the story die so quickly this year? Both B–52 strikes and elaborate lies are hard to conceal, so it is embarrassing for us in the press that the news did not explode in 1969. And the charges are so grave that it is more than puzzling why the full exposure of the facts did not even draw blood.

The first mention of the secret bombing occurred in *The New York Times* of May 9, 1969, where William Beecher cited "knowledgeable sources" as saying that American planes had "raided several Vietcong and North Vietnamese supply dumps and base camps in Cambodia for the first time." The story did not say how many raids were being carried out in Cambodia, or how regularly, or whether the raids meant an entire new bombing campaign. Instead, this rather offhand disclosure left the impression that there were some spot bombings going on and that we would hear more about it if something bigger were afoot.

Some reporters believe that Beecher, known as a Pentagon ally, actually intended to help the administration with the story by signaling a new "get tough" Nixon war policy that might make Hanoi negotiate. If so, Beecher was an overzealous flack because his mention of the Cambodia bombing served notice on the administration that the "special security" measures had failed and that Nixon's most closely held secret had already splattered onto newsprint. This story is now cited by Kissinger as one of the main reasons for the famous seventeen wiretaps, one of which was placed on William Beecher's phone.

Apparently, government officials liked what they heard Beecher say, for he was hired to cross the gray line and become Deputy Assistant Secretary of Defense for Public Affairs. In other words, he went over to the other side, where his job is now to help Jerry Friedheim fend off press inquiries. Whether his sympathies explain things or not, he did not follow up his scoop with information on the scope or significance of the bombing.

Newsweek broke the only other story during the fourteen-month campaign in a June 2, 1969, Periscope item entitled "The Secret Bombing of Cambodia." In four sentences, *Newsweek* capsulized the salient facts—the super-secrecy, the falsified battle reports, and the presidential responsibility for the orders. But even this tantalizing revelation failed to stir up a press inquiry. The next printed reference to the story came in the August 20, 1973, *Newsweek,* where the little paragraph from 1969 was reprinted to prove that *Newsweek* had been on top of the matter for four years. The fact that a cover story had remained submerged in the Periscope did not seem to mar the spirit of self-congratulation.

Other than these two isolated tidbits, the secret bombing story went nowhere in the press. Seymour Hersh of the *Times,* who was far and away the most thorough reporter on the story when it finally came out in 1973, says he can't imagine why reporters in Vietnam did not pry out the details by pumping the B–52 crews, searching for embassy leaks, flying over Cambodia, and the like. His best guess is that reporters did not believe that so unconstitutional a policy was possible: "I just don't think anybody could conceive of the United States systematically bombing a neutral country with which we are not at war."

Most reporters who worked on the story in 1969 advance just the opposite interpretation: bombings in Cambodia were so likely that they weren't even news. It was assumed that we were bombing all over Indochina, just as it was assumed that the body counts were inflated and that the light was not at the end of the tunnel. Lloyd Norman, the veteran *Newsweek* Pentagon correspondent who dug up the 1969 Periscope item, explains that the Cambodia story seemed like a very small part of the war in 1969. "It was just brushed off as another one of the facts of life. We're bombing the border areas. What's new? There was no great public uproar."

With this perspective on the raids, which were thought to be minor and sporadic rather than massive and sustained, reporters were content to investigate simply by asking the Pentagon what was going on. "We knew that the bombing was going on," says Norman, "and we kept asking . . . We repeatedly asked the Pentagon in those days about the reports of bombing in Cambodia. And as recently as last May I called and asked, 'When the hell are you guys going to give us the statistics on bombing in Cambodia and Laos?' " Norman finally got his statistics in July, just before the big story broke, and the numbers were falsified to show no bombing at all in Cambodia during the secret campaign. "The guy who sent me the stuff didn't know himself that there were all those omissions," Norman says and sighs.

William Thomas, editor of the Los Angeles *Times,* agrees with Lloyd Norman's view that the Cambodia story was not judged to be worth much investigative time in the climate of 1969. "I think several reporters probably made one good hard stab at it," he says. "They came up against a blank wall, and then had to go back and cover the rest of the war."

So much for 1969. Things were different in 1973, as parts of the press came out blazing in their best Watergate spirit. Sy Hersh hit with a big scoop in the Sunday *Times* of July 15, revealing that former Air Force major Hal M. Knight would tell the Senate Armed Services Committee how he had helped doctor reports to hide the Cambodia bombing in early 1970. Knight's confession had some of the cloak-and-dagger excitement that had given dramatic flair to the Watergate story. He told Hersh that he had worked at a radar installation in Vietnam, helping to guide U.S. planes to their targets. Every day, said Knight, an airplane would land at his base bringing secret orders for raids in Cambodia, which his subordinates would run through the computer to obtain coordinates and a flight plan for the secret mission. Knight's outfit would then divert the B–52s from their "cover mission" in South Vietnam and send them over Cambodia. Knight would report the cover missions as having taken place, and he would burn the secret orders and the computer material for the secret runs. Finally, he would call a phone number in Saigon and tell an anonymous listener that "the ball game is over." It was a role that Howard Hunt could have played comfortably.

Hersh wrote six front-page stories in the first seven days of the scandal—outraged senators, admissions that the raids took place, the magnitude of the campaign (three thousand sorties as compared with General Lavelle's twenty-five), denials from administration officials that they had had anything to do with a phony reporting system. The networks jumped on the story. ABC ignored the Knight testimony on July 16, but picked it up the next day, when the Pentagon admitted that the raids had taken place.

Soon, however, the media pattern became clear. Hersh would write every day on page one—overshadowed by Watergate, since the story broke in the same week that Alexander Butterfield revealed the existence of the Nixon tapes. He would dig a story out somewhere, calling people like Kissinger, Laird, and Wheeler for comment. The networks would run a story only when there was something to be photographed—either at the Senate hearings or at a Kissinger press conference. Sometimes ABC would have nothing while the other two networks ran the same story. On July 19, for example, NBC and CBS picked up that morning's Hersh story on Melvin Laird's denial that he knew of the false reporting system or who was responsible for the raids. ABC was silent. Similarly, on Monday, July 23, ABC neglected the story run by Hersh and the other networks—Senator Symington's charge that the money to pay for the secret raids was obtained illegally.

Some newspapers such as the Boston *Globe* and the Washington *Post* fell right in behind Hersh, but others virtually ignored the story. The Chicago *Tribune* ran two front-page articles the first week and then imposed a three-week black-out before an August 8 story on page 7 picked up the Senate testimony of George Moses, who described his participation in secret bombings more than seventy-five miles inside Cambodia, *after* the 1970 invasion. (The Pentagon confirmed this story on September 10.) The *Trib* then went back to sleep until August 11, when the Pentagon released a November 20, 1969, memo from Earl Wheeler to Melvin Laird asking clearance to continue the secret B–52 raids, with simultaneous sorties in South Vietnam to confuse the press. "Strikes on these latter targets," observed Wheeler, referring to the cover missions, "will provide a resemblance to normal operations thereby providing a credible story for replies to press inquiries." This memo, classified TOP SECRET–SENSITIVE–NOFORN–EYES ONLY–ABSOLUTELY FOR EYES OF ADDRESSEE ONLY, was not written for the general public, and it appeared to put Laird and Wheeler in a bind regarding their denials of involvement with the false reporting system. Not so, said Laird. He had ordered the concealment of the truth from the Congress and the press, but not the outright commission of a lie. If asked about the bombing, those few who knew were supposed to obfuscate, profess not to understand, divert attention, and otherwise search for the slimmest excuse to give a slippery answer—but they were not supposed to lie. They were to deceive without being dishonest, to be sneaky without being crude, to grasp at any polite evasion short of a dishonorable falsehood—all of which General Wheeler said he would have tried on the golf course, although the straight-shooting general said he would have lied if necessary.

The Laird story made the front page all over the country, but the *Tribune* ran it on page 14, with emphasis on Laird's defense: "Laird said the bombing was kept secret to protect the lives of American troops and because the Cambodian government would have condemned the raids and demanded a halt to them if they had been made public." The whole thing had a Watergate air about it, with big officials grimly walking a tightrope of legalisms that separated a lie from a "legitimate covert activity."

Nevertheless, the *Trib* dropped the story the next day without bothering to editorialize. That is not so surprising, but it is puzzling that *The New York Times* fell silent also. These papers, each of which often roars about stories that the other plays down, agreed that the Cambodia bombing story was dead.

Sy Hersh had mustered enough skill, passion, and Puritan discipline to keep Cambodia on the front page of the *Times* almost every day from July 15 to July 31, when he reported General Wheeler's Senate testimony that it was President Nixon himself who ordered the secret bombing and the special precautions against disclosure. Having treed the head raccoon, the press hounds had no more ground to cover or questions to ask. It was as if Nixon had personally gone down to the jail to bail out Liddy and his spooks, taking full responsibility for his hit men. The only remaining question was what anybody was going to do about it, and no one was making news on that issue. Hersh went off to report on the CIA's psychological profile of Ellsberg, and returned to the story a week later when the Senate served up more testimony —veterans speaking of hospital bombings, Moses on the deep raids, and Deputy Defense Secretary William P. Clements (who released the Wheeler-Laird memo). After four stories, culminating in the Laird revelations, Hersh left the Cambodia story for good. Thus the reporter who had put more energy and more copy into his first couple of dispatches than the Chicago *Tribune* devoted to an entire month of the scandal joined the *Tribune* on the sidelines, resigned but not indifferent to the demise of the issue. The networks and most other newspapers negotiated a middle course to the drop-off after the Laird story. They leaned heavily on the Senate hearings for drama and photogenic news, didn't bother to go filling in the journalistic cracks, and faded away when the hearings ended for the congressional recess.

*   *   *

I have surveyed the coverage in *The New York Times, Newsweek,* the Chicago *Tribune* and the Los Angeles *Times* in an effort to determine why this scandal bit the dust without a resignation or a lost stripe or even a reasonable amount of political chastisement. My best guess is that the story of the secret bombing fell prey to four great flaws of journalism: no build-up, no news peg, no sex and no hope. There is a normal amount of media sloth and dullness behind these categories, but it seems, on balance, that the coverage was dampened by iron laws more than by the human factor.

NO BUILD-UP

"If there are some disclosures yet to be made, then the story might take off. But if there aren't, it will just die. The whole story came out very quickly."

—William Thomas, editor, Los Angeles *Times*

Experience shows that there are three ways for a President to get rid of a brewing scandal. The first and most popular is to ride it out, saying as little as possible, until the jackals in the press and the political opposition get tired and move on to other things. The second is to confess to all the facts and say you're sorry. The third is to confess to all the facts and say you would do it again.

By most accounts, President Nixon got into trouble on Watergate by sticking to number one when he should have worked in some number two. By the time of the Cambodia disclosures, however, he had gone to school. So when the story appeared to die out after the Laird revelations on August 10, 1973, the President was not fooled. He knew the scandal had created more shock waves in the first month than Watergate had, and that there were still some unanswered questions on the familiar theme of his own personal view of the matter. The press might be playing possum, so the President decided to strike with a strong dose of number three. He took everyone by surprise and brought up the scandal himself—journeying to New Orleans, where he roused the woolhats of the Veterans of Foreign Wars with the proud announcement that he had personally ordered the secret bombing to save American lives in the war that he had ended but not started. He would do it again, he said. And furthermore, it was approved by the American people, such as the father who wrote in to tell the President that he had blamed his son's death on the President's failure to attack the Cambodian sanctuaries, but he no longer blames the President after learning of the clandestine bombing.

Nixon's emotional speech got big play at the Chicago *Tribune,* where the editors had been helping their readers forget the scandal. They were obliged to render their first editorial on the subject, which revealed their tortured position. As much as the *Trib* likes Nixon's war policies, said the editorial painfully, the President's speech avoided the focal issue of secrecy—secret war, secret bombings, secret reports, secret military cadres. The question is not why the bombing, but why the deception. After forcing out this censure, the editors went on to give thanks for the tumultuous reception Nixon received in New Orleans. Although the *Trib* editors seemed sorry that they had to reproach their man in print, they could rejoice privately that he was on politically solid ground.

At *The New York Times,* the editors found themselves in precisely the opposite situation, as they suffered from a classic Pyrrhic victory. They could flagellate the President all they wanted on the nonsense and evasions of the speech, but they were in a hopeless political position. Nixon had erected his battlements around the wisdom of his victorious war policy, and no newsman in his right mind would engage in a printed argument about the Indochina war. No one wanted to hear about it, and it didn't matter that the President had slanted the debate. The scandal was beyond disentanglement. So the editors at the *Times* came forth on August 24 with a long, passionate editorial denouncing the Nixon speech. They made roughly the same points as the *Tribune* editors, but they wrote with the thoroughness and finality of people who did not expect to return to the subject.

Nixon thus forestalled the possibility of a press build-up on the secret bombing. Before the media could make up their mind about the scandal, much less roll out the big artillery, Nixon forced a showdown and won. It takes a long time for a scandal to organize the press. In the *Times* of July 30, which broke the Cambodia scandal in less than a page, there were no less than eight full pages on the Watergate tape controversy—complete with constitutional analyses, a technical guide to the bugging, and so on—plus more than two full pages on the Senate testimony of witnesses like Kalmbach, and one full page previewing the testimony of Ehrlichman and Haldeman. It takes time and commitment for an institution to produce such coverage, and the Cambodia story was stopped up before it had even fermented in the brains of the columnists.

NO NEWS PEG

"I don't know that there's any news in it now . . . Who's going to sue President Nixon for bombing some peasants in Cambodia?"

—Clifton Daniel,
Washington bureau chief, *The New York Times*

To offset the Nixon offensive, the press needed an enormous amount of novel, exciting material to get the matter away from the Nixonian trap of a debate on war policy. But no one came forward to make the news. Senator Hughes of Iowa, who had carried the ball, announced that he was retiring from the Senate to give his life to the Lord, and this ruined him as a news source. No scandal can get anywhere on stories with the obligatory opening: "Senator Harold Hughes (D.-Ia.), who recently announced that he would retire from the Senate to do spiritual work, charged today . . ." Hughes was out, and nobody else cared enough to risk a political neck with the war already over and Watergate brewing away.

"I haven't heard any major politician in this town say anything about Cambodia lately," says Clifton Daniel. "Nobody's making news."

Of course, the news can sometimes get nudged along, but that requires great motivation on the part of the reporters. And most of them felt in tune with the presumed public attitude on Cambodia: so what? "I haven't seen a single piece of paper come across my desk saying let's do something about Cambodia," Daniel explains. "The problem is that there's a 'thank God the war's over' feeling," says Max McCrohon, managing editor of the *Tribune,* in agreement. Even some reporters who like abstract constitutional stories believe that the Cambodia scandal is old hat. The big issues —official lying, secret war, secret bombing—are the issues of the Pentagon Papers, and no one tried to *do* anything about them. The secret bombing is not newsworthy because it contains no fresh constitutional outrages.

The one possible exception here is the issue of the security cliques inside the military. This preoccupied the Senate Armed Services Committee, which had just completed an investigation of the Lavelle case, in which General Lavelle bombed North Vietnam on his own by ordering his subordinates to falsify the bombing reports. He told the pilots that it was all approved by higher-ups, and that the plan was so secret they could not discuss or check it out with anybody. Cambodia was bombed by the same method, except that the President *did* approve the secrecy and the raids—a fact which no one down the line could be sure of.

The Senate was concerned with congressional control of the military, as well as with adequate control *within* the military, but this question did not catch on in the press. It is far too complicated, say the reporters. So the public did not read accounts of the explosive fail-safe controversies at the hearings, such as the following exchange between General Wheeler and Georgia's Senator Sam Nunn:

NUNN: So Major Knight is sitting down here without any knowledge of what is going on, knowingly bombing Cambodia and reporting it as South Vietnam. And yet if you, as Chairman of the Joint Chiefs of Staff, had asked him what he was doing he would not have been able to properly respond and give you accurate information?

WHEELER: That is the way he should have responded. Whether he would or not, I can't say.

NUNN: How can you run an Army with an operation like that?

WHEELER: His next immediate superior is the man for him to break to.

NUNN: General, if there is one break in that link, the whole chain comes falling apart.

WHEELER: It wouldn't fall apart long, in my opinion.

NUNN: It has. In the case of Lavelle, it fell apart for quite awhile.

WHEELER: As I said, that too was corrected in due course.

NUNN: General, in an age of nuclear war, due course is not enough.

The hearings are dotted with these military questions, too abstruse for general consumption. In fact, the military nature of the Cambodia scandal hurts press coverage in several ways. The Pentagon is much less teeming with leaks and sources than CREEP and the FBI were for Watergate. The Armed Services committees have a firm jurisdictional grip on military investigations, and they are known for the gentlemanly, informal approach to disputes with the Pentagon. (Senator Nunn may ask tough questions, but he almost always votes with the uniform and avoids the soapbox.) Also, it is difficult to raise much blood pressure beating the drums against secrecy, because, as *Newsweek*'s Lloyd Norman observes, "the American public generally accepts secrecy in military affairs." Finally, the story is weakened because po-

tential wrongdoing is in the hands of the military command
and the courts-martial, instead of the Justice Department.
Nothing has stimulated reporters like the handcuffs and trial
scenes of Watergate, but there will be no such drama in the
Cambodia scandal because the military will not prosecute.
The Pentagon can be a hostile environment for human interest and hard news.

NO SEX

*"It just isn't sexy enough for the American public to get worked up
over."*
—Lloyd Norman, Pentagon Correspondent, *Newsweek*

The basic building block of Watergate has always been the
original arrest—a stickem-up affair with bugs, burglar's
tools, rubber gloves, mysterious cash, and walkie-talkies. So
the starting point of the scandal was the D.C. poky, and The
Question that rises above the constitutional issues has always
been whether the President was directly associated with that
undignified handcuffing, burned into the consciousness of
every tabloid-reading citizen. The fundamental mistake of
the white-collar criminals in the Nixon administration was
to get involved in a caper with the explosive blue-collar
connotations of *burglary*. Few voters are unable to com-
prehend a crime like that, and most have no trouble relating
to it negatively.

From this sound journalistic foundation, the Watergate
story pushed into a bonanza of scintillating items—laundered money, red wigs, dirty tricks, political espionage,
Perry Mason riddles, the trial, the dramatic letter, the stern
judge, the great shrink heist, NIXON BUGS SELF, Senator
Sam, on and on. Against this panorama of human drama, the
Cambodia scandal pits gray military automatons at work in
the distant reaches of the world. Many people check their
memory to make sure they haven't heard that story four or
five years ago, because over the last seven or eight years they

have become accustomed to that kind of activity as the soft ticking of the metronome of reality. In this case, it's no longer reality anyway, so why work up the discipline for sustained anger?

There's no question that the secret bombing lacks sex appeal, one of the primary raw materials of the press. What tidbits there are have been either overlooked by reporters or passed over for reasons of taste—General Wheeler testifying that the secret bombing, code name MENU, took place in areas of Cambodia designated as BREAKFAST, LUNCH, DINNER, SNACK, and DESSERT. Major Knight's cloak-and-dagger work was second-rate material compared to Watergate.

This issue of the entertainment quotient in journalism is a delicate one for editors. Certainly, they don't think the news and opinion side of the media should merely pander to the crass entertainment needs of the public. If they did, how would we account for all the impenetrable oatmeal on the editorial pages? No, the newspaper or network must stand for something and fulfill serious obligations, and most readers approach a journal like *The New York Times* at least partly with a sense of duty. A story like Cambodia obviously has to go on the duty side of journalism, which is unfortunately not the right channel for a mushrooming scandal. There are no clear answers in the balance between duty and the market, but well-established media should always guard against patronizing their readers by withholding weighty stories on grounds that Nixon used to make the bombing secret in the first place.

The only remote hope for pumping some life into the Cambodia story resides, ironically, in one of the least reported aspects—the possibility that one of the participants will be prosecuted for falsifying military reports. This admittedly occurred, and it is proscribed by Article 107 of the United States Code of Military Justice. At present, however, prosecution has been ruled out and the falsification justified as simply following orders. As Air Force Chief of Staff

George S. Brown told the Armed Services Committee: "For falsification to constitute an offense under Article 107, there must be proof of 'intent to deceive.' This is a legally prescribed element of the offense under the article and is negated when the report is submitted with orders from a higher authority in possession of the true facts." This means that you can lie to Congress and unauthorized superiors if ordered to by an authorized superior.

NO HOPE

"The fact of the matter is that we can't do anything about it."
—Clifton Daniel

Daniel is right: no prosecution means no scandal, which means no reform. The story has been overshadowed by Watergate, sealed off by the military, deflated by public boredom, and bowled over by Nixon. But the secret bombing is still undercovered relative to its importance, and the press has been undersensitive to the military implications of the Lavelle case and the secret raids. While the actual bombings should inflame those who opposed the war, the methods used raise essentially conservative issues—images of haywire plots and secret garrisons, defiance of the constitutional powers of Congress in a scheme so elaborate that even the classified secrets are lies.

The press can always resolve to do better, but it can't necessarily make any difference. Watergate showed that the media can surmount complexity, but Cambodia showed that it is helpless in the face of boredom—that the media can foster justice only so long as the story is prurient. This causes problems as nastiness learns to look dignified and impersonal. For years a drab machine was not even noticed as it poured out its atrocities on Cambodia—where Americans had neither friends, relatives, nor private property to care about.

October 1973

Fugue
for Tinhorns

A pianist who gets good fees and more recital dates than he wants told me one night a while back that he had spent the whole day wrestling with a short passage in a Charles Ives sonata that was so hard he thought Paul Jacobs could not play it at sight. Jacobs is an associate professor of music at Brooklyn College and the New York Philharmonic's pianist whenever the programs include Stravinsky's *Petrouchka,* Copland's *Appalachian Spring,* Shostakovich's *First Symphony,* or any of the few dozen other orchestral scores that have piano parts. Pierre Boulez was the leader of the avantgarde pack Jacobs ran with in Paris in the fifties until Leonard Bernstein hired him into the Philharmonic twelve years ago. "You're the one who plays all Schoenberg from memory," Bernstein said when they met. "How do you know that?" Jacobs asked. "Nadia told me," the conductor answered. That's Nadia Boulanger, eighty-seven, who was as *grise* an *eminence* in twentieth-century music then as Bernard Berenson in Italian Renaissance art.

And that's as many-headed a name-drop as ever gets fitted into such a tight space. But it is all I will offer here to support the claim that Jacobs knows a territory. His is the Schoenberg-Berg-Webern repertoire, which is far more discussed than studied—although not because the scores and recordings are inaccessible. Some of it was composed sixty-five years back, but 12-tone or tone row tunes still won't whistle. Mozart arias hang in the memory like "Adeste Fideles," but Schoenberg's *Five Piano Pieces*, Opus 23, are as easy to keep locked in the brain as any twenty-five pages of *Finnegans Wake*. Which makes writing reviews of recitals in that repertoire a risk-ridden night's work if Paul Jacobs is in the hall and checking what he hears against what the critics write.

He was in Alice Tully Hall at Lincoln Center October 23, 1973, when it was close to filled for the New York debut of thirty-six-year-old Marie-Françoise Bucquet. She is the sporty Parisian who started her career in New York last fall with not just one recital of twentieth-century piano music, but with four of them in a series of programs covering the territory from Schoenberg-Berg-Webern to Boulez-Berio-Stockhausen. All those seats in Tully could not be filled by armed force for such fare. But a real smoke-blowing promotion might do the trick, especially if the press could seem to be causing the stir instead of being stirred by it or by the lady on the top line of the program reading, "Alix Williamson Presents."

About half of Bucquet's first-nighters were promoted into coming by Alix Williamson and the other half were coming to see who had been promoted into coming. The objectively curious landed in the short line at the box office. Once inside Tully Hall they found the premises lightly papered but otherwise resplendent with big presences from the A-plus list Virgil Thomson called "The Intellectual Audience." Its members are the big presences who feel summoned to such recitals when the word has been passed that even bigger presences will appear, the biggest one in sight that night being Virgil Thomson himself.

Few debut recitals get more than a line in the week's listings, and unknowns playing unknowables often fail to get that shred. But two weeks before Bucquet's entrance, Alan

Rich, *New York*'s critic, pointed to a new Stockhausen-Berio record of hers and wrote that it was "enough to convince me not to miss these concerts . . . Miss Bucquet has a flair for this kind of hard work that goes beyond most of her colleagues." A week before the live show opened, *New York Times* critic John Rockwell fixed his endorsement on her Stockhausen-Berio disk as well as another she filled with Stravinsky pieces. "Miss Bucquet is clearly a pianist of stature with a mind of her own," Rockwell wrote, "and these two disks do succeed in whetting one's appetite for her forthcoming concerts."

Two days before the first of them, there was her picture in the *Times* surrounded by a short interview by Raymond Ericson, an old hand on the paper's music staff. Macy's had taken full-page ads in years past to bow in corporate tribute to the Metropolitan Opera, The New York Philharmonic, The Royal Ballet from London and other establishments of that rank; and a week before Bucquet played in New York, Macy's devoted a page to her. She was an hour-long guest in Robert Sherman's "Listening Room" on the *Times*'s radio station, WQXR, where the host and the guest passed the time admiring her records. Her picture had been emplaced in the vitrines outside Tully Hall months before she appeared to perform, and there she was again as a window display at Rizzoli's—the very toniest bookstore in New York. Alix Williamson made all that happen, and good for her; she's not in the aesthetic judgment dodge.

So many inflated reputations based on imported records have collapsed on the recital stages here in years past that the record industry is now armed with a cautionary jape about the species Promising Young Pianist. Goes this way: Another PYP arrives at his record producer's (i.e., tape splicer's) office to hear how 865 separate slips of iron oxide coating have been melded into one seamless toccata. As the tape unwinds, the PYP is mute with delight. "Marvelous, isn't it?" the producer-splicer intrudes. "Don't you wish you could play like that?"

Instead of dispatching John Rockwell with his whetted appetite to the Bucquet debut in Tully Hall, the *Times* sent Donal Henahan to decide whether Bucquet in the flesh measured up to the Parisian of the disk. Two days later, on October 25, he turned up in print to report that Bucquet had "put one on notice that she can get around the keyboard with the very best of contemporary music specialists. Further, she demonstrated a rare instinct for bringing out the lyrical aspects of nontonal works *without undercutting the design and structure of the music.*"

Leave Henahan with that and regard Alan Rich's assessment. "The combination of her masterful playing and an audience that was rapturously in tune with the entire evening," he wrote in *New York,* November 13, "made this one of the most triumphant recitals, and certainly one of the most spectacular debuts I have attended in eons." Along the way he emitted such whoops as "sensational artist" and "phenomenally gifted and *totally at home in new music.*"

Leave Rich with that and consider Paul Jacobs, who was not rapturously in tune with the entire evening, as Rich was, nor as convinced as Henahan that Bucquet could get around the keyboard with the very best of contemporary music specialists. Jacobs suffered Henahan's encomium in silence until Rich's appeared. Then he did a charitable thing. He called Rich and Henahan to offer them some instruction on the Schoenberg he knew and they didn't and they knew he knew they didn't. The performance Bucquet listed in the program as Schoenberg's Opus 11 was unrecognizable, he told them. The Opus 23 he recognized. That was because it contained, in his considered judgment, 10 percent of the right notes. "The rest of the time she just flailed around like a four-year-old banging away aimlessly at the keys," he said. Rich did not quarrel with Jacobs, of course, but he lamented his timing. "Why did you wait until my piece was in print to tell me this?" Rich asked, as Jacobs remembers it. When he had made the same points to Henahan, the *Times* man allowed that he would have taken the scores with him but the lights are so dim in Tully Hall that reading music there is often impossible. "I'm not trying to make a vendetta because it would be to my disadvantage," Jacobs said, "and I'm absolutely not jealous of anybody's career. If Van Cliburn makes ten thousand dollars a concert and I make two hundred and fifty, there is obviously some disparity between us. We do different things." He added: "What I resent is that music written in 1908, which should be in the public consciousness, is still such a mystery to the critics that they don't know when they are hearing something almost totally different from what Schoenberg wrote. Time will tell whether he is a composer the equal of any, and you may or may not like what he wrote, but Schoenberg certainly is one of the most influential figures in the history of music, and the critics might as well know something about him."

Jacobs was to play the Opus 11 at a Brooklyn College concert a few days later, and he invited both Rich and Henahan to come and hear what had been composed. With the lights up and the scores in hand, it would have been their chance to run a few retaliatory shafts through their tormentor. Seventy-five interested locals were in a hall seating five hundred, though neither critic showed up for a lesson from the master. After that a kind of *nolo contendere* calm set in between Henahan and Jacobs, while others at the *Times* took their turns at Bucquet.

Allen Hughes writing of Bucquet II on November 20 found her program of Stockhausen, Berio, Bussotti and Webern, which she and Alix Williamson subtitled "The New Piano in Europe," revealed nothing new about the piano anywhere. But he decided that the pianist was "at home with their musical and technical demands and that she made them a pleasure to hear and contemplate." Late in December, the *Times's* record editor, Peter Davis, gave the back of his hand to both a Stravinsky record Bucquet made and to her Stockhausen-Berio. That was after deploring her "washed-out tone and inability to give the notes real rhythmic or formal definition" in a recording of the complete Schoenberg piano music. Davis reminded *Times* readers that this unacceptable work was done by the well-publicized Parisian with the fuss now rising around her. "According to several outraged musicians present at her first concert," he wrote, "pages of Schoenberg's piano music were being desperately improvised on the spot and no one noticed it." At the *Times,* he meant, nodding at Henahan. Davis had heard from Jacobs.

Bucquet III, on January 13, 1974, a night of Berg, Stravinsky, Boulez and Bartók, was covered for the *Times* by Raymond Ericson, who found her disappointing. "She muddled through many passages, dropping or repeating measures, improvising in order to get a piece on track again," he wrote. "More disheartening was the lack of a basic rhythm and a constant nervous phrasing that made four totally different works sound colorless or alike." Ericson had it right, Jacobs said, even though the Philharmonic's pianist didn't get to the Frenchwoman's performance.

In *The Nation,* critic David Hamilton whacked away at Miss Bucquet's opening-night Schoenberg for its memory slips and cover-up improvisations as they were described to him by "a reliable witness" who was, of course, Paul Jacobs. Hamilton works at many stands—the *Times, The Nation, The New Yorker,* the *Musical Newsletter* and others. It was in *High Fidelity* that he found Bucquet's account of Stravinsky's *Waltz Pour Les Enfants* a failure. "I'm sure you know a child who can play it quite well," he wrote, cozying up to his readers, one of the most admiring of them being Paul Jacobs. "David is certainly one of the most conscientious critics around and one of the most intelligent," he told me when I sounded him out on the rest of the working class in which he found many failures. "Hamilton goes to rehearsals with the score to really find out something more about the music. Is there anybody else in New York who does his homework?"—he put the question to himself without any shoves from me. "Can't think of anybody" was the answer he came up with. But what of Ericson?

Only Alan Rich is in print on Paul Jacobs, a friend last

heard being fervent on the telephone. "I got a fervent phone call a while back from a friend who is a highly regarded authority on contemporary music," Rich wrote in the December 10 issue of *New York.* "Did I know, he asked, that Marie-Françoise Bucquet's playing of Schoenberg's piano music was full of distortions of rhythm and even of notes? I *didn't* know. As a critic I am supposed to know, from study and experience, about the outlines of any given style, and also what constitutes communication in the concert hall; Mlle. Bucquet's playing satisfies me on these levels. When I have heard the music of Schoenberg performed as often as I have the Beethoven sonatas, I will be ready to discuss specific distortions." And until then, presumably, pianists playing Schoenberg for Rich can rest assured that any old doodling will do.

Time printed not a word about the great uncovering of the music critics. *Newsweek* waited until most of the blows had landed before proposing the Legion of Honor and kisses on both cheeks for Bucquet. But before deciding on her reward, Hubert Saal, *Newsweek*'s music man, started the pianist pondering on her case and making it, word by word, seem worse. She admitted to a few memory slips at the recitals but insisted that she improvised nothing. "Anyone who could improvise Schoenberg would be a genius," she said modestly, before explaining why. "There are always two or three tone rows going on at once," she told Saal, who then neglected to remind her, or his readers, that not a piece Schoenberg wrote has more than one tone row. Just before he wanted the kissing to start, she tossed off another perception that he may have missed in his understandable haste. "Beethoven will survive me," he quoted her saying right there on page 75 of the February 4 issue. "But I'm always afraid that Stockhausen or Boulez or Xenakis won't." Out here in readerland that sounded like the lady appealing to herself to lay off contemporary music. If the appeal turns to pledge, there are composers she has named who would even join in the kissing.

I went over all this with Bucquet at the bar of The Ginger

Man during a long talk we had just before she left town. Her attitudes come and go, double back and contradict, and out of many things she said one hangs in the memory the way Schoenberg doesn't—not in mine anyway, and evidently not in hers, either. What she thinks, this pretty big operator from Paris, is that Paul Jacobs is a much better pianist in her repertoire than she is. After she had learned all about the ruin he had made of her stay here, she thought quite seriously about taking herself to him and getting some instruction on playing Opus 23. Maybe that's a reason *Newsweek* should give her a medal. And maybe she could have taken Rich and Henahan with her.

One last thing. Bucquet IV, on January 29, 1974, was passed altogether by the *Times,* and just about all of the populace. The pianist ended the night, the series, her big fling in New York, with Franz Liszt's fat, boring transcription of *La Marseillaise,* a supremely silly recessional. After which, *allons enfants,* not a one covered with *la gloire.*

March 1974

MICHAEL DORMAN

Plantation Justice in Lynchburg

Shortly after 7 P.M. on December 5, 1962, Annie Lee Carter, a white, fifty-nine-year-old spinster, left her apartment in Lynchburg, Virginia, and began walking to a prayer meeting at a Baptist church. Rain was falling, and, despite the hour the streets seemed almost deserted. When Miss Carter got within half a block of the church, she later reported, someone grabbed her from behind, dragged her beneath the limbs of a nearby fir tree and raped her.

The attack touched off a manhunt described as the most intensive in the history of Lynchburg, a city of 55,000 persons in the foothills of the Blue Ridge mountains. Miss Carter was able to provide only a vague description of her assailant, saying he was "a Negro with big ears." Nonetheless, three days after the attack, the police arrested Thomas Carlton Wansley and charged him with the crime. Wansley was seventeen years old, short, slender and black. He had never before been in trouble with the law. His I.Q. had been calculated at somewhere between 71 and 78, a range described as "mentally defective." He had dropped out of school after failing the seventh grade for the second time and had taken an eighteen-dollar-a-week job as a dishwasher at a small restaurant.

Wansley's arrest precipitated what some observers, including a federal judge involved in the case, consider one of the most flagrant examples of trial by newspaper in recent American history. As one result, Wansley has spent more than ten years behind bars—part of the time under a death sentence. The case is still in the courts at this writing, chiefly because of the behavior of Lynchburg's two daily newspapers, the morning *News* and the evening *Advance.*

The dailies are jointly owned by the family of the late Carter Glass, the former Virginia senator who served as Woodrow Wilson's Secretary of the Treasury. Glass, known as "the Unreconstructed Rebel" and "the Father of the Federal Reserve System," ruled Lynchburg as an oligarchy for more than four decades. And, since his death in 1946, his descendants have kept Lynchburg's power structure conservative and segregationist.

At the time of Wansley's arrest, the *News* and *Advance* were run by Glass's grandson, Carter Glass III, who held the title of general manager. Under his leadership, the papers were openly racist in both their news and editorial columns. Civil rights leaders were regularly branded as "agitators." The accomplishments of local blacks, if mentioned at all, were dismissed in a few lines. But crimes committed by blacks were given extensive play. The deaths of local blacks, no matter how prominent, could not find their way into the papers' obituary columns. They were noted only if paid classified ads were bought by funeral directors.

The Wansley case—representing as it did the classic theme of a black accused of raping a Southern white woman— prompted extraordinary news coverage even by previous Lynchburg standards. Shortly after the attack, but before Wansley's arrest, the *News* carried a story warning Lynchburg women against walking the streets alone after dark. It quoted a police captain who described Miss Carter's assailant as "a maniac" and said, "He must be caught before something more horrible happens." By that time, police were also attributing to Miss Carter's unknown attacker two previous unsolved cases—the reported rape of a Japanese-American woman and an attempted rape of a white woman.

When Wansley was arrested, the *News* spread stories and pictures on his capture across eight columns, with little pretense that he was presumed innocent until convicted. A boldface box accompanying the main news story began: "Commonwealth Attorney Royston Jester 3rd, who has worked unceasingly with police in their search for the Negro rapist that recently terrorized the city, commended Police Department efforts following the arrest of Thomas Carlton Wansley Saturday afternoon. Jester said: 'I am sure I express the heartfelt thanks of all the citizens of Lynchburg for the accomplishment of the Police Department in solving this horrible series of crimes recently committed upon several women of this community.'" The main news story also assumed Wansley's guilt, stating clearly unproved allegations as facts. One sentence referring to the assault on Miss Carter, for example, said that Wansley "held a knife to the throat of the middle-aged woman with a worded threat to kill her if she made a sound." Coverage by the *Advance* followed the pattern set by its sister paper. It published a picture of Wansley with a bold-face caption that said bluntly: RAPIST CAUGHT.

Following his arrest, Wansley was questioned intensively for five hours without being allowed to call his family or a lawyer. During that period, police claimed, he confessed committing the two alleged rapes and the attempted rape. Wansley denies the claim. He insists he told the police he had committed no crime, that he knew nothing about the rape of Miss Carter or the attempted rape of the other white woman. He concedes having sexual relations with the Japanese-American woman, Mrs. Kyoko Fleshman, but maintains she consented.

Since Wansley was only seventeen, he was originally handled as a juvenile and placed under the jurisdiction of Lynchburg's Juvenile and Domestic Relations Court. After being questioned by the police, he was jailed and interrogated further by the city's chief juvenile probation officer, Lee A. Read. Under Virginia law, Read's position toward Wansley was supposed to be parallel to that of a parent; Wansley was considered under his protection. Read telephoned Wansley's mother and summoned her to the jail, where he explained the three charges. Later, when Wansley's mother was permitted to see her son in Read's presence, she asked during a long conversation: "Buddy, did you do it?" Wansley replied, "Yes." He contends that his answer referred only to a question on whether he had sexual relations with Mrs. Fleshman. But the prosecution later maintained in court that the answer referred to all the charges against him. And, despite Read's semiparental role in the case, his account of the incident was admitted in evidence against Wansley.

The contention that Wansley had confessed to all the crimes was accepted and published as fact by the Lynchburg newspapers. They referred to him repeatedly as a "confessed rapist" or "the Negro rapist." When Wansley appeared in court for a preliminary hearing, the *News* reported that he was confronted there "by one of his women *victims.*" (Emphasis added.)

Although Wansley was a juvenile, he was denied the right to be tried as such. After a hearing, Juvenile Court Judge Earl Wingo—giving no reason for the decision—ruled that Wansley would have to stand trial as an adult in Lynchburg Corporation Court. The decision was crucial, since it meant that, if convicted of the rape charges, Wansley could be sentenced to death. If tried as a juvenile, the most severe punishment he could have received would have been confinement in a reformatory until he reached twenty-one.

Wansley was indicted in January 1963 on charges of raping Miss Carter and Mrs. Fleshman and of stealing Miss Carter's purse, containing twelve cents and two bus tokens. The charge of attempted rape of a third woman was ultimately dismissed. Reuben Lawson, a black attorney from Roanoke, Virginia, became Wansley's defense lawyer—the first of several who would eventually handle the case.

On February 8, 1963, two months after his arrest, Wansley went on trial before Corporation Court Judge O. Raymond Cundiff on the charges of raping and robbing Miss Carter. No court stenographer was present to record the proceedings. Lawson argued that it would be unconscionable to try a death-penalty case without a stenographer, since the absence of a transcript would severely impede any appeal of a possible conviction, but Judge Cundiff overruled his objection. An all-white, all-male jury was quickly chosen.

Miss Carter testified in detail about the rape and robbery. But when asked if she could identify Wansley as her assailant, she admitted she could not. She said he "looked like" the attacker, but that she was "not too sure." Policemen testified that Wansley had confessed the crimes—a contention disputed by Lawson. Aside from the contested confession, no evidence was presented to connect Wansley with the crimes. Wansley did not testify.

Commonwealth attorney Jester told the jurors in his summation that if they failed to convict Wansley and sentence him to death, it would mean Lynchburg residents "can't walk safely upon the public streets." The jury deliberated for an hour and forty-one minutes, then gave Jester the verdict he had sought. It convicted Wansley of both charges—sentencing him to death in the rape case and twenty years in prison in the robbery case. Judge Cundiff scheduled Wansley's execution in Virginia's electric chair for June 7, 1963. The entire trial had taken less than a day.

The following week Wansley was tried on the charge of raping Mrs. Fleshman, a mother of four. Mrs. Fleshman testified that he had raped her in the bedroom of her home. Although she contended she had tried to resist him, she conceded that two of her children had remained asleep beside her throughout the purported attack. Wansley took the stand to testify that he had known Mrs. Fleshman for some time and that she had readily consented to have intercourse with him. He said that, after having relations with him, Mrs.

Fleshman asked him to repair a broken slat in her bed, which he said he did. Following that, he testified, the two of them sat and talked in her kitchen for more than an hour. When he left he promised to return in a few days with a package of her favorite cigarettes, he said.

The second trial was also heard by an all-male, all-white jury that was asked to render a death sentence. Judge Cundiff, in his instructions to the jurors, cautioned them that Wansley could be freed on parole if they gave him any sentence less than death. They quickly returned with a verdict of guilty and a sentence of death.

Defense attorney Lawson died before he could file any appeals. By that time, Dr. Martin Luther King, Jr., had taken an interest in the case. He asked New York civil-liberties lawyer William M. Kunstler, who often represented Dr. King and other civil-rights leaders, to become Wansley's attorney. Kunstler agreed and was joined as co-counsel by Philip Hirschkop, a civil-liberties lawyer from Alexandria, Virginia, and Charles Mangum, a Lynchburg attorney. All volunteered to serve without fees. They filed appeals of all three convictions with the Virginia Supreme Court. Wansley's scheduled execution was stayed by the appeals. Meanwhile, he was kept in the state prison at Richmond.

Kunstler's entry into the case set off a concentrated campaign of vilification in the *News* and *Advance*. The campaign centered on what the newspapers claimed was Kunstler's record of connection "with Communist-front organizations and efforts." On August 31, 1964, after Kunstler had appeared at a Lynchburg rally intended to raise funds to pay Wansley's court costs, the *Advance* carried a lengthy story headlined: KUNSTLER HAS RECORD OF COMMIE FRONT LINKS. The story began:

> William M. Kunstler, New York attorney who spoke here Sunday in behalf of the Wansley Defense Fund, has on numerous occasions been linked with Communist-front organizations and efforts. Information into the

more recent activities of Kunstler has been made available from the files of the House Committee on Un-American Activities through Rep. William M. Tuck of Virginia's Fifth District and a member of the committee.

Additional sources of information cited in the article included an American Legion publication, *Firing Line,* and a self-styled "Americanism" organization in Port Chester, New York, calling itself the Citizens Alert Committee. Among other allegations made against Kunstler in the story, which stretched more than twenty-six column inches, were the following:

On June 20, 1960, Kunstler's name appeared as one of the signers of an advertisement in *The New York Times* asking clemency for Morton Sobell, still serving a 30-year federal prison sentence for espionage. . . .

On April 21, 1961, Kunstler was a speaker at the "Rally to Abolish the House Un-American Activities Committee" held in New York. . . .

In the March 1962 issue of *The Southern Patriot* (page 4) a photograph showed Kunstler and other individuals at a reception in New York. . . . *The Southern Patriot* on June 17, 1947, was tagged a Communist-front publication by the House Committee on Un-American Activities. . . . The photograph's caption identified Kunstler as an American Civil Liberties Union lawyer who handles many southern civil rights cases. The House of Representatives on Jan. 17, 1931, cited the American Civil Liberties Union as "closely affiliated with the Communist movement in the United States and fully 90% of its efforts are on behalf of Communists who have come into difficulty with the law."

The Congressional Record, May 1, 1962, listed Kunstler as among the signers of *The New York Times* advertisement, Feb 22, 1962, attacking the House Committee

on Un-American Activities and seeking its "abolition."
Interestingly, that advertisement was photographically
reproduced and published in the Mar. 4, 1962, issue of
The Worker. . . .

The article went on to cite as "evidence" against Kunstler
the fact that his wife had served as Westchester County, New
York, coordinator of a civil-rights march on Washington. In
virtually every subsequent news story dealing with the case,
the *News* and *Advance* inserted a sentence—usually in boldface type—that said: "Kunstler has been linked on numerous
occasions with Communist-front organizations and efforts."
Beyond that, almost any time Kunstler's name appeared on
the Associated Press wires in connection with any *other* case,
the papers made it a point to carry the story with an editor's
note pointing out that he was Wansley's lawyer and repeating the Communist-front allegations. Sometimes, the wire
story would contain only a single obscure reference to Kunstler and the editor's note would run several times as long as
his mention in the story.

One *Advance* article, for example, bore a three-column
head that read: WANSLEY LAWYER DEFENDS SNCC ON
CHARGES OF PLANNING RIOTS. The story carried a three-
paragraph, boldface precede that began: "(Editor's note—
William Kunstler of New York, mentioned in the story below, is an attorney for Lynchburg Negro Thomas Carlton
Wansley. . . .)" The precede went on to say that Wansley
was a "convicted rapist" and repeated the Communist-front
charge against Kunstler. The AP story that followed, which
was eleven paragraphs long, concerned a Nashville federal
court hearing in which the Student Nonviolent Coordinating
Committee (SNCC) was challenging Tennessee antiriot laws.
It contained only one sentence, in the ninth paragraph, referring to a question asked by Kunstler—who represented
SNCC.

Another *Advance* story, running fourteen paragraphs,
concerned the late Representative Adam Clayton Powell's

fight against being denied his House seat. Kunstler, one of Powell's several lawyers, was mentioned in only two sentences near the story's end. But the article contained a two-paragraph, boldface editor's note describing his role in the Wansley case and the Communist-front allegations. When Kunstler entered the case of the late Jack Ruby after Ruby had been convicted of murdering Lee Harvey Oswald, the *News* wrote its own 18-inch story, headlined: WANSLEY'S LAWYER WOULD REPRESENT OSWALD'S SLAYER. The article began: "The attorney of a twice-convicted Lynchburg rapist is in Dallas in an effort to represent Jack Ruby in an upcoming sanity hearing for the man who killed the assassin of President Kennedy." Again, the story repeated the Communist-front charges.

While the Lynchburg newspapers continued their attacks on Kunstler and Wansley, the Virginia Supreme Court overturned Wansley's convictions on September 11, 1964. The court ruled that Judge Cundiff had violated Wansley's rights in both the Carter and Fleshman cases. In the Carter case, it held that Cundiff had improperly jeopardized Wansley's right to an appeal by refusing to have a court stenographer present during the trial. In the Fleshman case, the court ruled that Cundiff had given unfair instructions to the jurors when he told them Wansley would be eligible for parole unless sentenced to death. The appeals court returned the cases to Cundiff's court for retrial.

Although the appeals court decision concerned substantial issues, the Lynchburg newspapers attributed the ruling to mere "procedural errors." The *Advance,* for example, reported: "Wansley's appeals to the state court had centered more on legal technicalities than on his guilt or innocence." When the cases were returned to Lynchburg, the prosecution ultimately decided to dismiss the charge that Wansley had raped Mrs. Fleshman. That left him facing only the charges of raping and robbing Miss Carter. Despite the reversal of the convictions and the dismissal of the Fleshman case, the *News* and *Advance* continued to call him a "twice-convicted rapist." Since Wansley then stood convicted of nothing, his lawyers asked Cundiff to release him on bail while awaiting retrial on the Carter charges. Cundiff refused, although he had previously released on bail a white man convicted of raping a Negro. He explained the white man's release by saying, "That was statutory rape of a prostitute." The so-called "prostitute" to whom he referred was eleven years old.

Wansley's lawyers also asked Cundiff to transfer the retrial to another Virginia city on the ground that the Lynchburg papers' coverage of the case had been so prejudicial he could not get a fair trial there. In support of their change-of-venue motion, they submitted affidavits from one hundred and sixty-four Lynchburg residents who said the "extraordinary amount of inflammatory and prejudicial" coverage made an impartial trial impossible in the city. Cundiff conducted a hearing on the motion in August 1965. Among the witnesses subpoenaed by the defense were Carter Glass III and several editors and reporters of the *News* and *Advance.* All agreed that the published allegations against Kunstler were based on information from Glass's personal files. Kunstler's questioning of Glass contained the following exchanges:

QUESTION: What brought me to your attention?
ANSWER: Your Communist and Communist-front activities.
Q. Why me?
A. Because I have accumulated a file on every Communist and Communist-front individual that appeared in our newspaper. . . . I am interested in the background of all Communists and Communist-fronters.
Q. Are you stating I am a Communist?
A. I said I am interested in the Communists.
Q. If you think I am a Communist, say so honestly.
A. I don't know, sir. I haven't seen the records of the Communist Party.
Q. All right, sir. Neither have I, so we're even. If I am not

a Communist, I must be a Communist sympathizer, is that correct?

A. Your record shows that conclusively to me. . . .

Q. Do you have any information personally about me other than what you say you got from reading *The Daily Worker*—which I don't read but you obviously do—or from the congressional reports, which I do read, or from the files or reports of your congressman or the Senate Internal Security Committee? Outside of these hearsay reports, do you have anything in your own knowledge about me?

A. I don't know you, sir.

Q. You have never investigated me yourself, have you?

A. I have not, sir.

Q. You are relying on what *The Daily Worker* says, are you not, about me?

A. In part.

Q. You are relying on what Senator [James] Eastland might say?

A. In part.

Q. And what Representative Tuck might say?

A. In part.

Q. So all of your information—lock, stock and barrel—is hearsay. As a lawyer, you know this, do you not?

A. That's correct, sir. . . .

Q. Did you furnish the reporters from your files information which in turn got into the newspaper and has furnished the background information for each of these stories?

A. Yes.

Q. Then I understand you correctly are the original source of information?

A. The original source of information was my files. . . .

In arguing his change-of-venue motion, Kunstler told Judge Cundiff that the Lynchburg papers had attacked him in an attempt to "destroy" Wansley. "That is the only purpose of printing this material," he said. "It has no news value relevancy to the case other than the attempt to destroy this man's life. And that's why it's being used here. And Mr. Glass, as he says, uses his so-called subversive files in this as a racial case—a capital-crime case—in order to make every man who sits in the jury box suspect this man is being defended from Moscow. . . . I have never seen or read of articles so deliberately designed to prejudice a client of mine, and I have been with some very controversial clients."

Cundiff denied the motion for a change of venue and another motion that he disqualify himself, on grounds of prejudice, from presiding over the retrial. The *News* then published an editorial—headlined RED HERRINGS—that repeated the Communist-front allegations and accused Kunstler of trying "to use the Lynchburg newspapers as whipping boys to divert attention from the crimes of which his client is charged."

A second trial on the charges involving Miss Carter ended in a hung jury in October 1966. A third trial was scheduled for March 1967. By that time Wansley—who still stood convicted of nothing—had been behind bars more than four years. Cundiff again refused to move the trial to another city or disqualify himself. When the third trial got under way, Kunstler and Hirschkop questioned prospective jurors closely about their attitudes resulting from news coverage of the case. More than sixty prospective jurors were questioned, virtually all of whom said they read one or both of the Lynchburg papers. Most of them, including several eventually seated as jurors, said they believed the allegations against Kunstler. Some said they would consider Wansley guilty until proved innocent. Once again the jury was composed entirely of whites.

In this trial, Miss Carter—contradicting her previous testimony—said she was now able to identify Wansley as her assailant. Asked by Kunstler to explain her change of mind, she conceded her identification was based on the many times she had seen Wansley in court and viewed his picture in the newspapers. It was at this trial that Probation Officer Read testified for the first time about overhearing the conversation in which Wansley told his mother he did "it." Kunstler demanded a mistrial, claiming such testimony was improper in view of Read's supposedly semiparental role toward Wansley. When the motion was denied, Kunstler contended —as Wansley has consistently done—that the statement to his mother referred only to his relations with Mrs. Fleshman. The jury deliberated five hours before finding Wansley guilty on both charges. This time he was sentenced to life imprisonment on the rape charge and twenty years on the robbery charge. The defense appealed, and Wansley remained in prison

Following the third trial, the *News* and *Advance* were subjected to sharp criticism from both inside and outside Lynchburg. *Time, Newsweek, Life,* the Washington *Post,* among other publications, wrote scathing pieces about the papers' coverage of the Wansley case and of racial issues in general. A Washington *Post* editorial said: "The atmosphere in Lynchburg is what lawyers mean when they talk of 'trial by newspaper.' When a city is inflamed, the fairness of the court proceeding is always in question." In Lynchburg, the campus newspaper of Randolph-Macon Woman's College also assailed the coverage of the case by the *News* and *Advance.* The local papers responded by calling the *Post* "an extreme socialist publication" and by accusing the campus newspaper of "parroting to perfection the Communist line."

Perhaps the most serious blow to the prestige of the *News* and *Advance* came when sixty-seven of Lynchburg's most prominent citizens issued an open letter making clear that the newspapers' racial policies had grown too extreme even for the city's conservative white power structure. The open letter accused the papers of fomenting "frustration and bitterness" in the black community. "To persist in these policies can only be destructive of the general morale as well as the reputation of our community," it said. The *News* characteristically answered the letter with an attack of its own, accusing the letter's signers of a plot to take over the papers. In an editorial, the *News* described the open letter as an invitation to outside racial agitators.

Meanwhile, the papers continued their campaign against Kunstler and Wansley. On June 2, 1967—while Kunstler was seeking a new trial for Wansley—the *Advance* published its longest attack on Kunstler to date. The article, headlined KUNSTLER CONTINUES TO BE LINKED WITH COMMIE FRONT ORGANIZATIONS, filled almost four columns on one page and most of another column on a jump page. It began: "Attorney William M. Kunstler of New York has continued to be linked with Communist front organizations and efforts since he took over the legal defense of convicted Negro rapist Thomas Carlton Wansley and turned the case into a national racial cause célèbre." Then followed another listing of Kunstler's supposed left-wing connections, many of which once again repeated previous allegations.

While Wansley remained in prison, Kunstler, Hirschkop and Mangum appealed the new convictions through the Virginia state courts. The main points in their appeals were that the trials had been "conducted in what was clearly a prejudiced atmosphere"; that the Lynchburg newspapers had deliberately tried to create such an atmosphere; that the grand jurors who indicted Wansley had been improperly chosen since the grand-jury list did not contain an adequate number of blacks; that the probation officer should not have been permitted to testify about the supposed "confession"; and that Judge Cundiff should have disqualified himself. The Virginia Supreme Court, which had reversed the previous convictions, upheld the new ones. The defense lawyers then asked a U.S. District Court in Richmond for a writ of habeas corpus overturning the convictions on the grounds appealed in the state courts—especially the charge of prejudicial publicity. On January 1, 1973, Federal Judge Robert Merhige, Jr., reversed the convictions in a decision that excoriated the *News* and *Advance.* Merhige wrote:

The record before this court is shocking as to the nature and amount of prejudicial pretrial publicity given the matters by the Lynchburg press. The court finds that said publicity emanating from the Lynchburg newspapers was both inflammatory and highly prejudicial to the petitioner [Wansley] as well as to one of his counsel, William Kunstler. Reference to his counsel obviously contributed to the totality of circumstances making the trial one violative of the principles of a fair trial. . . . As to the petitioner himself, the newspapers consistently referred to him, prior to the third trial, as a "twice-convicted rapist," even though Wansley's two rape convictions had been overturned

After reviewing the papers' repeated allegations against Kunstler and the record of the questioning of prospective jurors, Merhige wrote: "In such an atmosphere, the court finds that as a matter of law it is well nigh impossible for prospective jurors to possess the 'indifference' required for an impartial hearing . . . The trial court's refusal to grant a change of venue was fatal to Wansley's right to a fair and open trial." Merhige also upheld defense contentions that racial discrimination had been used in selecting the grand jurors who indicted Wansley and that Probation Officer Read's testimony had been improper. The prosecution appealed Merhige's decision to the U.S. Fourth Circuit Court of Appeals.

When Lynchburg's Judge Cundiff again refused to free Wansley on bail—saying such a release would "endanger the safety of every woman in Virginia"—he was overruled by Judge Merhige. The federal judge ordered Wansley released on $10,000 bond. Thus, on January 17, 1973, Wansley became a free man for the first time in more than ten years. He had entered prison as a boy of seventeen; he left it as a man of twenty-eight.

He had educated himself behind bars, earning both junior-high and high school equivalency diplomas. He had also become a leader of a group of Virginia convicts seeking to reform the state's prisons. As a result of a lawsuit brought by the group, Virginia's prison director had been ordered by a federal court to pay Wansley and several other convicts $21,265 for subjecting them to "cruel and inhuman punishment." The punishment described by the court included bread-and-water diets, arbitrary use of tear gas, extended periods of solitary confinement, "placing prisoners naked in a hot, roach-infested cell and taping, chaining or handcuffing inmates to cell bars." When Wansley was released on bond, Merhige placed him under the supervision of J. J. Franklin, an ex-convict who runs a rehabilitation program in Richmond. Wansley works there in a community center on behalf of a prison-reform group, the Prisoners Solidarity Committee.

I interviewed Wansley at the community center in March 1973. He is a slender man with an erect carriage who wears horn-rimmed glasses and keeps his hair in a semi-Afro cut. He looked stylish that day in a blue and white turtleneck sweater, blue and white checked bell-bottom slacks and tan ankle-height boots. Hanging from his neck was a medallion depicting a tribal African's head, which he explained was made "by a white guy in The Walls who wanted me to have it."

For a man whose I.Q. had been described as in the "mentally defective" range, he spoke articulately about events of the past ten years. His conversation was sprinkled liberally with such terms as "restructuring society" and "reeducating the public." Asked about his reaction to being released, he said, "I walked around in a daze for two days. Every time I walked up the street, I kept turning around and looking for a guard. I couldn't believe I was out."

He said he planned to devote his life to prison reform and to "restructuring society." As for Lynchburg, he said, "I think Lynchburg's a nice place. There's nothing wrong with Lynchburg. The power structure there just has to be restructured; it's got to get away from a lot of false beliefs—such as racism. People there don't know they have prejudices, but they do. Reeducation has to be done to give people true values—rather than fantasies. I couldn't really hate the Lynchburg power structure because that would be a complete waste of time. But I can't love it, either, because it perpetuates false ideas. It's almost like a monarchy. Those people sit in their towers and look down on everyone else."

He said he was not worried about the prospect that he might have to stand trial still again. "I'd have doubts if I was tried in Lynchburg, because of the newspapers there," he said. "But if I was tried someplace else, I don't think a judge would even send the case to a jury."

The chances of another Lynchburg trial are minuscule. The prosecution's appeal of Merhige's ruling was argued before the Fourth Circuit Court on May 8, 1973, and the panel of judges reserved decision. No matter what their ruling, legal experts say Merhige's criticism of the Lynchburg newspapers and of Judge Cundiff was so severe that any potential future trial would almost certainly be moved to another city. As for the Lynchburg papers and their officials, they have consistently refused comment on Merhige's ruling. Carter Glass III has bowed out as general manager and been replaced by his cousin, Powell Glass, Jr., another grandson of the late Senator Glass. Powell Glass, staff members say, is "not quite so far out" as Carter. As one long-time editorial employee put it: "The charges of racism made against us during the Wansley case—when Carter was in charge—were probably true. We're a little more moderate now."

Perhaps. But, if so, the news apparently has not seeped down to the papers' readers. A random sampling of Lynchburg opinion disclosed recently that few readers interviewed by this writer realized Carter Glass had stepped down and fewer still saw any discernible policy changes in the papers. "Looks like they're the same papers I've been readin' for thirty years," said one resident. Lynchburg itself is growing, with new industry and an impressive new bank and office building on Main Street. Some token homage has been paid by the city government to blacks' needs. But one typical Lynchburger whose ancestors helped settle Virginia summarized the situation this way: "It's the same ol' town, still run by the same ol' families, with the same ol' newspapers. Nothin' much changes around here over the years."

June 1973

For Thomas Wansley and those who felt he had been unjustly treated, there was a sad sequel to the story. The U.S. Fourth Circuit Court of Appeals, while agreeing that the Lynchburg newspapers' coverage of the case had been prejudicial, eventually ruled that Judge Merhige had overstepped his authority in reversing Wansley's convictions. The appeals court overturned Merhige's order and reinstated the convictions. Virginia authorities immediately took Wansley back into custody. Wansley's attorneys appealed the case to the U.S. Supreme Court and urged Virginia Governor Linwood Holton to grant Wansley a pardon. The Supreme Court declined to review the case. And Holton denied the pardon, but ordered Wansley placed in a program under which he could spend part of his time working on a job outside prison. After Holton left office in January 1974 Wansley was removed from the program because of a minor infraction of prison regulations. At this writing, he is a trusty doing field chores at a state prison farm.

How the Press
Stopped Biaggi

During the week in March 1973 when John V. Lindsay faced
reality and formally removed himself from the 1973 mayoral
campaign, I found myself on a radio talk show with John
Hamilton, then a member of the editorial board of *The New
York Times* and the man who molded much of the *Times*'s
opinion on local issues. We were discussing the other mayoral contenders and when Mario Biaggi's name came up,
Hamilton's hackles rose visibly, perhaps even audibly. He
zeroed in on all those nasty rumors that had trailed Biaggi
for years and most of the other reporters on the program
agreed that they might well present a problem for Biaggi. But
the very fact that so few of those dark tales ever had been
pinned down also suggested that there might be more smoke
than fire. Just wait, Hamilton seemed to bristle. You'll see.

Well, we saw. For more than a month that spring, while
Watergate dominated the national scene, the big New York
story was Mario Biaggi: his appearance before a federal
grand jury back in 1971, his invocation of the Fifth Amendment on various questions of finances and personal and political associations and his repeated lying about that appearance. The ensuing wrangle over what Biaggi said pushed

most other campaign issues into the background and the final disclosure of his grand jury testimony probably fatally undercut an otherwise solid shot at City Hall by the conservative cop-turned-congressman.

Was it a triumph for *The New York Times* and New York *Daily News* which broke the story on April 18, 1973? Of course. But their first front page pieces also prompted a small squall of debate and self-criticism within the journalistic community. Even some dedicated Biaggiphobes began to feel that the congressman's rights were being infringed. The unfettered operation of the press—with a somewhat surprising assist from the courts and the U.S. attorney—also shook up some of the traditional concepts of secrecy and sanctity generally associated with the grand jury system. "I don't think it was one of the proudest moments in American journalism," says WNEW-TV's Gabe Pressman, a veteran New York newsman who followed the Biaggi affair closely. "It was our obligation to run the story," argues *Times* managing editor A. M. Rosenthal. "How could we possibly justify not running it?"

How the *Times* and *News* went after the Biaggi story, how they penetrated the veil of grand jury secrecy and how they viewed the legal and ethical problems involved in the process is a revealing story in itself. For one thing, each newspaper took a significantly different approach. While the *News* tried to force the truth out through official channels—by having the candidate, the Conservative party (whose nomination Biaggi had locked up) or government officials make the testimony public—the *Times* launched a good, old-fashioned effort of its own to get the story on page one. As it happened, the *Times* scored a scoop of several hours, although with at least one glaring error on the number of questions that Biaggi had refused to answer. The fascinating question is whether the difference in approach was merely a matter of journalistic preference, or a reflection of basic differences in political orientation—the *Times* being hostile to Biaggi while the

News was somewhat predisposed to the law-and-order Democrat, at least at the outset.

Sensitive investigative stories always demand a certain delicacy in handling. "I was not asked about my sources," says *Times* reporter Nick Gage. "All Gelb [*Times* metropolitan editor Arthur Gelb] asked me was, 'Are you sure?' He was taking a big chance. One mistake on a story like this and you're through in this business." Gage, thirty-three, born in Greece and raised in New England, had been an investigative reporter at Cowles *(The Insider's Newsletter),* AP, the Boston *Herald Traveler* and the *Wall Street Journal.* At the *Times,* he had broken big stories about organized crime, government investigations and, most recently, had exposed the curious case of the Metropolitan Museum's Euphronious krater. Because of a pending investigation into grand jury leaks in the Biaggi case, Gage was extremely reluctant to discuss his own investigation in any substantial detail. But he did suggest that the techniques he developed produced the necessary corroboration without breaking any law. And Gage says that he "never worked on a story as hard to get—where people talked less" than the one on Biaggi.

Gage is a man of striking inventiveness and chutzpah; he boasts about bluffing most of the krater story out of art dealer Robert Hecht at their very first meeting. For the Biaggi story he composed lists of potential sources that included members of the grand jury, the assistant U.S. attorneys involved— even relatives of these and others who might know the story. Gage hunted through public records, hoping to come across misfiled papers that might give him a clue (a happy accident that helped him once on a story for the *Wall Street Journal),* and he made several attempts to overhear the assistant U.S. attorneys during lunch at a local restaurant (it didn't work). He later drew a rebuke from the U.S. Attorney's office for asking one of the assistants to pump another for information —and for putting out the word that he would appreciate receiving a copy of the grand jury transcript sent anonymously. A report filed by former U.S. Attorney Whitney North Seymour—after Biaggi's testimony was made public —called the *Times* reporter's methods "improper and potentially illegal." Says Gage: "They are standard procedures in my reporting practice . . . When you're struggling, you try anything."

There were other leads. Denny Walsh, the former *Life* staffer who then did investigative reporting for the *Times* out of Washington, provided some contacts in the U.S. Immigration Service, but their confidence proved nontransferrable. Gage did get some information from other investigations of Biaggi—including the report prepared for former Representative James Scheuer, who once thought of challenging Biaggi—but they were filled mostly with rumor or second-hand versions of events inside the grand jury room. Gage also found himself falling heir to a string of tips from Biaggi's political enemies, most of which proved useless or at least unverifiable.

Where did Gage finally pin down his story? It is probably not the place of a journalism review to reveal a reporter's sources—the confidentiality of which it would surely defend if the reporter himself were brought before a grand jury. But it is known that knowledge of what went on inside the grand jury room passed through the U.S. Attorney's office to other branches of the Justice Department, the Internal Revenue Service and perhaps even the White House. (John Caulfield and Anthony Ulasewicz, the former New York cops who played Holmes and Watson for John Ehrlichman, were known to have delved into Biaggi's history—and possibly into federal files on him as well.) With so many people involved, the likelihood of leakage is enormous, despite the denials sworn to by two score government employees in the official investigation later conducted by Seymour's office.

That investigation (self-touted as highly "imaginative") did come up with two government employees who allegedly passed Gage information that they said they had obtained from "nongovernmental" sources. And one word around the

Times is that Gage focused a good deal of his own effort on sources in the private sector. Friends and associates of Biaggi, including principal adviser Laurence Marchini, were said to have known and talked about his testimony with various people from time to time. There are no constraints on information that comes from a grand jury witness himself —or from those he has made privy to his testimony.

The *Times*'s interest in Biaggi has fluctuated over the years. *Times*man Charles Grutzner, now retired, looked into some rumors about the Bronx congressman back in 1969 and 1970 but could not come up with sufficient corroboration. Then, last October, reporter Martin Tolchin surfaced the story that Biaggi was one of several congressmen called before a New York federal grand jury looking into the welter of private immigration bills introduced every year on behalf of aliens trying to remain in the United States. Shortly after that story ran, the *Times* says, Tolchin received an anonymous tip that Biaggi had taken the Fifth Amendment during his grand jury appearance. Questioned about this by Tolchin, the congressman said he had answered all questions on immigration; he refused to go beyond that in the interview. The matter was apparently dropped. When Biaggi began to gain prominence in the pack of City Hall hopefuls, he was asked about his grand jury appearance again by *Times* reporter Tom Buckley, who was preparing profiles of the likely contenders. Buckley reported Biaggi's claim that he "replied fully to all questions put to him."

In January 1973 Arthur Gelb put Gage on the Biaggi case, although it still apparently rated less than top priority on West 43rd Street. Gelb shipped Gage off to Europe right in the middle of his investigation in order to get the story behind the acquisition of the controversial krater. By the time Gage returned to the newsroom, the *News* was on to the Biaggi story, too. "I was hoping for a few days' rest," Gage recalls, "but Gelb came by and asked, 'What about Biaggi?' "

In the end, Gage learned that Biaggi had actually made two grand jury appearances and that it was at the second—

not focused exclusively on immigration matters—that he took the Fifth. Armed with this knowledge, he confronted the congressman, but instead of bringing up the second appearance straight away, Gage asked first about a number of charges that he knew Biaggi could easily deny. As the congressman began feeling more confident, Gage inquired whether he had been asked about a certain matter at this second grand jury appearance—Gage knew he hadn't—and Biaggi breezily denied it. After several more irrelevant questions, Gage asked again about the second appearance. Yes, there was one, Biaggi replied, but the particular matter Gage had asked about earlier had positively never come up. And that confirmed the second appearance.

By Monday, April 16, Gage had confirmed the whole story to his satisfaction, asked Biaggi specifically if he ever took the Fifth (the congressman denied it) and finally turned in his copy. The editors took a day to go over the piece and ordered it set in print on the afternoon of Tuesday, April 17. It was pure coincidence, the *Times* insists, that this was the same day the *Daily News* had invited Biaggi back to its offices for a confrontation before running its own Fifth Amendment story. In any case, the first edition of the *Times* was exclusive with the story that night. "We didn't even know he was over at the *News* that day," says Arthur Gelb. "We were kind of gloating over the story. They didn't match it until their final edition."

There were few second thoughts at the *Times* about the nature of the story or the way Gage had broken it. "I don't see any objections to a reporter calling up any potential source," said Rosenthal after the Seymour report was issued. "How do you get a story anyway? Obviously, we don't ask a reporter who his sources are or how he's going about getting his story. But I consider that the *Times* is responsible for the methods our reporters use and there our standards are quite clear: we don't pay for stories, we don't masquerade and we don't tap."

"The important thing to understand about the Biaggi

story," says Rosenthal, "is that this was not a question about
whether a person has the right to take the Fifth Amendment
but whether a public official has the right to lie—and to lie
in a context that was essential to the electoral process." (The
Conservative party had specifically asked Biaggi about his
grand jury testimony.) "We went through weeks of discussion here," Rosenthal told me, pacing across his office den.
"And the point is that once you have the information, what
is a newspaper to do? There are only two options really—to
print or not to print. In almost every instance of major
controversy you will find people—both well-motivated and
self-seeking—who say you should not print. But generally
speaking I believe that the long-run benefits to society come
with printing. Should we have spiked the Pentagon Papers?
You're not Solomon or a judge . . . You're a newspaper."

"To print or not to print." Those were the options as seen
at the *Times*. But across town on East 42nd Street, the *Daily
News* had carved out a third route. While its team of investigative reporters worked to pin down the story, the paper
tried using what information it had to prompt others to
spotlight Biaggi's public perjury by obtaining release of his
grand jury testimony through official channels. Had the ploy
worked as planned, there would have been no need for a
News story quoting only unnamed sources on what was supposedly secret testimony. Perhaps there would have been no
need for a story at all if Biaggi was actually telling the truth.

Was this gingerly handling dictated by the fact that Biaggi
was the natural *News* candidate? Sources at the paper are
quick to point out that no endorsement was planned for
1973's Democratic primary and there were no official
editorial discussions about endorsement. Managing editor
Mike O'Neill, a rumpled-looking UPI alumnus with a slow,
sure manner, warns against jumping to the conclusion that
Biaggi would have been the *News* candidate, although there
was certainly no philosophical antagonism towards him. Another politically sensitive source at the *News* judges that
Biaggi, indeed, was probably more in tune with the paper's

editorial thinking than any other contender. But during the course of their investigation of the story, *News* editors say, they became convinced that Biaggi was lying to them and the question of philosophic affinity became moot.

Like the *Times,* the *News* had pursued various earlier reports on Biaggi with little success. And they did not successfully follow up on the *Times* report in October 1972 about Biaggi's grand jury appearance. The *News* tip about his taking the Fifth Amendment came in a January 18 luncheon at which the editors were questioning another mayoral candidate—a man who had heard of the incident but could not confirm it. One of the first to be told about the new lead was Sam Roberts, a political reporter only five years out of Cornell ('68) but already a top hand at the *News.* A month earlier, Roberts had lunched with Biaggi and asked about all the rumors trailing him. "Let's be practical," the congressman said then. "If I had anything to worry about, I wouldn't be running."

On January 21, a Sunday, Roberts was among those waiting to question Biaggi at a special session in the News Building's seventh-floor conference room. The congressman called reports about his taking the Fifth "completely inaccurate," but balked over discussing the matter in detail. Then Biaggi, law partner Bernard Ehrlich and press secretary Mortimer Matz (a *News* veteran himself) moved out to the paper's deserted Special Features section to prepare a one-and-a-half-page typed statement that concluded: "I again categorically state that I answered each and every question before the grand jury on immigration matters and did not involve the Fifth Amendment in connection therewith." Asked if he had *ever* taken the Fifth, Biaggi huddled with his aides for ten or fifteen minutes more. Then, recalls Roberts, "He said no and shook his head with that look of grim determination he has."

The *News* editors were suspicious but, like their counterparts at the *Times,* not yet ready to give the Biaggi story top priority. Roberts checked sources in New York but also

remained tied up with a series on banking; another investigative reporter, William Sherman, was assigned to go through
all the pertinent immigration bills, but he was also working
on a Medicare series. Dick Oliver, assistant city editor for
special investigations, directed the operation and pitched in
on the reporting himself, but after two months what the *News*
had was mostly secondhand reports.

In March 1973, with the story not solid enough to print,
Oliver and Roberts sat down to map a new plan of action.
First they would run Biaggi's carefully crafted statement to
the *News* under the noses of various high government officials "hoping for a reaction, an indignant response . . . something," says Roberts. Then, since the date was fast approaching past which the Conservative party could no longer shed
Biaggi as a candidate, they went directly to the Conservatives. Their argument was that the party leaders might be
embarrassed by future disclosures and that they might have
been misled by Biaggi; the idea was to have them put pressure on Biaggi to get the testimony made public.

The notion was unprecedented, but not without promise.
Some weeks earlier, managing editor O'Neill had talked with
then U.S. Attorney Whitney North Seymour—not about the
facts of the case, he says, but about the legal restrictions on
grand jury minutes. "We simply investigated with him what
was possible—how one would go about getting the release of
such minutes for overriding public reasons," says O'Neill.
"He gave me a copy of the appropriate sections of the federal
court rules and he pointed out the extremely limited circumstances under which these minutes could be released."

According to Rule 6 (e), grand jury testimony can be
released (1) to "the attorneys of the government for use in the
performance of their duties," (2) on the orders of a court
"preliminarily to or in connection with a judicial proceeding," and (3) to a defendant "upon a showing that grounds
may exist for a motion to dismiss the indictment because of
matters occurring before the grand jury." None of this was
specifically applicable to the Biaggi case, obviously, but the

thinking at the *News* seemed to be that Biaggi was coming under a form of public indictment by virtue of all the rumors and impending stories and that conceivably he might have the right to request disclosure of the minutes to clear the air. Seymour maintains that he ventured no opinion on the outcome of such a request by Biaggi. But the *News* editors came away with "the feeling and some hopes—though no actual commitment," according to O'Neill, "that this would not be opposed by the U.S. Attorney's office." (Indeed, when Biaggi made his first transparent request for a limited judicial review of his grand jury testimony, Seymour insisted on release of the full transcript with all names other than Biaggi's deleted.)

Some Conservative leaders were initially receptive to the plan, but on March 10 the party turned it down. State Chairman J. Daniel Mahoney told the *News:* "If you have information to which we're not privy, it seems you ought to go to Biaggi." Sam Roberts had done just that several days before, but Biaggi was not interested in applying for release of the testimony. State authorities also were approached, on the grounds that a false statement by Biaggi to the Conservative party—to clear the way for his nomination—might be deemed a violation of the state election law. But these officials, too, demurred, telling the *News* that a complainant with proper legal standing would be required. The state's hands-off reaction does not square with subsequent charges that Governor Nelson Rockefeller was the man pulling the strings behind the scenes to cause Biaggi's embarrassment. Given Rockefeller's often-Machiavellian manner, of course, it doesn't prove that he wasn't either.

Some of the *News* people involved with the story thought they should go ahead and print it then. They had gotten additional corroboration from authoritative sources—including one "law enforcement official" in Washington who rendered a "hearty guffaw" after reading the Biaggi denial. Of these sources, Roberts says, "They knew they were doing something illegal perhaps . . . their mood was something on the order of 'who's Biaggi trying to kid?' " And as Biaggi looked stronger as a candidate, that indignant attitude grew stronger, Oliver recalls. Still, the paper's editors decided to try one more confrontation with Biaggi himself.

On April 17, Biaggi was told that the *News* would run the story next day. Once again he denied it—saying in response to specific questions that he had never taken the Fifth Amendment, never refused to answer questions on the grounds they were not germane, never refused to testify at all. "We asked him why he didn't petition the court or Seymour's office to have the minutes released," recalls Roberts. "But he said he would not. He talked about the sanctity of the grand jury and said, 'You don't believe me.' I walked him down to the car and he insisted he was telling the truth. I stood on 42nd Street and almost literally pleaded with him. I said, 'Christ, if you're telling the truth, why not clear things up? For your sake, not mine!'"

It was 4:40 P.M. Upstairs, in O'Neill's office, the editors realized that it was too late to make the next day's first edition (deadline: 5:00 P.M.). They talked about going ahead for the later editions with a story saying Biaggi had lied about the Fifth Amendment or, more circumspectly, with a piece that said that despite all the rumors about Biaggi's having lied, he refused to settle the question by requesting release of the minutes. In the end, however, they decided to spend yet another day checking the story. "We were fairly sure, but after all this was a grand jury appearance we were talking about, and there were a lot of stop-Biaggi forces at work around town," says Roberts. "We were not interested in getting a beat," says Mike O'Neill. "There was a genuine concern about this story."

Any possibility of scoring a beat vanished at 10:00 P.M. when the first edition of the *Times* arrived with the Biaggi story on the front page. The *News* city desk immediately called O'Neill, Oliver and Roberts at home but the 10:40 deadline for the three-star edition was already passing as Oliver strode into the office to start writing. He put his piece together from information already in the house plus fresh material that Roberts was getting in urgent phone calls made from his East Side apartment. Most important was the advice from *News* sources that the *Times* lead was wrong about the number of questions Biaggi refused to answer; the *Times* said at least thirty, but actually it was sixteen. Oliver's story was on the press by 2:30 A.M. for the paper's final edition—the biggest run of the night.

Next day, the *News* followed up with a story about one of the key questions on which Biaggi had taken the Fifth: the $7,200 consultant's job at an advertising agency arranged for his daughter Jacqueline by Martin Tannenbaum, the late Democratic wheeler-dealer. *Times*man Gage says he had no information on that point when he wrote his story, and he concedes that he misinterpreted some information from one source to come up with the erroneous thirty questions. But he was first nonetheless, and the *News* would have to find consolation in its greater accuracy and an accolade from U.S. Attorney Seymour for all those backstage efforts to surface the story officially. "What the *News* did was terribly honorable," Seymour told me, "and the irony is that they were scooped. I think they paid the price for responsible journalism."

Regardless of who broke the story, reporters who worked on it for both the *News* and the *Times* found themselves under some criticism—even from friends and colleagues. Hadn't they been guilty of illegally receiving grand jury information? Wasn't it a man's right to testify secretly before a grand jury? And wasn't it also his right to take the Fifth Amendment? The most serious complaint on that last score came to the *Times* from the paper's own Washington bureau in a letter to Abe Rosenthal signed by some twenty staffers, including top investigative reporter Seymour Hersh. The crux of the criticism was that Gage's original story had not sufficiently emphasized that taking the Fifth Amendment is a constitutional privilege whose use should not imply any wrongdoing.

"If it was a complaint, it was a complaint lodged in affection and loyalty and to portray it otherwise would be totally false," says Eileen Shanahan, one of the original half-dozen Washington *Times* persons who found themselves objecting to the story over lunch on the day it ran. "It was merely a matter of people feeling free enough to write to their boss and say, Gosh, the *Times* didn't live up to our own best standards of care on that one!"

Self-criticism in journalism needs to be nurtured, but that particular complaint about Gage's story seems a bit overdrawn. In his fourth paragraph, the reporter wrote: "The Fifth Amendment guarantees the right of an individual to refuse to answer questions that might tend to incriminate him." The luncheon bull session that spawned the letter to Rosenthal actually began with some soul-searching about stories that looked "inadequately sourced," a valid area of sensitivity in Watergate, D.C., at that point in time, when new scoops surfaced daily on the basis of grand jury leaks. And the *Times* folk might understandably be even more sensitive because so many of those scoops belonged to their national competitor—the Washington *Post.* Indeed, their rage at Gage, to overstate it, looks like a textbook case of transference.

Biaggi did some complaining himself, of course. In paid TV time on four local stations, he charged that he was the victim of "a plot of attempted political and character assassination" and he named the plotters: "boss Alex Rose" of the Liberal party and the *Times.* The *News* came in for some rough treatment, too, when the Biaggi camp apparently helped to arrange a press conference at which ex-convict James Forella was supposed to accuse *News* reporter Bill Sherman of offering him a bribe. Forella was involved in the now famous 1959 incident during which Mario Biaggi, then still a policeman, shot and killed a young gunman inside a Cadillac convertible. Biaggi people tipped TV reporters to the story and apparently provided two beefy escorts to bring Forella to the WCBS-TV studio. Under the camera's eye,

Forella backed off; he claimed Sherman had harassed him (the reporter denies it) but never made the promised charges about being offered large sums of money or anything else he wanted.

Gabe Pressman, who arranged an exclusive TV interview with Biaggi (during which the candidate admitted he had "misled" the public), is one of those journalists with mixed feelings over the Biaggi affair. He is particularly disturbed by the obvious lip-licking of some of his colleagues as Biaggi's admittedly shabby attempt to use the federal court was turned back on him to provide grounds for the ultimate publication of his grand jury testimony. "In the immediate mayoral situation, I guess it was better that it got out," says Pressman of the Fifth Amendment story, "because we got a better picture of the man. But to the extent that it shook up and weakened the tradition of grand jury secrecy and to the extent that it gave us a picture of the vindictiveness of the federal courts, I think it was disquieting."

Most of those involved in the Biaggi story emphasize that it was the congressman's lying that got him into trouble— not the fact that he took the Fifth. But the notion that Biaggi could have prevented all the front-page publicity by admitting his action when the story first leaked out is a little hard to accept. If the newspapers themselves didn't follow up that story—Gage, for instance, says he would have used the information as a stepping-off point for further investigations into Biaggi's affairs—the candidate's opponents surely would have. Burt Neuborne, the American Civil Liberties Union lawyer who filed an amicus brief against disclosure of the grand jury record, has an even wilder idea. He suggests that Biaggi might have used the publicity to his own advantage by presenting his invocation of the Fifth Amendment as another skirmish between Congress and the Executive branch—thereby winning over the city's liberals. "But taking the Fifth is still slimy and reprehensible to him," shrugs Neuborne. "After all these years he still sees the Constitution more as something to hide behind than to wrap yourself in."

*　　　*　　　*

If Watergate wasn't enough to dramatize the fact that there is no such thing as absolute secrecy these days—especially for government officials and even inside a grand jury room—the Biaggi case did. The ACLU's Neuborne would upgrade the procedural safeguards of grand jury secrecy so that no citizen is easily put in the bind that Biaggi got himself into. But Neuborne agrees with practically all the reporters and editors who worked on the Biaggi story that "once a free press got the facts, it was obliged to print them."

The provisions for grand jury secrecy—even the Fifth Amendment itself—are unquestionably basic elements of a constitutional framework designed to serve the public good. They are not to be treated lightly. But a responsible press also serves the public good, and its wide latitude of freedom is firmly rooted in that same constitutional framework. It is an obviously untidy system and one rich in controversy when something like the Biaggi story comes along—but it seems to work.

August 1973

MADELINE NELSON

Money Makes the Press Go 'Round

Banking establishments may or may not be "more dangerous than standing armies," as Jefferson suggested, but at the very least they would seem to be news. And Chase Manhattan, perhaps the most visible and powerful bank in the world, would seem to be big news. At the end of 1973, Chase had assets of $36.7 billion, and that's just the beginning. The bank holds another $10 billion in custody. It is the trustee for some 1,400 public bond issues worth several billion more. It is the paying agent for $20 billion in public debt. Moreover, Chase holds $15 billion in trust for widows, workers, pension funds and doubtless, the Rockefeller boys, the youngest of whom, fifty-nine-year-old David, is probably the most powerful banker in the world.

David absolutely fascinates the media. In December of 1973, CBS pursued him around the world as he gave a dinner for Prime Minister Heath, shook hands with President Pompidou and wined and dined with Premier Kosygin. Back home in Westchester County, David splashed about for the cameras in his Pocantico Hills pool with some high-rolling Chase customers. When the nation's newspapers and magazines are not recording Chase's quarterly reports, they eagerly dog its chairman for pronouncements on Important Matters. As David Rubin points out in an article on Chase Manhattan's public relations operation ([MORE], March 1974, p. 18), the molding of David Rockefeller into a World Business Statesman is no accident. It is a carefully orchestrated plan to take the heat off the bank itself. And it works.

Given the middle-class mentality of most reporters and editors, David Rockefeller would probably be a media darling without the PR machine. After all, he has all that money. But his bank has even more, and nobody seems much interested in all *those* billions and what impact Chase has on the society. Hard questions on the subject are almost never asked by the financial press. I will get to some of them momentarily. But lest my case against the media seem overstated, here is how *The New York Times,* the *Wall Street Journal, Business Week, Newsweek* and *Time* covered Chase Manhattan in 1973.

In all of 1973, *Time* found only one story on Chase important enough to cover, the naming of Chase as U.S. correspondent for the Bank of China. Run as an "Eyecatcher" in the business section, the story began with the kind of gush that typifies coverage of the bank and its chairman: "Genial David Rockefeller, the quintessential capitalist, visited China, chatted amiably with Chou En-lai for two hours and came home last week with a deal." The three-paragraph piece, which included a half-column-wide picture of David, called the move "a coup for Rockefeller" and ended: "Indeed, the communists, who like to deal with the topmost people, are captivated by the very name of Rockefeller."

Newsweek chose a different event for its single 1973 Chase story, the bank's new branch in Moscow. Headlined A COMRADE AT CHASE, the two-column story had Rockefeller "greeted by Premier Alexei Kosygin and feted with caviar and champagne when he arrived to open the first office of an American bank in the Soviet Union in some 50 years." After six paragraphs on the problems and profits of dealing with the Russians, the magazine concluded: "Its new address, for those interested in contacting their comrades at Chase, is 1 Karl Marx Square." The accompanying picture showed Chase's Moscow chief standing in Red Square.

Business Week covered the Moscow and China moves along with a third story, a two-plus column piece on a seven-year-old Chase labor dispute in Japan—a story different not only because no one else covered it but also because Rockefeller was not mentioned. *Business Week*'s Moscow piece, CHASE MOVES INTO 1 KARL MARX SQUARE, had Rockefeller in the second sentence: "The Chase's globetrotting Chairman, David Rockefeller, flew into Moscow for the opening and stopped in for a meeting at the Kremlin Palace with Soviet Premier Alexei Kosygin." A two-column-wide picture of that meeting topped the six-paragraph story. In its China coverage, *Business Week* said the agreement was "a relationship he [Rockefeller] hardly lifted a finger to get," giving as a partial reason for his success his "status as leader of the U.S. business establishment."

Although it did not cover Chase separately, *Business Week* did include figures on the bank's trust holdings and comments from Chase officials on various bank problems in its thirty-plus-page special on banking (September 15, 1973). While accepting as inevitable the increasing concentration of power—"The U.S. banking system very clearly is headed in the direction of still fewer, but bigger, banks"—the section raised some basic questions on trust policies and even banks' responses to social issues.

The *Wall Street Journal* covers Chase's day-to-day news for investors and businessmen. Four times a year (in 1973 on January 17, April 17, July 18, and October 17), the paper prints the quarterly earnings report as issued by the bank. The July story covered the figures on increased assets, loans, net income for the quarter and the half, all dutifully compared with the same figures for the year before. The only explanation came from the bank: "Chase said the quarterly increase in operating net was attributable to gains from international activities." Beyond that, the *Journal* reports, without flourishes, new big loans such as $86 million to Russia for a truck factory (March 9), $49 million to Spain for a power plant (May 23), acquisitions such as a new Albany bank (February 2), a new Canadian bank (October 5), and new vice presidents. When the Chase tried to buy its own finance company, the *Journal* story dealt only with investor details: "The proposed transaction which was agreed to in principle yesterday would involve the exchange of up to 2.8 million shares of Chase for the outstanding stock of Dial."

The *Journal* downplayed Chase's splashier '73 moves, putting the opening to China on page 8, then devoting only five of the ten paragraphs to that subject. (The other half of the piece dealt with a Federal Reserve Board order to Chase to divest its interest in a British bank, a subject not mentioned in the headline.) When the bank attempted to encourage interests in its stock, the *Journal* put the story on page 11 with the headline, "Now Chase Is Seeking Friends of Its Own, Preferably Investors." The piece began: "Chase Manhattan Corporation which has sustained years of sluggish earnings threw what could be called a coming-out party for more than 200 stock analysts in an unabashed pitch to gain investor interest in its stock." Its reporter found the analysts "skeptical."

The New York Times banking reporter, John Allan, got a different impression. Devoting the paper's Sunday Wall Street column to the meeting (CHASE WOOS THE ANALYSTS), Allan wrote of the bank's "strenuous effort to make investors like its stock." After a "well-modulated performance" in which "Mr. Rockefeller, scholarly and soft-spoken, outlined the Chase's overall management philosophy," the analysts "stayed for cocktails and roast beef." Allan reported that if "the initial response [a 4¼ point rise on Thursday] is a true reflection of analysts reaction, the outlook for Chase improved immensely from the meeting." He failed to note the Chase stock was up only 1¼ for the week.

In general, the *Times* financial page covers the same information as the *Journal* with as little explanation. In a September 19 story (BIG BANKS CONTINUE TO MOVE TO 10% PRIME RATE), the paper simply listed the banks that had raised their rates, including Chase. The difference between the papers is that the *Times* devotes more space to Chase news. Where the *Journal* will lump the bank's earning reports with the reports of other banks on inside pages, the *Times* gives the bank a separate story, usually on the first page of the financial section.

The *Times* put the China agreement on page one (CHASE AGREES TO BE AGENT FOR BANK OF CHINA IN U.S.), and offered the following social note: "Mr. Rockefeller, who was accompanied by his wife Peggy; Francis X. Stankard, senior vice president; Joseph V. Reed, Jr., vice president and Mrs. Reed, visited four cities and met with Chou En-lai and other Chinese officials." The piece ran twenty-seven inches, not including a column-wide head shot of Rockefeller that ran inside. The middle-class editors of *The New York Times* most often merely fawn over the wealthy. But in contemplating David Rockefeller they and their reporters are positively pop-eyed with awe. A review of 1973 coverage indicates there must be a David desk somewhere on 43rd Street.

David appeared briefly on February 2 in a routine announcement of a Chase loan to Poland, but that was just a prelude. Three weeks later, in the middle of the front page of the Sunday business section, spread across the full eight columns, was David's "An East European Diary." Four pictures showed Rockefeller with officials of Hungary, Yugoslavia, Rumania and Poland. It had been "a fascinating, rewarding and exhausting visit," the last because "In less than nine days we were to have some fifty meetings with officials of these four countries." The article outlined the various possibilities for U.S. companies to make money in Eastern Europe; but those who wanted a glimpse of the summit, Rockefeller style, were not disappointed. "We were particularly honored and delighted . . . to have a luncheon hosted by Dr. Bruno Kreisky, Chancellor of Austria . . . On the second day, a Saturday, we had the great pleasure of flying to the island of Brioni for a conversation with the President of Yugoslavia, Marshal Tito . . . Our second day in Rumania was highlighted by an excursion to the fascinating monasteries in Moldavia with their unique exterior frescos dating from the 15th century." For anyone who was not familiar with Eastern Europe, the *Times* provided a two-column-wide map with arrows charting Rockefeller's journey. The article ran over forty inches, not counting the pictures.

David's next major, though much shorter, appearance was on May 14 when he made a speech criticizing tax reforms. "Mr. Rockefeller said that Congressional proposals to reverse or eliminate corporate tax reductions . . . 'would turn the clock back.' " Eight days later the *Times* quoted him on Soviet trade when Chase opened its Moscow branch; but for the paper, China, not Moscow, was the big story.

David's China coverage began on June 1 with an announcement in the People and Business column that Rockefeller was going. His arrival in China made it to the Notes on People section on June 27. When he met with Chou En-lai, the *Times* ran it as a Sunday World News Brief (July 1), reporting that while Rockefeller would not give any details of the two-hour meeting, he would say it had been "wide ranging . . . we discussed a whole range of possible future contacts." The trip itself was "basically exploratory" and "enormously educational." For readers who missed the Sunday item, the *Times* followed up with a five-column-wide picture of Rockefeller and Chou at the top of page 3 of the Monday paper. The picture had a two-line caption but no article.

The announcement of the Chase-Bank of China agreement made the front page on July 5, beginning: "Chase Manhattan Bank will represent the Bank of China in the U.S. under an agreement concluded by David Rockefeller, Chase Manhattan's chairman, during a ten-day visit to China." The chairman's picture was back on page 44—David's, not Mao's.

That was the last David Rockefeller coverage from China, but not the last mention of Rockefeller and China. When the Bank of China revalued its currency, the *Times* ran the story with a three-column-wide picture of Rockefeller in China although the currency switches had nothing to do with Chase or Rockefeller. As a final touch, David himself wrote an August 10 Op Ed page piece on China. He admired the "national harmony" and the "social and economic progress," but added that (count 'em) "three major questions remain in my own mind." They were: can individualism and creativity be contained; can the decentralized economy adapt for technology and foreign trade; can both sides live with their differences.

Even before the China coverage was over, the *Times* was back to following Rockefeller through his more mundane chores. He announced a new Rockefeller University council "to spread understanding of the University" on July 9. During August, Rockefeller joined two committees, the International Industrial Council, August 8, and an advisory committee on monetary reform, August 23. He gave his "well-modulated performance" for the stock analysts on September 12 and joined the Urban League's Equal Opportunity Day dinner committee on September 23.

On election day, November 6, the *Times* sought "Words of Advice, Wisdom and Warning for the Next Mayor" from, among others, Shirley Chisholm, Helen Gurley Brown, William Buckley, Zero Mostel and the brothers Rockefeller, David and Nelson. From David: "I think the most important thing is to unite and bring together all the communities in the city to work together toward a common objective. At the moment, unfortunately, there are a lot of groups which feel they are in conflict with other communities. It is a very difficult thing to do."

The crown jewel in the *Times* 1973 Rockefeller coverage was Tom Buckley's feature, "A Long, Crammed and Very Typical Day in the Life of David Rockefeller," which ran on the split page November 7. The sixty-five-inch piece begins:

"The man who runs the garage at the Chase Manhattan Bank Building had been keeping watch. When he saw David Rockefeller leave the Federal Reserve Bank of New York, 100 yards or so to the west of Liberty Street, he shouted, 'O.K., Chester.' The chauffeur, Chester Erb, drove the maroon Cadillac limousine up the ramp from the basement. It was waiting at the curb with the doors open when Mr. Rockefeller, trailed by his bodyguard, Tom Swanzey, strode up."

Rockefeller is a man of great importance, as Buckley keeps showing. In the limousine, an aide discusses problems, some of which "danced and shimmered with the genuine luster of great affairs." The aide reports: " 'We've heard from the Prime Minister [of Japan] . . . He said that even if Mr. Kissinger is in Tokyo, it won't interfere with the dinner he is giving for you.' "

David, Buckley informs us, is "regarded as a spokesman for enlightened American capitalism and as a symbolic figure." After more than thirteen inches establishing Rockefeller's importance, Buckley adds that "Rockefeller is encircled by an aura of power." Then he waits four more inches before revealing that on the day of the interview "the aura was scarcely glimmering, Mr. Rockefeller being on his way to Albany to officiate at a cocktail party celebrating the opening of an office of the bank there."

Eleven more inches of details of the plane ride to Albany and Buckley finally gets to the question of how Rockefeller runs his bank: "if less relentlessly acquisitive, perhaps, than his grandfather, [he] still must guide Chase Manhattan Bank as a business institution rather than as a charity." Or a duck pond.

With that, the article returns to Albany and then to the details of David's day: when he got up, seven-thirty; how long he exercised, five minutes; what he had for breakfast, "orange juice, a protein cereal with skim milk and black coffee," and finally his home. "To enter the Rockefeller house . . . was to step into Ali Baba's cave. The butler stood in the doorway. A Degas danced on one paneled wall, a

Toulouse-Lautrec jockey mounted on another."

Rockefeller "seldom says anything that slows down, let alone stops the presses," Buckley writes, as he proves in his concluding David quote: "The implication again is that I have some supreme view of things that is overriding, is presumably for my interest against other people's. To me that is not a very fair or reasonable approach. All I can say is that I try to exercise good judgment and to be guided by the same moral principles that others are." The people at Chase liked Buckley's piece so much they had it copied and sent to the Bank's officers.

The *Times* barely broke stride as it and David moved arm in arm into the new year. On January 1, 1974, there was David on the split page again telling us of his New Year's resolutions. "In terms of East-West initiatives, we got a good start in 1973, and this year we want to do a number of things to round it out." And why not?

In early January 1974, a Senate committee issued a 419-page report, *Disclosure of Corporate Ownership.* The Washington *Post* put the story on the front page of its Sunday, January 6, issue with an inside-page eight-column headline 8 INSTITUTIONS CONTROL MOST OF LARGEST CORPORATIONS. The piece ran a total of fifty-four inches and a shorter, sixteen-inch follow-up ran on Monday. The report found that six banks, five in New York City, including Chase, hold controlling interest in eighty-nine major companies. With the exception of Morton Mintz's coverage in the Washington *Post,* most of the media barely mentioned the report, though it contained a wealth of previously undisclosed information. *Time* gave the report a fair summary in a two-column business section story. *Newsweek* and *Business Week* did not cover it at all, though in fairness to the latter, it had covered the issues raised in the study extensively in a June 2, 1973, cover story on institutional investors and again in its September 15 banking issue.

The *Journal* put the story on page 2 of its Monday, January 7, edition, emphasizing the legislative impact (MORE DATA ON INSTITUTIONAL STOCKHOLDING URGED IN SENATE COMPANY–OWNERSHIP STUDY). In a textbook example of understatement, the *Journal* said: "Many believe the tendency of these financial institutions to invest large amounts of money in the securities of a relatively few big prestigious corporations has created some economic and regulatory problems." The eleven-paragraph article gave little more than a quick summary of those problems, in one paragraph, and a few examples, in three paragraphs, all drawn from the report's eleven-page introduction. As a follow-up, the *Journal* ran an eleven-paragraph story on Tuesday: BANKS CRITICIZE SENATE STUDY'S PROPOSAL THAT THEY TELL MORE ABOUT STOCK HOLDINGS. Predictably, the bankers denied they have excessive control.

Predictably, too, the *Times'* coverage was worse. Though it is a New York City paper and the report dealt with New York's biggest financial institutions, the *Times'* total coverage was an eight-inch Reuters dispatch (SENATE REPORT HITS BANK STOCKHOLDINGS) run in the financial pages on Monday. Reuters picked up a minor point in the report, never mentioned the major finding that the eight institutions can control some of the country's largest companies. Five days later, the *Times* gave Chase nine inches for the report on its annual earnings, a story that included, among the figures, information on where they were revealed (at the annual bank officers' dinner at the New York Hilton) and who hosted the dinner (David Rockefeller and Chase's president).

In the long list of unexplored bank stories, the Senate report is perhaps one of the most important, not so much for what it says as for the questions it raises about the banks' power to control the giant corporations. At the heart of the report and of the financial community's concern are the bank trust departments and their stock-buying policy. The consequences of that policy are complicated but the policy itself is simple: buy only large blocks of stock in large corporations. The number of really large corporations is limited; the number the trust departments concentrate on, even more limited. At the end of 1972, for example, Chase had almost $400 million in IBM stock, Morgan Guaranty held $2 billion and the other top-eight trust departments held another $6 billion among themselves. The system is fine for the favored few, but it spells possible disaster for the rest.

When a company wants to raise money for expansion, for improvements, for pollution controls, the best way is to sell stock. If a trust department favorite does this, it has few problems, for its stock price is high enough to absorb new stock without lowering earnings. For the rest—estimated at 90 percent of the companies in the nation—the risks are great. If a company whose stock sells at ten times earnings wants to sell 10 percent more stock, it must increase its income by 10 percent to maintain earnings. Should their income rise 8 percent, earnings per share will fall, investors will be wary, stock prices may go down. The other ways of raising money—loans or bonds—increase the company's debt. The money crunch, analysts fear, may lead to company shutdowns or takeovers by foreign investors.

The money with which this two-tier system, as the financial press calls it, has been built is not the bank's; it is pension-fund money and money held in trust. The practice of investing in just the bluest blue chips, however solid it may look, is trapping the trust departments, and more importantly, jeopardizing the pension funds. If Chase had to sell its large holdings to get cash, it could not do so without a drastic drop in stock prices. The result is that the pension funds, rich on paper, would be much poorer if converted to cash because the market can no longer absorb huge blocks of stock.

The banks themselves are partly to blame for the market's inability to absorb big stock sales, the practices of institutional investors having driven most small investors out of the market in search of some investment where everyone else does not get inside information and leave the small investor holding worthless stock. To paraphrase Russell Baker, the small investor feels that if the ship is sinking, and the lifeboats are in the water, look out, small investor, the banks have all the seats. Since acting on inside information is illegal, the banks quite naturally deny that it ever happens. The loan departments, they say, never talk to the trust departments even if the loan people find out a company in which the trust department has big holdings is about to go under and leave the bank's trust accounts with an embarrassing loss.

This is exactly what happened in the demise of the Penn Central, except for the part about the embarrassing loss. From the first of May 1970 until the railroad filed for bankruptcy on June 19, Chase Manhattan's trust department sold 418,000 shares of Penn Central stock. During that time, Chase's loan department was one of several negotiating with the government to *save* the company. If that weren't enough, the chairman of the Penn Central was a director of Chase. The charges of using inside information weren't proved (they rarely are, since corporate confessions are unusual and bankers are bright enough not to put that kind of thing in writing), but the charges were serious enough so that Rockefeller himself went to Washington to deny them.

When the *Times* devoted its Sunday Wall Street column to the problems of trust departments (BANKS STIR CONTROVERSY AS A STOCK MARKET FORCE—October 7, 1973), the guest columnist wrote forty inches without once naming a single bank or the size of the holdings. On the possibility of inside information, he observed: "One suspects that well-managed banks that recognize what can be lost by crossing the lines of traditional demarcation do so with great trepidation." On the problems of nonfavored companies trying to raise capital: nothing. On the problems of holdings so large they cannot be sold without severe losses: nothing.

Dire as the effects on the market are, actual bank control of corporations may be more serious. Technically, banks cannot own companies unless their business is closely related to banking; but under the Bank Holding Act of 1970, control of 5 percent of a company's stock is considered "presumptive control." With that as a measure, Chase controls twenty-seven corporations listed in the Senate report, including seven airlines, six railroads, CBS and ABC. This figure is probably high because, except for the broadcast companies, the holdings may include stock for which the bank does not have voting rights. Nevertheless, smaller holdings, the Senate report says, still give the banks considerable leverage over company policies.

Exactly how often they use that leverage is a well-protected secret, but the study indicates that banks rarely vote against management; disputes with management are more likely to result in selling shares. Since the effect of having one of your company's big stockholders dump its stock can be a drastic decline in stock prices, few corporate heads risk the battle or need to be reminded that banks control loan money as well. One company that crossed the banks, Leasco, got the full treatment.

Leasco's sin may have been the worst imaginable: the upstart conglomerate tried to take over a bank—in this case New York's Chemical Bank. Although the trust departments of Chase, Continental Illinois and Chemical itself had been buying Leasco stock before the takeover attempt became known, its stock quickly lost 25 percent of its price. Into the battle came David's big brother, Nelson, who called on the legislature to give the superintendent of banking power to approve takeovers. The official reason for this was to keep the Mafia and other undesirables out. (The bill passed.) Even Nixon's Justice Department got into the act, launching an investigation of Leasco. The conglomerate beat a hasty retreat. The banks may be ready to loan companies money to swallow other companies, as Chase did with Gulf and Western, but not to swallow one of their own.

Banks, in truth, have little to fear since, as the Senate report documents, they are on the top of a money pyramid. They own everyone below them and they own each other.

Twenty-two of Chase's top thirty stockholders are bank trust departments. Chase even owns 1.5 million shares of its archrival, First National City (which in the past has been controlled by another branch of the Rockefeller family).

Another critical area of bank control over corporations that the Senate report, the Penn Central investigations and others have long questioned is interlocking directorates. In the Penn Central case, the railroad shared directors with nine banks. During the seven years before it filed for bankruptcy, the railroad paid $215 million in dividends while the company lost $2.5 million over the same time. One reason the House investigators of the Penn Central collapse suggested for the directors' seemingly irrational continuance of dividends was that the directors' banks' trust departments held large blocks of stock in trust and depended on that dividend income.

The present Chase board interlocks with Exxon, ARCO, and Standard of Indiana; it shares directors with GM and Chrysler (Henry Ford sits on the bank's International Advisory Committee). Chase also controls large blocks of stock in each of those companies. Do those shared directors give Chase an ear or a voice in those companies or are those the only men in the country qualified to sit on the Chase board, as Rockefeller has suggested? When a stockholder raised the issue of possible conflict of interest at the Chase 1972 annual meeting, the *Times* described the stockholder as a woman "who perennially plays the role of gadfly," noting that the challenge was greeted by laughter.

For most corporations and individuals, a bank's most immediate power over their lives is the decision on who gets loans. At present, the American banking system is fragmented. If one bank refuses to give a loan, others may agree. Smaller community banks are often more sympathetic than the big banks. The system of local banks continues, in part, because until recently statewide branch banking has been limited and interstate banking virtually unknown. But the barriers are coming down. In 1976, New York will permit statewide branch banking and Rockefeller says Chase Manhattan Corporation, the holding company which owns the bank, is "moving rapidly toward establishing Chase throughout the state." The new banks Chase is buying have subtle names like Chase Manhattan of the Northern Tier so no one will doubt what they really are; technically they are now separate banks, but in '76 they will merge with Chase.

"It is a matter of big banks largely in big cities taking over big banks in little cities. In other words, the movement toward statewide domination in banking over a period of time by a few big banking systems," says Benet Gellman, counsel to the House Banking and Currency Committee. Bankers look beyond that to even bigger control. *Business Week* quotes bankers as predicting nationwide banking with domination by no more than a dozen big banks no later than the end of the century, possibly within ten years. When statewide banking, let alone national banking, becomes a reality, what is to stop Chase from taking money deposited in New York City and funneling it into the suburbs? As fewer banks exist, who will make the crucial decisions on who gets loans, what areas will flourish, what kind of housing gets built? During 1973 the papers recorded each new Chase acquisition as if they were isolated incidences. On February 25, the same day the *Times* ran Rockefeller's "An East European Diary," the business section also devoted its Sunday business roundup to statewide banking without including New York.

Then, of course, there are the poor. Banks, including Chase, refuse loans to the poor but give loans to finance companies, which gladly loan to poor people at twice bank interest rates. In 1973 Chase tried to go one step further and buy its own loan company, Dial Financial, with offices in thirty-three states. In his speech to the stock analysts, Rockefeller said, "Dial will put us in the consumer financing business." But, the bank is already in the consumer loan business according to its 1972 annual report, which lists $442 million in such loans—almost $150 million more than Dial. The difference between Chase's consumer loans and Dial's is that even credit card interest is limited to 18 percent while Dial loans can carry interest of well over 20 percent. The *Times* and *Journal* carried stories on the proposed acquisition, covering it as they would a new branch opening, just the facts, with no attempts to raise questions or get dissenting views. On January 30, 1974, however, Chase got a dissenting opinion, the one that mattered. The Federal Reserve rejected the bank's application to acquire Dial, though the reason was reduction of competition rather than a concern about usury. The Chase president said he was "appalled" by the "shocking decision."

Not surprisingly, banks are quite adept at using power to get even more money for their own use. Most employers, for example, don't send employees' withholding taxes off to the government; they ask their bank to shift the money into the bank's tax account where the bank earns interest on it until the Federal Reserve withdraws it, one to thirty days later. Banks don't pay interest on this, they simply earn it. Presumably this money compensates them for services they provide the government without charge, such as cashing government checks and saving bonds. The sums are far from trivial: in 1971, Chase held an average daily balance of $181 million in interest-free federal income taxes, and similar arrangements exist with the state and local governments. The banks claim they make no money on the accounts, that they barely compensate them for the free services; but every time Congress has suggested collecting interest and paying banks for the services, the banks have killed the efforts.

Chase Manhattan, of course, is not the only large bank in the nation. And David Rockefeller is hardly the only powerful banker. Nor, for that matter, is the banking establishment the only corporate force that the media treat gingerly. On the contrary, the private sector in general is almost never covered with any toughness or real understanding of the critical impact business decisions have on the country. Since banks in general, and Chase Manhattan in particular, are at the core of the economic system, the press ought to mobilize its own "standing armies" to investigate the terrain, rather than falling for David Rockefeller's claim that "to the extent that we have power we use it wisely and in the public interest."

March 1974

PROFILES

J. ANTHONY LUKAS

"Say It Ain't So, Scotty"

QUESTION: Good morning, machine. Please identify yourself.

ANSWER: I am the 1973 model of the electronic truth detector, Uniquack.

QUESTION: Very good, machine. Now tell me, who is the only man in the world this past year to have exclusive interviews with Chou En-lai, Henry Kissinger and Arnold Toynbee?

ANSWER: James Barrett Reston of *The New York Times*.

QUESTION: Uh-huh. And whom did the *Saturday Review* call "an American journalistic statesman sought by prime ministers and world leaders"?

ANSWER: James Barrett Reston.

QUESTION: And who is the only American newspaperman included in the volume entitled, "The Hundred Most Important People in the World Today"?

ANSWER: James Barrett Reston.

QUESTION: And when A. M. Rosenthal, the *Times* managing editor, plays a favorite parlor game in which guests pretend they are God and declare whom they would appoint as President of the United States, whom does Mr. Rosenthal choose?

ANSWER: James Barrett Reston

QUESTION: He must be quite some guy, this Reston.

ANSWER: He sure is. After all, he invented me.

QUESTION: Oh, really? What for?

ANSWER: Well, he called me his electronic truth detector, but really I was his electronic bullshit detector. When he ran into enough, he'd pile it all up in a column and turn me loose. Oh, we used to have some fun!

QUESTION: You don't have fun any more?

ANSWER: Not much.

QUESTION: How come?

ANSWER: Oh, Scotty and I were buddies when he was just a reporter. Since he's become a Journalistic Statesman, I don't see him much any more.

When I was a young reporter on the Baltimore *Sun* in the late fifties, Scotty Reston was the man I wanted to be when I grew up. In fact, almost everybody on the *Sun,* or for that matter on any other paper, wanted to be Scotty Reston. Around the magistrate's desk at the Eastern Police Station or over a Bohemian beer at Obryckhi's Crab House, we would chatter excitedly about his latest scoop or chuckle over the way his dyspeptic computer, Uniquack, deflated Eisenhower's verbosity. In that era, scornful of Ike's bumbling babbitry but still profoundly respectful of national power, Reston was the apotheosis of the Washington Correspondent: scrappy but eminently respectable; brassy yet reflective; tenacious and still charming; irreverent but responsible. That marvelous moniker, "Scotty," conjured up the image of a tough little terrier, trim, well-groomed and welcome at the best tables in town—where he claimed, not the bones, but the choicest morsels—yet alert, unmuzzled and never hesitant to nip at even the best-booted heel.

Above all, he was renowned for his "scoops"—already a slightly archaic concept, redolent of "The Front Page" or the

World city desk; but Reston revived the term, lending it weight and dignity by the sheer scope of his exclusives. His first and best known was a whopper—the full position papers of the allied powers attending the 1944 Dumbarton Oaks Conference. Day after day, as other reporters seethed with frustration, Reston ladled the spicy broth from his secret cauldron onto page 1. And there were many more to come: the "Yalta Papers" (shared with the Chicago *Tribune* only because the *Trib* found out about Reston's scoop at the last moment and demanded equal treatment); the documents in the Oppenheimer case; the last public statement (in a letter to Reston) of Josef Stalin; the first interview by Premier Aleksei Kosygin with an American correspondent.

"He is quite simply the greatest reporter of our time," says his longtime friend Tom Wicker. "He's particularly good at getting men in power to give him interviews, to give him documents, to tell him what happened—or what they think happened." Anyone who has ever seen Reston go after a big story on deadline will never forget it. "One of the most effective telephone men I've ever seen," Arthur Krock once said. "He's a master at extracting information from a guy who doesn't want to talk," says Wicker. "He'll pretend to know more than he does. He'll unload A and B on the hapless son of a bitch and get him to come across with C."

Wicker, who succeeded Reston as the *Times* Washington bureau chief, concedes that a bureau chief's nightmare goes something like this: a phone call from New York forty-five minutes before deadline: the Akron *Beacon-Journal* has a story that Henry Kissinger is meeting with Castro in a Guatemalan hill resort to carve up the Southern Hemisphere. Get that story.

"What do you do in a crunch like that?" I ask Wicker.

"Call Scotty," he says. "You don't waste that kind of resource. If anybody can get through to the White House and find out what's happening, Scotty can."

Since most of us realized we would never be Scotty Restons, the next best thing was to go to work for him. So like eager rookies in spring training, we flashed our skills, hoping to catch his eye. Indeed, Russell Baker recalls: "Reston saw himself then as general manager of the Yankees, a recruiter of talent, a watcher of the farm system. In my early days on the paper he used to call me in and ask, 'Who's good? Who've they got on the Baltimore *Sun,* the Atlanta *Constitution,* the Charlotte *Observer?*' " I remember my awe when Reston reached down and plucked my friend David Halberstam off the Nashville *Tennessean;* and the exaltation eighteen months later when my own call came, Emmit Holloman's slow drawl crooning across the line from Washington: "Mr. Reston would like to see you this week. Would that be convenient?" Would that be convenient!

Destined for almost immediate assignment to the Congo, I spent only three months in Washington and never became a permanent part of the remarkable bureau Reston was assembling at 17th and K streets. But since he had recruited me, I always considered myself one of "Scotty's Boys." In *The Kingdom and the Power,* Gay Talese has described that "special breed of men, an almost Restonian species: they were lean and tweedy journalists, usually quite tall, educated at better universities, and brighter than they first seemed to be." An exaggeration perhaps, but we did consider ourselves a special outfit, a kind of Praetorian Guard, and wherever we chanced to meet in later years, at Sardi's or the Caravelle bar, we would ask after each other and then, warmed by a few drinks, quietly reaffirm our pride in being "Scotty's Boys."

Reston has a great capacity to stir allegiance among those who work for him. In part, this is because he never seems to resent others' achievements. Baker recalls that Reston once said of another *Times* editor: "He's scared to be surrounded by good people. I always feel that if I'm surrounded by good people it'll make me look better." Harrison Salisbury remarks on Reston's knack for becoming a father figure to younger men, in much the same way as, years earlier, he had been almost a son to older men like Arthur Krock and Arthur Hays Sulzberger.

The warmth and loyalty which he engendered both below and above—particularly his intimate relationship with the Sulzberger family—sped his rise within the *Times* hierarchy: to bureau chief in 1953; associate editor in 1964; executive editor in 1968; vice president in 1969; and in 1973 to a seat on the board of directors. The *Times* has made him a wealthy man. In 1970, the last year for which published figures are available, he received $96,395 in salary and fees, $30,000 in "supplemental remuneration," and had built up "deferred compensation" in stock valued then at $857,648 (less now, for the price of *Times* stock has slipped sharply). He also owns outright *Times* stock valued in December 1972 at nearly $170,000. He has two offices, one in New York and one in Washington, spacious and impressive enough for *Esquire* to photograph. Although the term makes him uncomfortable, he is certainly, as the *Saturday Review* puts it, "a journalistic statesman who has arrived."

Richly deserved as these rewards may be, they have taken their toll. A Journalistic Statesman does not have much time or energy left for reporting.

At its best, in the fifties and early sixties, Reston's column was a projection of his reportorial talents. Analysis has never been his strong point, and certainly not philosophy. ("Scotty has journalism's best legs," says Russ Baker. "He's not Aristotle, he's Alexander. He's got to be out striding around the world.") What he did best in those years was to illuminate a situation through high-level reporting. He could get to the "experts" or the actors in a drama, sit down and talk with them, find out how they saw the issues, then write about it in a breezy, colloquial style. "I think I know where the brains are in this town," he once said. "I pick 'em. When I pick enough of them, I can write an analytical piece about whatever the problem is."

But as he had less time—and perhaps inclination—to report, Reston began disparaging "the old-fashioned scoop artist" who liked to play "cops and robbers" with government officials (precisely the rough rodeo act in which he won his own golden spurs). He scorned "police blotter journalism," the tendency merely to "transfer the reporting habits of the police court and the county court house to the great capitals of the world." Instead, he called for a more "thoughtful" journalism which would explain "what it all means."

Soon he developed a striking metaphor for this viewpoint: "On the surface the waters are ruffled and confused, but deep and powerful tides are running underneath." And, he decided, a columnist's task was to contemplate the tides, not report the waves. In recent years this has become Reston's most persistent theme—the need to get our minds off the day-to-day headlines and concentrate on the sweeping longterm changes which are transforming our lives. As he put it in 1963:

> We are in trouble because we have not kept up with the needs of the age. Change is the biggest story in the world today, and we are not covering it adequately; change in the size and movement of our people; change in the nature, location and availability of jobs; violent change in the relations between village and town, town and city, city and state, state and nation, and, of course, change in the relations between the empires that are rising . . . unless we report these changes, our people will not adapt to them, and every civilization must either adapt or perish.

One can hardly argue with this. But the theme has been repeated so often in Reston's columns over the past decade (one friend suggests it is his "slow-day column") that I wondered where it came from. So during a long interview in the study of his Washington home, I asked him. He walked across the room to his cluttered desk where he picked up a well-thumbed copy of *The Essential Lippmann* and proceeded to read this passage from "Drift and Mastery":

We are unsettled to the very roots of our being. There isn't a human relation, whether of parent and child, husband and wife, worker and employer, that doesn't move in a strange situation. We are not used to a complicated civilization. We don't know how to behave when personal contact and eternal authority have disappeared. There are no precedents to guide us, no wisdom that wasn't made for a simpler age. We have changed our environment more quickly than we know how to change ourselves.

Reston balanced the graceful sentences like crystal goblets which might shatter in a moment's carelessness. For he holds Lippmann in respect bordering on awe. They have known each other for years, many of them as neighbors when Lippmann occupied the former deanery of Washington Cathedral a few blocks down Woodley Road from Reston's place. In 1959, Lippman's seventieth year, Reston and Marquis Childs edited a volume of appreciation in which Reston marveled at the stately grandeur of Lippmann's career: "Half in the noisy pit and half in the quiet study, a duality of engagement in the world of public affairs and disengagement from the world of affairs into the world of books and political philosophy, of reason and meditation on ultimate values."

During my interview with him, Reston emphatically denied that Lippmann was his journalistic model. "He's a beautifully educated man and I'm not well-educated at all. He's a very orderly man. I'm terribly sloppy. He imposed his private life on the news. I'm tied to the ticker. I've never thought of myself as another Lippmann."

Yet others have made the comparison. In a 1961 article on Washington columnists, *Newsweek* noted that President Kennedy "concentrates most intently upon a trio of sages": Lippmann, Joe Alsop and Reston. Later, John K. Jessup wrote in *Life:* "Lippmann, the born mandarin, can be said to have brought philosophy down from its mountain to the sweaty forum of public events; whereas Reston, moving in the opposite direction, has elevated city-room journalism into political and social criticism of a high order." And when Lippmann retired as a newspaper columnist in 1967, speculation on who would inherit his mantle as pundit-in-chief focused most frequently on Joe Kraft and Reston.

"That kind of talk couldn't help but affect Scotty," says one *Times* editor. "Almost despite himself, he wants to be Lippmann's successor." In any case, Reston continued to drift steadily away from reporting in his columns and toward the "political philosophy" and "meditation on ultimate values" he had once detected in Lippmann.

This tide reached its high-water mark in 1968–69 when the Sulzbergers prevailed on him to take over as executive editor, partly to run both the Daily and Sunday news departments but primarily to resolve a fierce power struggle underway in New York. Though a step up for Reston the Institutional Figure, the new job was something of a disaster for Reston the Journalist. It meant leaving Washington, the city which had nourished his creative energies for nearly three decades ("I can no more imagine Reston leaving Washington than the Pope leaving Rome," Bob Donovan of the Los Angeles *Times* remarked on hearing the news).

New York fascinated him, but he never felt at home there. He could still interview his Washington sources on the phone, of course, but somehow he seemed to do less and less even of that. Linda Greenhouse, his news clerk that year, recalls that "writing the column seemed to be a terrible chore for him during that period. He had all these mandatory meetings from which he would have to wrench himself away, lock himself up in a room and write under great pressure." And the columns showed it—lofty, above the fray, moralistic, and often downright banal. Since his return to Washington in 1969, they have regained a bit of their lost concreteness; but they still ring with empty, windy sentences like these:

- "The discontent that is shaking the world cannot be dealt with by politics alone or at the periphery of public life but must get closer to the central and intimate places of personal life and moral conduct." (June 6, 1971)

• "You cannot go across America these days without realizing that the nation is in the midst of another vast physical transformation, and without wondering where all this is leading." (March 22, 1973)

• "The more the American people get, the more they seem to grumble about what they don't get, but at least this Thanksgiving even most professional grumblers would probably admit that the world is now in better shape than it was a year ago." (November 22, 1972)

Every once in a while—notably on his trip to China last year—he plunges anew into real reporting and we get flashes of the old Reston: his famous five-hour interview with Chou En-lai (" 'Please don't eat the lotus leaves,' Mr. Chou said") and the lively account of his own appendectomy at the Anti-Imperialist Hospital in Peking ("Doctor Li lit two pieces of an herb called ai, which looked like the burning stumps of a broken cheap cigar, and held them close to my abdomen while occasionally twirling the needles into action").

Savoring dispatches like those, one wonders whether the crest of a great reporter's career ought necessarily to be a column. It wasn't always so. Adolph Ochs, the *Times*'s founder, abhorred opinion in his paper and the *Times* didn't have a political column until Arthur Krock snagged his in 1933 (joining a relatively small corps of capital columnists headed by Lippmann and David Lawrence). But today, a hard-driving, scoop-scoring political reporter sees a column as his only just reward.

But why? Each morning, on editorial and op-ed pages across the country, Alsop and Kraft, White and Fritchey, Bartlett and Phillips, Wills and Thimmesch, Evans and Novak, Buckley and Kilpatrick masticate the same tasteless bit of Washington gristle chewed over by their colleagues yesterday and the day before. Most of them write as if their world were bounded by 1600 Pennsylvania Avenue, Capitol Hill, Foggy Bottom and Langley, Virginia, seemingly unaware that something may also be afoot at the Federal Trade Commission or the Bureau of Indian Affairs, much less in overcrowded prisons, understaffed hospitals or crumbling neighborhoods across the land. Even those columnists with broader horizons—notably Tom Wicker and Tony Lewis— often seem wasted in their 700-word grooves. Should the ultimate product of exceptional talent like theirs be impassioned screeds into whose margins we scrawl, "How true!"? Reston once wrote: "News is more powerful than opinion." In a year whose most significant journalism was produced by two Washington police reporters it is difficult not to agree.

But there is a deeper paradox in Reston's career: his very triumphs as an institutional figure may have contributed heavily to his obsolescence as a columnist. For beyond reporting, Reston's major assets as a columnist were bright writing, access to expertise, and a feel for "the inside story." Yet these are the very qualities which Reston has so vigorously sought to inject in the *Times*'s general news coverage over the past twenty years.

Twenty years ago, Reston's lively, informal writing stood out from the soggy swamp of *Times* verbiage. For he brought to political coverage the brisk, droll style he had developed as a sportswriter on the Springfield (Ohio) *Daily News* and with the Associated Press (the sports pages then being the only part of a newspaper free enough from the textbook formulas so a writer could develop a distinctive style). Reston's outright forays into humor, including Uniquack, largely ceased in 1962 when Baker began his satirical column across the way ("Why have a bush-leaguer do it when you have a pro on the page?" Reston explains). And since then better writing has pervaded so much of the paper that Reston's own style no longer seems anything special.

Likewise with expertise. In the fifties, Reston had an unparalleled ability to "get to the man who knows." But he was also among the first to recognize that the age of specialization required a new specialization among reporters. Thus, he hired men like Ed Dale and Dick Mooney to report economics; John Finney on science; Jack Raymond on military affairs, and so on. Today, there is very little expertise in Reston's column one cannot read more fully elsewhere in the paper.

All too often in the fifties, the "inside story" was told only around the bar after work because reporters couldn't find a way to get it in the paper. Russ Baker recalls: "As a reporter, I often felt I couldn't tell the reader all I knew about a story. You had to channel your information between those bare column rules with all the conventions of sourcing and 'objectivity.' So Scotty was invaluable. While we had to write 'Joe McCarthy charged . . . Ike replied . . . ,' you could flip over to Scotty and get it all in perspective." Reston wrote the bar talk.

But, partly as a result of his efforts, the *Times* has loosened up considerably. More interpretation is allowed in news stories. The "news analysis" column is available to reporters on complex stories. Very rarely these days does one get an "inside story" from Reston that doesn't appear elsewhere in the paper first.

"There was a time when the political column was important to American journalism," says one Washington reporter. "But journalism is so much more subjective now, a reader soaks up so much more of what a reporter knows, that there isn't much role left for the columnist any more. To make a column compelling now you need strong whiskey; spritzer isn't good enough."

And that is part of the problem, for Reston often goes down like Gator-ade these days, a pastel shading of opinion so carefully hedged that one isn't sure just what he thinks. His columns on Watergate, for example, have been models of circumspection—particularly toward the President himself. As late as March 24, 1973, he was treating the whole matter as a relatively minor aberration ("Politicians have a way of doing fairly well on major questions and then stumbling into trouble over secondary issues"). On April 19, after the case had broken wide open, he was still ready to assume the President's own innocence ("He is too intelligent to approve such risks in an election against George McGovern which was never in doubt. Also, in fairness to him, he is too smart to get involved in raising funds laundered through Mexico, or recruiting C.I.A. characters to bug Larry O'Brien's telephones").

Or, if he takes a strong position one day, he takes an equally strong position on the other side several days later. In November 1972 he praised the President for being "more generous, more composed and more serene" than ever before. In early February 1973 he denounced him for "an insensitivity to people in trouble, if not an actual strain of cruelty."

In part this reflects an understanding of the complexity of human affairs. "Having raised a family," he told me, "I know that most readers live in ambiguity. Yet somehow when they read a columnist they don't want ambiguity. They want you to be either Bill Buckley or Tony Lewis." In part, it comes out of a strong sense of fairness and balance: if you knock 'em down one day, pick 'em up and brush 'em off the next.

But it also stems from the ad hoc, improvised nature of his judgments. "It would be flattery to suggest that I have a clear, simple, coherent philosophy," he said in our interview. "I don't." (One friend compares Reston's method to the technique in calculus for locating a point on the arc of a circle. "He hits first on this side, then on that side, thus gradually defining the boundaries of a point without ever really establishing it.")

Linda Greenhouse, now a *Times* reporter, thinks it comes from an acute awareness that he is read by powerful men. "He takes that responsibility very seriously. He thinks the best way to get politicians to listen to him is to appeal to their better nature. He thinks they'll respond to sweet reason whereas castigation would only turn them off." And inevitably he must protect the many powerful readers who are also his sources. Some years ago, John Kenneth Galbraith, reviewing a Reston book, wrote: "Over the years he has learned to treat all people in the manner of a newspaperman who must one day go back and see them again . . . He should now indulge himself more often in the added pleasure of plain and candid and categorical speech."

But perhaps it is just not in his nature. One member of the Washington bureau says, "There's something in Reston that makes him instinctively go for the middle ground. It's the instinct of the politician who just naturally gravitates to the center where the power and the influence and the money lie. He doesn't calculate it. It's in his glands."

In our interview, I asked Reston what he considered the keynote of his reporting over the years and he replied unhesitatingly, "Profound skepticism of power." But others do not see it that way. Russell Baker says "Scotty may be skeptical about the men who wield power, but he's very respectful of power." And another long-time bureau member says, "I don't think he's skeptical either of government or of men in government—except in their role as politicians, and that largely in a Mr. Dooley way."

One Washington reporter says, "Reston is the classic example of the journalist who tacitly accepts that his mission is to convey what the great men think. He doesn't put his own intellectual perceptions forward. The materials he deals with are the perceptions of other men."

Reston's skepticism seems most restrained when dealing with foreign affairs. And perhaps he trusts sources as he does because foreign affairs was his first political beat and has been his main focus of interest ever since.

His views on the relations between press and government in foreign policy were outlined in his 1966 lectures to the Council on Foreign Relations, later published as *The Artillery of the Press*. The title derived from Reston's statement that "the rising power of the United States in world affairs, and particularly of the American President, requires not a more compliant press, but a relentless barrage of facts and criticism, as noisy but also as accurate as artillery fire." But as he spelled out his view, the press corps' guns seemed strangely muffled.

Reston pinned his hopes for an enlightened foreign policy on a "remnant" of wise and intelligent citizens, "an expanding minority" composed of "the best elements in the press, in networks and government, in the schools, colleges, universities and the church, in business, commerce and finance." Thus he felt "the responsible government official and the responsible reporter in the field of foreign affairs are not really in conflict ninety per cent of the time. When they do their best work, they are allies with one another and with 'the remnant' in the nation that wants to face, rather than evade, reality."

The consequence of an alliance between government and press can be found in Reston's own successful efforts to tone down the *Times*'s 1961 story about the imminent Bay of Pigs invasion. Likewise, Reston knew that the United States was flying high-altitude reconnaissance planes over the Soviet Union but suppressed the fact for more than a year until one of the planes was shot down in 1960. And David Wise's book *The Politics of Lying,* says the *Times* Washington bureau, while headed by Reston in 1961, killed a story about the secret training of Tibetan guerrillas in the Colorado Rockies after the Secretary of Defense's office called to say it would violate "national security." Reston does not recall the incident, but he is on record as saying that "the old principle of publish-and-be-damned, while very romantic, bold and hairy, can often damage the national interest." (Reston favored publication of the Pentagon Papers which, he argued, were mostly history and therefore could not damage the national interest).

Such an alliance may have seemed defensible in the midst of the cold war. But it was a strange argument for Reston to advance in 1966 at the peak of the Vietnam agony.

"Scotty's form of reporting presupposes that you are dealing with an honorable entity," says one editor. "But as government became less honorable in the sixties, as the Vietnam war led Presidents and Secretaries of State to lie systematically not only to the press but to themselves, Reston's reliance on government sources no longer worked very well. His instinct was always to give them the benefit of the doubt, and he got taken.''

Perhaps he was right to trust William Fulbright, Mike Mansfield or John Gardner, whom he saw often in Washington. But what of Robert McNamara, William Rogers and Henry Kissinger, who also rank among his best sources? When I sat down in his study for my interview, Reston said, "Henry Kissinger sat in that chair just the other night." In an administration where Kissinger is one of only two reliable sources on foreign affairs, Reston's remarkable access to him is certainly invaluable. But there are those who think he has been used by Kissinger as often as he has used him. Leslie Gelb and Anthony Lake, in their February 1973 article in [MORE], concluded that Reston had been misled by Kissinger in Paris in December 1972, resulting in the columnist's overly optimistic page-one story saying that the last remaining obstacle to a peace agreement involved the sovereignty of the Saigon government and if that could not be resolved to Thieu's satisfaction, the United States would sign without him. Kissinger apparently went around Washington saying that Reston misunderstood him—something Reston very rarely does. Yet, on March 11, 1973, we found Reston again in print with a column of inside information—reportedly from Kissinger—about Hanoi's massive violations of the Vietnam peace treaty. There are those in Washington who think he was being used again.

David Halberstam feels Reston stumbled in the sixties because he could never bring himself to accept what Vietnam had done to America. "Scotty was pretty good on the war itself," Halberstam says. "I don't think he was ever really fooled, and long before a lot of other people, he realized it was going irrevocably wrong. But he wouldn't take what he knew and carry it the whole way. He kept saying, 'The war is bad, but America works, the system works.' "

Reston does believe the system works; he has his own life before him to prove it. In 1972 he was one of eleven Americans to win the Horatio Alger Award for rising to greatness from humble beginnings. And indeed all the elements of the Great American Success Story are there: born the son of a poor factory worker in Clydebank, Scotland; emigrated to Dayton, Ohio, with his family at the age of eleven; worked there as a kitchen boy, newspaper deliverer, and caddie; told by his mother "make something of yourself "; and he did. "I came here as a poor immigrant boy," Reston told me, "and what a marvelous life I've had of it."

And since Reston is a sentimental, romantic, pious man, perhaps it is not surprising that he should regard the System, as he grew up in it, with something approaching reverence.

There is reverence, of course, for God. "The religious foundation of our common life—no matter how much we divide over creeds and sects and their relation to the state—is not 'forgotten.' We may not believe, but we believe in believing" (April 2, 1969). Raised in a devout Scotch Presbyterian family, encouraged to become a minister, he takes his Calvinism seriously. But not solemnly. Russell Baker recalls standing next to Reston on the night John Kennedy received the Democratic nomination in Los Angeles: "A minister was up there on the podium intoning, 'We will beat our spears into pruning hooks' or some gibberish like that, and Reston leans over to me and whispers, 'He's got it all fucked up.' "

There is reverence for country, for his adopted land. Sometimes that is expressed in outright patriotism: "The United States went to war today as a great nation should—with simplicity, dignity and unprecedented unity" (December 8, 1941); and sometimes in a remarkable sense of place, rare in a man accustomed to the anonymous marble of official Washington. He is fond of citing a Christopher Morley aphorism: "To be deeply rooted in a place that has meaning is perhaps the best gift a child can have." And Reston is deeply

rooted in at least two places, besides Washington, of course
—not Clydebank and Dayton, but Fiery Run, Virginia, and
Martha's Vineyard, where he maintains houses and often
retires for a quiet Thanksgiving or Christmas to begin columns with folksy sentences like, "The neighbors down this
mountain road are pleased with President Nixon's agreement
in Moscow."

There is reverence for the past and reverence for the future. He loves the simple graces of the nineteenth century
when he can still find them: "The old Currier and Ives America of the Thanksgiving Day prints has not wholly vanished"
(November 22, 1959). And he has boundless faith in what is
yet to come: "It will be a long time before there is peace and
goodwill everywhere in the land, but there is enough of it to
keep us going in the right direction" (December 22, 1968), an
optimism so persistent and so often flung in the face of facts
that one editor has dubbed his columns "the bright side of
chaos."

There is reverence for women and the home. Reston has
a perennial column about the brave little women behind the
powerful men in Washington. "Back of the candidates are
their women, with all their love and doubts about their guys,
and their anxiety about their children" (January 16, 1972). In
part, this reflects Reston's relentlessly traditional view of the
woman's role. Eileen Shanahan, the *Times*'s able economics
reporter in Washington, recalls Reston's surprise when he
walked into the bureau late one Saturday evening some years
ago and found her doing her regular turn on the news desk.
"You shouldn't have to do that," he said, to which she
replied, "Chivalry has no place on the job." (Shanahan adds
that otherwise Reston treated her as "a full-fledged bureau
member without reservation," and she, unlike some others,
feels Reston has become "modernized" on the women's issue). But in large part his views on the matter probably
reflect his marriage to the former Sally Fulton, who for
nearly forty years has devoted her full energies to her "guy"
and their three sons. The day of our interview, Reston had

just gotten back from a speaking trip to Buffalo. As we swung through the door, Sally Reston was coming down the stairs. She stopped for a moment, broke into a warm smile and sang out, "Hey, it's the Buffalo flash!"

There is reverence for *The New York Times.* On December 24, 1962, in the middle of a strike against the *Times,* Reston wrote, "Dear Santa: All I want for Christmas is *The New York Times* . . . Somebody struck the *Times* in the belief that it's a newspaper, but that is obviously ridiculous. The *Times* is a public institution, like the Yankees or Barney Baruch." To me, he put it more simply: "I'm kind of goofy about this paper." And he knows just how to use the power of the *Times* in getting a story. "He really feels the *Times* is equal to any other institution," says Wicker. "So when he sits down with Dean Rusk or Rogers it's like our Secretary of State meeting their Secretary of State."

There is reverence for ideas. He has campaigned for decades to get them into the paper. "Ideas are news," he argued. "We are not covering the news of the mind as we should." Largely as a result of his efforts, the *Times* assigned Bob Reinhold and Israel Shenker to "news of the mind" beats and inaugurated the Op Ed page, where intellectuals, among others, could express their views directly. And long before that he was working to encourage some of "the best young minds" in the universities to join the *Times* and to make sure they got the scope and time to do serious, thoughtful work when they got there. Later, when some of those men got restless, Reston tried unsuccessfully to devise a way for them to stay with the *Times* on a contractual basis while doing still more serious, long-term work outside. He argued for development of "a new class of public servants, who move about in the triangle of daily or periodical journalism, the university or foundation and government service," pointing to "a growing and hopeful breed" of such men— McGeorge Bundy, Arthur Schlesinger, Jr., John Kenneth

Galbraith, Theodore Sorenson, Richard Goodwin and Douglass Cater, among others.

But Reston proved vulnerable to men like those. "The tough-mindedness which he might bring to a politician," says Halberstam, "he never seemed to bring to eggheads and ideas." Precisely because he is not essentially a man of ideas (he was a mediocre student at the then mediocre University of Illinois), he has an exaggerated awe for those who are. His columns are filled with pithy quotes from Alfred North Whitehead, Paul Valéry and Lippmann which he either culls himself from the fifty-four-volume *Great Books of the Western World* in his office or sends his news clerks to dig out of the library. And every chance he gets, he will seek out "the thoughtful people"—Toynbee, C. P. Snow, Jean Monnet or John Gardner.

Those columns have a distinctive ring, like this one on Hamilton Fish Armstrong: "There are so many noisy voices in the world these days, including the shrill and urgent voices of columnists, that it is seldom possible to hear the quieter thoughts of wiser and more thoughtful men." And it helps too if the thoughtful men also happen to be gentlemen of the old school, as evinced in these words from what may be the quintessential Reston column (March 16, 1973):

> It seldom happens in these hairy, youthful days that anybody chooses a wise old gentleman for a critical job, but President Nixon has done it again by picking David Kirkpatrick Este Bruce of Virginia to be the first official U.S. representative to the Communist Government of China . . . still spare and handsome, white-haired, cautiously slow, but alert and elegantly courteous . . . If, occasionally, they [Chou and Mao] want to talk about the fundamental questions of the coming world order, Bruce will be equal to their questions . . . Now suddenly he has been called back again to go to Peking, and he

and his lovely wife, Evangeline, who was a student of Chinese history at Harvard with John Fairbank . . .

Ah, Harvard! His reverence for ideas seems to focus on the graceful old university by the Charles. When he began choosing "clerks" from the universities in the sixties, a disproportionate number came from Harvard—Steve Roberts, Craig Whitney, Iver Peterson and Linda Greenhouse (Radcliffe '68). When Nixon appointed three new cabinet members— Eliot Richardson, Caspar Weinberger and Roy Ash—what struck Reston as most significant about the appointments was that all three had gone to Harvard. And when student unrest came to Harvard in the spring of 1969, only the crustiest Harvard alumni rallied to the support of President Nathan Pusey as he did.

Reston did not care much for the student rebels anywhere. "He saw that whole era as a return to incipient Yahooism in which students were trying to get involved in things which should be left to serious and substantial men," says Russell Baker. But Harvard sent him into a real dither, and finally into a bitter public feud with the "liberal caucus" in the faculty who he felt had let President Pusey down. One column ended with a revealing observation: "The Harvards have been telling us for generations that they were just like other people, only better. And now both points are in dispute." The events in Cambridge proved so disconcerting to Reston because he really did believe the Harvards were better.

There are those who feel Reston's evolution of late is a bit like that of his friend Hubert Humphrey (of whom he wrote in 1968, "If Presidents were elected by the thousand best-informed men in Washington on the basis of who would make the best President, he would be No. 1 at last"). Both men were symbols and spokesmen for the great American liberal center in the fifties. But largely as a result of the Vietnam war, the liberal center shifted during the past decade and their constituencies shifted leftward with it.

Some of those who have worked for and with Reston over the years may wish that he were a little less cozy with power, a little less reverential toward the System, a little more outspoken about the evils they detect in American society. But they still revere him for his immense kindness, decency, generosity, professionalism and integrity. "My career would have been nothing without him," says Halberstam. "He was like a blocking back for me." So what they feel more than anything else these days is a sense of loss. "Those of us who honor and love him wish that he were still walking with us," says Halberstam. "It's like what Chicago fans felt in 1919 about Shoeless Joe Jackson. Say it ain't so, Joe. Say it ain't so, Scotty."

May 1977

Portrait of an Outsider

Neil Sheehan spent a year waiting—waiting for the Justice Department to strike, dealing with lawyers instead of writing, waiting for the Pulitzer Prize to come, which it did not, and marking the tenth anniversary of the day when he first arrived in Vietnam. Those are ten long years in which he held doggedly to the subject, in season and out of season, despite other assignments, ten years in which we all thought we would have gone on to other stories, other sorrows. His history, it seems to me, tells something about the particular journalism of the war and of our generation.

He was twenty-five years old when he first came to Vietnam, airlifted in by UPI from the Tokyo night rewrite desk when Mert Perry resigned to become a stringer for *Time*. What recommended him to his employers was the size of his salary, then seventy-five dollars a week. He was totally green and a born natural reporter. I came on the scene for *The New York Times* about three months later and I still have a letter from Homer Bigart, my predecessor, evaluating restaurants, briefing officers, colleagues, and which said: "the young kid from UPI is going to be very good." It was Bigart who gave him his education. Sheehan had arrived in Saigon, had looked around and had decided that the best way to learn journalism was simply to follow Bigart around all day and do whatever he did. It was not a bad way to start. If there is a greater reporter than Homer, a man with a surer sense for fraud, I do not know him. It was an odd friendship. Bigart, the veteran reporter at the height of his powers and shrewdness, hating the war, the assignment, sensing everything that was going to go wrong, and Sheehan, young, energetic, loving everything because it was new and fresh.

Sheehan believes that their friendship started when he gave Bigart something usually rare for Homer, a rocket. It had been on a Saturday and Sheehan had filed a story about two hundred Vietcong being killed in the Mekong Delta by waves and waves of attacking government troops. It was, Sheehan says in retrospect, the one really bogus story he filed from Saigon. The story arrived in New York just before deadline for the *Times* Sunday edition, and the editors fired off a rocket to Bigart. So that night about 3 A.M. in Saigon, Sheehan was awakened by a call from Homer. "Mr. Sheehan. This is Homer Bigart. I have a cable here from my employers in New York. They seem to believe that there are two hundred dead Vietcong in the Mekong Delta." Sheehan's voice, very small at the other end of the phone, noted its assent about the victory. "Mr. Sheehan," came Bigart's voice. "Get dressed. We are driving to My Tho . . . And, Mr. Sheehan, there better be two hundred bodies down there." So they drove to My Tho that night and there were not any Vietcong bodies and on the way back Sheehan was despairing. His first big story and it was a clinker; his career in journalism was now clearly over; surely by the high standards of American journalism he would now have to resign. Bigart consoled him. "Don't let it get to you, it happens to all of us, I've done it a few times myself." And, of course, the final important message: "Don't let it get you down, kid . . . But just don't do it again while I'm here."

They made one more trip to My Tho which was unusually instructive to the young Sheehan. It was supposed to be a long weekend of combat, many battles and many famous victories. Only it did not turn out that way. On the first of three days there were a few Vietcong killed. On the second day nothing happened. And on the third day again a massive operation was launched and again nothing happened. On the way back to Saigon Sheehan was extremely depressed.

"What's the matter, Mr. Sheehan?" Bigart asked.

Well, said Sheehan, the problem was that he had come down here and spent three days, and there was no story. Three days wasted without a story.

"But there is a story, Mr. Sheehan," Bigart said. "It doesn't work. That's the story."

That was his education, all from this extraordinary reporter, who brought the cumulative sense of his long career to that assignment, who had sure instinct for the softness of it all. It was not just the sheer excellence of his reportorial ability, but the fact that he had stayed the outsider; his ability and success had not made him a member of what he had originally criticized. And his iconoclasm did not just extend to the government of the United States, to ambassadors and generals, it included as well the people who ran the great newspapers of America. He had an intuitive sense of their limits and their timidity. To be with him was to have one's own doubts about management confirmed. Much of this rubbed off on many of us. We learned that people in management—no matter how friendly they were and how well they used our slang and our terms, even if they had come from our ranks—were to be watched carefully like Good ambassadors or Good generals. Bigart's sense of institutions, what they did to good men, was very good, and far ahead of the times.

Sheehan, too, was an outsider then, and he is an outsider now, but with all the style, education and resources of the insider. Which made him somewhat different in the era of the late fifties and early sixties. That was a time when American journalism was going respectable; it was consciously raising the educational level of its reporters, which was a good idea and long overdue. The new breed was better educated, had been to Harvard and Yale or thereabouts, was sophisticated, had taken the right courses in the history of foreign policy, but there were problems as well. First, there was something of a drop-off in sheer digging; the new breed was hired after all, primarily to think and interpret, not so much to dig. Second, the new breed was perhaps too willing to accept the basic norms of American government and foreign policy—those norms, of course, having been set at the very colleges we were all graduating from. (I have long suspected that one reason for Jack Kennedy's remarkable success with the Washington press corps was that he was so much like it in education, dress, style, clothes, humor, books read, general political assumptions.)

Sheehan was different. True, he was the product of Harvard and he had even been on the *Harvard Advocate,* which was a bit effete (though he had once drunkenly thrown a typewriter out of the *Advocate* window, which was not effete). But there was still the raw Irish edge to him. If he had been brought to Harvard as a potential recruit to the system and he had, like the rest of us, hovered on the edge of conversion, then Vietnam would take care of that. It was for him and for many of us the issue of deconversion; the more we learned about Vietnam, the more skeptical we became, first about Vietnam, then about the U.S. government in general. But he was not yet converted in 1962 when he arrived; he was still raw, he had not been tempered in any genteel city room, a process which took the edge off many reporters; instead he arrived in Vietnam with plenty of edge and the experience added more. He did not accept the assumptions of the U.S. government or its foreign policy; he knew he had everything to learn, and he had the most relentless kind of energy I have ever seen.

I thought then and I think now that he had the best overall sense of the war. Of us he was the first to see—it hardly seems revolutionary now, but it was an important link then—that so much of the failure and frustration in the South was connected to the legacy of the colonial war, that we were in the French footsteps more than we knew. (When we would go out to the airport to see another American dignitary arrive and give the requisite propaganda speech about inevitable victory, Neil would nudge me and say, "Ah, another foolish Westerner come to lose his reputation to Ho Chi Minh.") He did not win the Pulitzer Prize in 1964, and for most of us who were out there that year it was somehow inconceivable that Mal Browne (of the AP) and I could win and Neil did not. In a way he got lost in the shuffle. UPI was particularly bitter about not getting its share of Pulitzers and had put all its efforts behind Merriman Smith that year for his coverage of the Kennedy assassination, so Neil was left out.

He moved that year to the *Times* and soon returned to Vietnam. I thought his reporting in those days was first-rate. He was not as flashy as some, but he was one of a handful of reporters who had a sense of the fabric of the society and still wrote about the Vietnamese and how the war affected them. Others were writing about the American build-up and somehow that seemed more dramatic, though Neil was concentrating on those questions which eventually spelled defeat for the Americans. But matters did not work out particularly well for him on the *Times* in general; he was not exactly their kind of man. He was in effect dogged and slow (he does not write quickly, which is a surprise since he is as quick in story reflex as anyone I know), and journalism is a profession for those who are facile and quick, who are ready to pick up when told to pick up and let go when told to let go. Neil does not pick up as quickly as some, and more important, he does not let go as easily as others.

But the problem with the *Times* is a larger one: the *Times* is a good newspaper, but it is so large that it is more than that; it is essentially an institution, and institutional norms, rather than journalistic ones, have become dominant. An institution, any institution, is not at ease with people who vary from the norm, who have too much passion or commitment, and who repeatedly cause problems. This is true in journalism as well, though the profession itself is supposed to be outside of and alienated from other institutions. Instead, at every level of the society it inevitably begins to parallel the society. The *Times* will handle itself very well when it is confronted by a direct challenge—the riots at the 1968 Democratic National Convention, the coming of the Pentagon Papers—but it will not by and large seek challenge, and those who repeatedly do fall into a kind of journalistic limbo.

The *Times* wanted Sheehan to do investigative reporting. But investigative reporting is complex; it takes time—weeks sometimes—before there is a tangible lollypop to put on the front page. Sheehan feels that the paper would give him the go-ahead, but then more often than not would ask him to fill in on another assignment, to help out at the Pentagon that day, or take a breaking story on another beat because a reporter was on vacation. He wanted to go back to Saigon in 1968 and report once more, but the assignment didn't come through—though his background, knowledge and tenure made him uniquely qualified for the job.

So he remained in limbo. The *Times* management, for example, was less than enthusiastic about the publication in the Sunday book review of Sheehan's essay on war crimes, which in terms of journalistic achievement and initiative was perhaps superior to the publication of the Pentagon Papers, and which in terms of that quality most often heralded at publisher's conventions—freedom of speech within a democracy—was a truly remarkable act. It is one thing to publish documents about a bad war seven years after the fact; it is quite another thing to touch on war crimes in the middle of the reevaluation of the war. Indeed, there is a special irony in the fact that the article that is generally believed to have linked Sheehan and Daniel Ellsberg—the piece on war crimes—was one which embarrassed the *Times* brass.

But there is a larger irony. Sheehan's war-crimes piece was initiated and sponsored by the book review, which typifies the journalistic accommodation to change that has taken place over the last five or six years. Since the dew-line of change has been more cultural and attitudinal than directly political, the great journalistic institutions have responded by turning over the back of their books, the critical areas, to editors, writers and critics generally sympathetic to the counterculture, while the front of the book, the *serious* area, has been left to serious men who still hold to the old assumptions and myths. Mindless statements from the White House are taken seriously and treated seriously. In essence this is true at the *Times,* the Washington *Post, Newsweek* and *Time;* in effect it gives them all split personalities. (It must be somewhat jarring for the serious men who have lied so seriously for so long and been treated so respectfully by these publications to write their memoirs and see them savaged by the new generation holding power at the back of the book.)

Upon publication of the Pentagon Papers, Sheehan was to lose an entire year as a reporter, a year in which his life was totally disrupted, his capacity to operate as a professional journalist crippled. There were first weeks and then months and then more months of long sessions with his lawyers going over every detail of the incident point by point. And then after several months of this, just when he thought he could get back to work, there would be interruptions again —a neighbor saying that the FBI had been by to see her with photos of different people, asking if these people had visited the Sheehan house. Or finding that his bank statement had been subpoenaed by the government. Or discovering that an old friend on the West Coast had been visited by the FBI. And then always a long session with his lawyers finding out what had been said. Keeping up with government. So each time there was a call it simply wiped out the day, or the week; for almost a year his concentration was destroyed. There were several serious tips from Justice Department friends that he might be indicted on a given day, and over a period of time he mentally steeled himself for the fact that he might have to go to jail and found himself in his mind explaining to his daughters why he was going off. As far as the journalistic profession was concerned, he bore the full brunt of the tension between working reporters and the government on the Pentagon Papers issue.

Yet all of that was part of the price of a singular personal triumph—a reporter staying with a single story for ten years. And yet again he does not win the Pulitzer Prize. I do not understand these things, why he is ignored and the *Times* selected (if he wins, the *Times* wins, too). Is it callousness? Is it a way of getting even with an audacious reporter? Surely the story was not, to say the least, assigned by an editor (if anything the Pentagon Papers seem to me an indictment of established American journalism, in that the question of the origins of the war was the most pressing of our time and yet no editor assigned it). Is Sheehan's enterprise in this seen as less enterprise than that which went into at least half of the Pulitzers? And were the papers that easy to come by? After all, *no one else came up with them.* In a way, the Pulitzer for the *Times* is confirmation that there is a double standard of integrity, one for reporters, one for newspaper executives. It is unthinkable for a reporter like Sheehan, knowing of the papers, not to want to publish them. Yet by the standards of the Pulitzer jury, it is clearly thinkable for news executives not to want to publish. Why else recognize *their* "courage"? (Indeed, for the world of journalism to have known that the *Times* had had a shot at the papers and turned them down would have destroyed the reputation of every executive there.)

Much has been said, of course, about the Pentagon Papers simply being "handed" to Neil Sheehan. Yet even for someone like me who does not know the details of the Sheehan-Ellsberg relationship—a relationship that remains secret because the Justice Department now hovers above—there is considerable evidence of Sheehan's legwork. Ten years of dedication to one story, in fact. Moreover, it was an unusual bit of legwork that led to the war-crimes essay in the first place. Sheehan had been given a book to review, a book on war crimes by Mark Lane, and the whole thing had smelled wrong. So he took the trouble to do a few things that neither Lane nor his publisher had bothered to do. He dug into the book and checked out fact after fact. And when he was through he had demonstrated that much in the book was simply not true. By turning a *book review* into an investigative piece, Sheehan began the chain of events that led ultimately to the Pentagon Papers. From Bigart, he had developed a very good nose for fraud, and he has used it well.

August 1972

The Prince of Gonzo

"Aaarrgggghhh." The strangled croak of the deadly gila monster jolted from its sullen stupor. "Eeeeacccckkk." The warning screech of the poisonous reptile about to strike. "Who the hell is it?" shrieks Hunter S. Thompson.

"Uh . . . it's Tony Lukas . . . I'm sorry to wake you, but you told me to call when I got in, and it's twenty past noon."

Another hideous groan in the earpiece of my pay phone at Washington's National Airport. Then a mumbled apology: "One of my depraved and degenerate nights. Sorry if I shouted at you. Afraid I blew it with the White House a few hours ago. Some nitwit secretary called about my flight on the President's press plane and I yelled, 'What the fuck is it?' She hung up. Oh well. I'll meet you at the pool."

A half-hour later, I find the National Affairs Editor of *Rolling Stone* floating on his back in the Hilton's pool spouting water in the air like a malevolent sperm whale. He scrambles out, six-feet-three of bullet sleekness shedding gallons of chlorinated water, tosses on a salmon sports shirt and white tennis shoes and escorts me to a table at the poolside cafe. The languid waitresses ignore us, so he saunters to the bar and brings us each back a Bloody Mary, with grapefruit juice on the side for him. "Can't start the day without grapefruit. Cuts right through all the booze and dope from the night before. Usually, I order a crate of them and slice 'em up with a machete."

He downs two more grapefruit juices and two more Bloody Marys to go with his tropical fruit plate and cheeseburger as we sit in the sun gazing up at the Hilton's glistening white façade. All around us are efficient-looking types with badges identifying them as delegates to the Liquified Natural Gas Convention at the hotel. Recalling his acid contempt for most hotels along the campaign trail (he once denounced Milwaukee's Sheraton-Shroeder as a "Nazi pigsty" where the management would only deal with you if "your breath smelled heavily of sauerbraten"), I asked him how he had managed to survive eight months of transient existence. "It's a horror show," he says. "I can't even stand going down to the lobby or restaurants. More and more I just sit up in my room ordering all this bizarre, exotic shit from room service and denouncing them if they don't have it."

When he first took the *Rolling Stone* political assignment last winter he was supposed to be based in Washington like all other respectable political correspondents. He rented an office in the National Press Building but never moved in, preferring to share a cubicle with the New York *Post* ("I let them use my well-stocked refrigerator and all those free records—better than rent"). With his wife Sandy and his eight-year-old son Juan he moved into a comfortable old house in a wooded section near the District line, but he lasted only a few months. "I detested this town, just couldn't stand living here." Sandy and Juan have since moved back to Woody Creek, Colorado, while Hunter goes on living off room service in pigsties across the land.

He is back in Washington this week in late September 1972 on a double mission: looking for the "villain" in the McGovern campaign and trying to get onto Nixon's press plane for the President's trip to New York and California. So far he hasn't made much progress on either front. "The McGovern thing got off so well and collapsed into such a complete wipeout disaster that you have to fix the blame on somebody. I take some different McGovern guy out drinking every night, but so far I haven't found the villain. I'll track the bastard down, though, until my feet start dripping blood."

He's had even less success with the White House. During the 1968 campaign, Hunter was one of the few correspondents to get a private audience with Nixon, sharing the back seat of his car in New Hampshire on the proviso that they talk only football. But when he got to Washington this year, Nixon's press people steadfastly refused to grant him White House credentials ("A music magazine doesn't need a man up here," he was told). And in recent months he has written some rather uncomplimentary things about the President (comparing the Nixon campaign to "six months in a Holiday Inn" and the Republican convention to "a bad pornographic film"), and his British illustrator, Ralph Steadman, went him one better—portraying the President as some kind of vile, filth-spewing piranha fish. "I would understand by this time if they didn't think I'd make the best company for the President"—Hunter chuckles—"but all I want them to do is say so. Refuse me. Ban me from the plane. Then I can blast them. But that's just what they won't do, the canny bastards. All I've gotten for seven days is the silent treatment. Hell, the plane leaves the day after tomorrow. I guess I better get upstairs and start making some phone calls."

Up in his room on the Hilton's top floor, the first thing I notice is a rash of papers scotch-taped to the bathroom mirror. There is a letter from Lewis Lapham, managing editor of *Harper*'s, turning down Hunter's proposal for a piece on the Auburn-Alabama football game; a memo from Hunter to Gary Hart, the McGovern campaign director, advising him to accept John Lindsay's offer to campaign for McGovern ("Fuck his lack of popularity. Send the bastard out on the hustings immediately"); and several lists with items like "shirts to hotel laundry," "cash check," "swim?" "Booze—case W.T.," "Mac speakers," "Volvo tires," "Call Semple (Ziegler)," "Stearns—Buchanan."

I raise an eyebrow and Hunter explains: "After one of my debauched nights I'm totally wiped out. Unless I have that stuff right in front of me, I don't know what I'm doing." The tires, the shirts, the swim and the check are self-explanatory. "W.T." is Wild Turkey, Hunter's favorite bourbon, a quart of which stands half empty on the dresser. "Mac" stands for McIntosh, the best stereo speakers available, $1,050 and up. ("I'm a sound freak," Hunter says. "My sound system out in Woody Creek is so powerful it broke the plate-glass window; now I want to make it even more powerful.") But what's all that about Semple, Ziegler, Stearns and Buchanan?

Hunter smiles a sly, good-old-Southern-boy grin (he is, after all, a good old Southern boy from Louisville, Kentucky, although he is loath to admit it—even to himself). "That's my White House strategy," he says. And it's a pretty wild strategy. Semple is Robert Semple, the *New York Times* White House correspondent, a very straight, very preppy, Yale-educated journalist who seems like just about the last reporter in Washington for Hunter S. Thompson to call on in a situation like this. But Hunter and Semple were colleagues briefly sometime ago on the *National Observer* and they've kept in touch—at some physical and psychic distance—over the years. Hunter has asked the clout-wielding *Times* man to intervene for him with press secretary Ron Ziegler and Semple has agreed to try. But what about "Stearns—Buchanan"? That is even better. Stearns is Rick Stearns, the McGovern strategist, and Hunter has learned that he is a close friend of Pat Buchanan, the Nixon speechwriter. So McGovern's house radical is calling Nixon's starchy conservative to try to get the lunatic *Rolling Stone* correspondent on the President's plane. Only Hunter S. Thompson could have engineered a three-cushion shot like that.

The middle man in all this is Gerald Warren, the assistant White House press secretary, so the first thing Hunter does up in the room is to place a call to Warren who of course isn't in, as he hasn't been in to Hunter S. Thompson for the past week. Hunter leaves word, then slams the phone down mumbling about "those little secretaries with their sing-song, Pepsi-Cola, ad agency voices." He strides to the refrigerator, breaks out a Ballantine, pops a Marlboro in his horn filter, and slaps a Rolling Stones cassette into his Sony. And there he sits on the bed, beer in one hand, cigarette in the other, phone juggling back and forth or cradled under the chin, and "Jumpin' Jack Flash" jumpin' on the Sony. It is 4 P.M. and Hunter's working day has begun.

"This is the time I usually get started," he says. "Days are for detail work. Nothing important ever happens during the day. Nobody ever tells me the truth in their office. I have to get them on neutral ground at the very least, which usually means a bar. And I never start writing before midnight. By that time I'm usually pretty spaced out on booze and speed —I've eaten enough speed this year my brain should be fried to a cinder, like a piece of bacon. I'll put some music on the Sony—usually Herbie Mann's "Memphis Underground" if I'm into serious politics, but if I want Gonzo Journalism then usually something with a more jerky rhythm like the Stones or the Grateful Dead. And I'll stay with it until I'm burnt out, usually about dawn." (Many of Hunter's pieces begin with dawn rising outside some hotel room. Tim Crouse, another *Rolling Stone* correspondent who has spent a lot of time with Hunter this year, describes him during those early-morning writing binges as "this great bird, this huge dactyl, with his arms like wings out to his sides, his fingers poised over the keys. Very erect, very excited. He'll rip out a burst. Stop. Wait for it again. Then rip off some more.")

By now it's five o'clock and Hunter still hasn't heard from Gerald Warren. He calls again and this time Warren's secretary asks him to hold. He holds for four minutes. "Ah, it's their new technique—put me on permanent hold." He hangs up, gets another Ballantine and starts pacing the floor, really angry now. "Come on, Warren, you mother-fucker! The horror of all this is that I've never even wanted to cover these bastards. I don't like them." Abruptly, he grabs some binoculars and silently sweeps the horizon. "God, what a scene! It looks like Pittsburgh. Churches and government buildings. If you added banks, you'd have total corruption."

At 5:48 the phone rings. "Yes, Mr. Warren. I've had a difficult time reaching you." Pause. "Oh, fine." When he puts the phone down, Hunter looks very pleased with himself. Like Alexander Graham Bell, he shouts, "It worked! It really worked!" He celebrates with a third beer. Then he puts on blue hip-huggers, a red Italianate sports shirt and white loafers. "Everything I'm wearing comes out of this one shop in Miami. In New Hampshire I was wearing my usual stuff— jeans, lumber jackets, sneakers—and I got thrown out of several restaurants. So when I got to Miami I said, 'Okay, if you bastards want a suit I'll really get you something.' But this isn't my style." As if to prove that, he pulls a green and gray lumber jacket on over his mod duds and drapes an Aztec medallion around his neck ("I don't function well without it," he explains. "A karma kind of thing").

Then we're off on Hunter's quotidian search for villainy at McGovern headquarters. In the subterranean reaches of the Hilton complex, we clamber into his big Volvo 174 with the "Keep Big Sur Beautiful" sticker on the bumper, and plunge into the rush hour maelstrom. Gulping his fourth Ballantine, which he had stowed away in his kit bag, Hunter grumbles, "Worst traffic in the world. The street pattern here is a perfect metaphor for what's happened to the Bill of Rights. It all made perfect, logical sense when it was laid out years ago. Then they put in all these cross grids and got all fucked up."

Stowing the car in a lot next to McGovern Central on K Street, we pass a BMW motorcycle chained to a fence. "Nice bike," he mumbles. Hunter is a bike freak. He owns three of them. His first book, *Hell's Angels* (1966), is a first-hand report on the California motorcycle gang; his second, *Fear and Loathing in Las Vegas* (1972), is nominally about Hunter's trip to cover the Mint 400 motorcycle race; and through that book, some of his other recent writings and, one suspects, much of his fantasy life, churns an incredible monster bike called the Vincent Black Shadow ("two thousand cubic inches, developing two hundred brake-horsepower at four thousand revolutions per minute on a magnesium frame with two styrofoam seats and a total curb weight of exactly two hundred pounds"). One suspects Hunter loves bikes not merely as machines but as vehicles for the outlaw band. It was precisely his affinity with the outlaw style which makes his Hell's Angels book such a good one. Indeed, today, he is the quintessential Outlaw Journalist.

Once inside the eight-story McGovern catacomb, it is clear that Hunter not only knows his way around but is respected, even loved, by these people. "Hi, Hunter," says a girl in jeans. "Well, if it isn't Hunter S. Thompson, the eminent pundit," jibes a mustachioed functionary. Of course, he has been following the McGovern campaign longer than all but a handful of reporters (he recalls a frozen gray afternoon during the New Hampshire primary when he was one of only six reporters on the McGovern "press bus"—and Tim Crouse was one of the others). His interview with McGovern, while both relieved themselves in a hotel urinal, has become an insiders' classic. From the start, he obviously liked the McGovern volunteers. "They are very decent people," he wrote back in March. "They are working hard, they are very sincere." And by and large he liked and respected their candidate (in that same piece, he called him an "honest man," who gave "straight answers" and said "all the right things").

Indeed, Hunter was one of the first political reporters in 1972 to sense the dedication and organizational ability of the McGovern campaign during the primaries and in a May 11, 1972, piece—when McGovern still had only 95 of the 1,508 delegate votes he needed in Miami—Hunter predicted he would win the ballot on the first nomination. On the other hand, he also saw very early that McGovern lacked something crucial, which he called "one dark kinky streak of Mick Jagger in his soul." In an April 13, 1972, article, he went on to write prophetically, "Kennedy, like Wallace, was able to connect with people on some kind of visceral, instinctive level that is probably both above and below 'rational politics.' McGovern does not appear to have this instinct. He does not *project* real well." And, perhaps most important, Hunter perceived very early that despite all the pizazz of the New Politics, McGovern—as he wrote in his March 2, 1972, piece—"is really just another good Democrat."

For Hunter that is a terrible indictment. As he says, his political consciousness was born on the afternoon of August 28, 1968, at the corner of Michigan and Balbo in the city of Chicago. The flailing nightsticks, the blood, the naked hatred and—most particularly—the cynicism of most of the "good Democrats" gathered there drove him nearly wild. For two weeks afterwards, back in Aspen, he couldn't talk about Chicago without breaking into tears. And that led directly to his renowned "freak power" campaign for sheriff of Pitkin County. Originally, the campaign was designed as a wild, frightening diversion—so that by comparison Hunter's friend Ned Vair would seem a moderate and win election to the County Commission. Hunter's platform was indeed pretty wild: renaming Aspen "Fat City"; ripping up the streets with jackhammers and planting grassy sod instead; disarming the sheriff's deputies; and savagely harassing business and real estate exploiters of the valley. But as thousands of "freaks" and not-such-freaks rallied to his campaign— which was really animated by a deep love of his beautiful valley and a passionate hatred for its commercial despoilers —for one crazy moment he thought he just might make it. He didn't, but he came pretty close, close enough to make him and his friends begin wondering whether they couldn't transfer "the politics of madness" to the national level. That, he says, is what led him into political coverage. "I wanted to learn something about big-time national politics and see whether some of our ideas might work up here."

But most of the time big-time politics has simply revolted him. "The only thing worse than going out on the campaign trail and getting hauled around in a booze-frenzy from one speech to another is having to come back to Washington and write about it." Or, more typically, a gut eruption like: "How long, O Lord. How long? Where will it end? The only possible good that can come of this wretched campaign is the ever-increasing likelihood that it will cause the Democratic party to self-destruct." And he saves his vilest eruptions for the "good Democrats"—men like Mayor Daley, Scoop Jackson, George Meany—whom he called "a gang of senile leeches." Ed Muskie, he wrote, "talked like a farmer with terminal cancer trying to borrow money on next year's crop." And Hubert Humphrey was "a treacherous, gutless old ward-heeler who should be put in a goddamn bottle and sent out with the Japanese current."

And so it was profoundly depressing for Hunter to see McGovern proving his worst suspicions of the spring—backing off his boldest positions, sucking up to Mayor Daley, kowtowing to Brooklyn Democratic leader Meade Esposito, apologizing, temporizing, playing the "good Democrat" game. "McGovern could have won this time if only he'd followed the strategy his own man, Fred Dutton, laid down in his book—tapping the new forces abroad in the land. Dutton understood that it's only at times like these—when you come in with a wild card—that you can play on your own terms. They started that way. But McGovern— or somebody around him—lost his nerve. And I'm going to find out who."

The search doesn't prove very fruitful that day, either. Everybody at McGovern Central is too depressed about the new polls showing their man many points behind. Hunter tries to find Pat Caddell, McGovern's pollster, but everywhere he goes Caddell has just left. "That bastard," he grumbles, "he's like a fucking lizard slithering from floor to floor." Finally, he traps the lizard in his office and quietly, skillfully, grills him on the day's grim statistics. Later, he tapes a note to Rick Stearns' chair, telling him he got on the Nixon plane, and joshes for a few minutes with a bone-weary Gary Hart. (Hunter's rapport with the McGovern staffers is impressive, but Marty Nolan, the Boston *Globe*'s Washington correspondent, explains it this way: "Hunter pays more attention to the McGovern people than anybody else. He tells anecdotes about them, makes personalities of them, quotes them at great length. And since so many of the McGovern staff are in politics as an ego trip, they love all that and go on talking to him—at their peril.")

It's getting on towards 9:00 P.M. That's when the Kansas City Chiefs and the New Orleans Saints are due to start playing on ABC Monday night football. Hunter is also a football freak, and he absolutely, positively wants to see that game. We prowl the desolate boulevards of downtown Washington hunting for a bar with a color set and end up in the dank, dreary cellar of Bassin's Lounge, two blocks from the White House. The set there is color all right, but the signals barely seem able to penetrate the layers of macadam and concrete between us and the street. We get a muddy Missouri River of a picture with the New Orleans catfish and the Kansas City carp wiggling through the muck. But New Orleans is putting up a surprisingly good fight against the favored Chiefs, so we decide to say. Hunter orders a Würzburger, I a Heineken.

"Jesus, I love football," he exclaims. "Last Monday I flew into New York from Denver and I realized the game was on. So instead of catching the shuttle straight down here as I'd planned, I went to this scurvy bar in Queens filled with truckdrivers and longshoremen. It was great!" Hunter orders another Würzburger.

"You *know* Nixon's watching on a better set than this one," he muses. "Yesterday, watching on the old black and white set up in my room, I got this sudden flash I ought to call the White House and ask whether I could come over and see the game with the President. We really did have a pretty good talk last time. He's a goddamn stone fanatic on pro football." Hunter orders another Würzburger.

On the other side of the room, some white-haired guy sits down at the piano and starts banging out tunes like "When the Saints Come Marching In" and "When Irish Eyes are Smiling." There are only six other people in the bar and we're all watching the game, and it's quite clear that the old guy is playing just as loud as he possibly can in some horrid spite because we aren't listening to him. Hunter is seething. "That bastard represents everything I hate about this town," he growls. "The fucking forties mentality." (Hunter has a volcanic temper. He generally keeps it under control, but when it erupts it is evidently an awesome phenomenon. He is reported to have ripped a door off its hinges at the Democratic convention. Sidney Zion, the former *Scanlan's* editor, recalls another such incident. Hunter wrote three pieces for *Scanlan's* during its short existence in 1970 but then bitterly feuded with the magazine over money. This summer he and Zion met in an elevator at the Fontainebleau and Zion recalls: "He was just livid. His face got red, the veins stood out in his neck, and he shouted—with all these terrified people cowering in the corners—'I'm going to kill you, you bastard, I'll mace you.' ") I was afraid Hunter might do something like that to the piano player. Instead, he ordered another Würzburger.

I am trying to keep pace with Hunter's chugalugging. But it's tough. He's already downed six Würzburgers and is halfway through his seventh. The alcohol doesn't help the abominable set: vermillion amoebae are beginning to mate with gangrenous globules. Hunter concedes, "This is the low point in my viewing history." We adjourn to Anna Maria's, an Italian restaurant which has two virtues: it stays open late, and it serves Hunter's favorite hors d'oeuvre—garlic bread spread with sliced green peppers. To wash that down he orders a double Margarita.

I ask Hunter to explain what he has been trying to do in his *Rolling Stone* pieces this year. Just what is Gonzo Journalism? He chuckles. "Gonzo all started with Bill Cardosa, who used to be editor of the Boston *Globe* Sunday Magazine. I first met him on the Nixon press bus in New Hampshire in 1968. This very straight guy in a gray overcoat—could have been a *New York Times*man—sat down next to me. He leans over and says, 'You the guy who wrote the Hell's Angels book?' I said I was. 'You get high?' he asked. I said I did, but I must have been looking nervously around because he said, 'Don't worry, these fuckers are all so square they won't know what you're doing.' So there we sat smoking dope on the Nixon press bus! Then Cardosa left the *Globe* and the next time I heard from him was after I wrote the Kentucky Derby piece for *Scanlan's*. The Derby piece was a breakthrough for me. Maybe because it was set in my hometown and I had to confront all my early life—you know I was a real juvenile delinquent back there, got picked up on a phony rape charge, all that. Anyway, the Derby piece was the first time I realized you could write *different*. And after it appeared I got this note from Cardosa saying, 'That was pure Gonzo journalism!'

"I'm not sure what it means. Some Boston word for weird, bizarre. But to me it means intense, demented involvement. I use it very often to contrast with 'Professional Journalism,' which I guess I don't have too much respect for." (Hunter first became disenchanted with conventional journalism while writing about the Hell's Angels, whom he felt were badly misunderstood and grossly sensationalized by most Professional Journalists.) "I have lots of respect for some of the professional reporters I've met on the campaign this year —Jim Naughton of *The New York Times,* Dave Broder of the Washington *Post,* Jules Witcover of the Los Angeles *Times.* I use their stuff all the time, which means I have some of the best leg men in the world working for me. But I wouldn't want to do what they do, and most daily journalists don't even approach their skill. Not because they don't have it in them, but because it's never asked of them. Most newspapers are satisfied to work through the old, worn-out formulas—the five w's, objectivity, all that." I ask whether he feels part of the New Journalism. "Not really. I like what Wolfe does—all that detailed re-creation of events and moods. But he isn't involved. Not even Mailer gets involved the way I do. Hell, in Chicago, while I was down at Michigan and Balbo getting beaten up, Mailer was in a bar looking down on the scene." (Tim Crouse says he would have a hard time placing Hunter in any literary tradition. "His favorite book is *The Great Gatsby*. He loves the precision and compression of Fitzgerald's writing. But the writer I'd compare him to most is Twain—because everything he writes is so very serious and so very funny at the same time.")

Others are less complimentary Marty Nolan wonders whether "it's really necessary to wade through three thousand words of why he's having so much difficulty grinding out the piece. When Hunter is clicking he's very good—particularly in catching mood and nuance—but when he's bad, he's tedious." Others say he often gets his facts wrong. Ron Rosenbaum of the *Village Voice* specifically contests Hunter's version of an incident involving him in Miami Beach. And a reporter who asked not to be identified said, "Hunter is a genius, but like all geniuses he doesn't like to be held down by mere facts. I get the impression he takes some liberties."

Certainly Hunter takes liberties. But he is constantly surprised when others take them at face value. Both in person and at the typewriter, he is a great put-on artist. It's part of his reportorial technique. "I get some of my best stuff by provoking people. I'll go up and tell someone he's a fascist. Whether he is or isn't, I inevitably learn something from his reaction." But in his articles he expects people to sort out dreary fact from merry fantasy. In one piece, he had Frank Mankiewicz jump out of the New Hampshire bushes and whack him over the head with a shoe. In another, he solemnly reported that Ed Muskie has been taking "massive doses" of a West African drug called Ibogaine that produces tearful breakdowns, delusions and total rage. "Do you know, some pretty sophisticated reporters actually believed both of those bits. So I've started telegraphing my punches a little more or following them with a phrase like "My God, what makes me write crazy stuff like that?"

But the keynote of Hunter's writing is the pervasive sense of imminent apocalypse. Cars are always "screeching" and "fishtailing"; Hunter almost blows up Nixon and his staff by lighting a Zippo too near an airplane gas tank; a blue indigo snake is beaten to death in the marble lobby of a New York publisher; the campaign begins to feel "more and more like the second day of a Hell's Angels picnic"; and hearing young voices wailing in the night must sound to an Old Guard candidate "like camping out in the North Woods and suddenly coming awake in your tent around midnight to the horrible snarling and screaming sounds of a werewolf killing your guard dog somewhere out in the trees beyond the campfire."

Over his second double Margarita, I ask Hunter about all that and he says, "Yes, I do believe we're heading toward apocalypse—the collapse, the total shame and impotence of the American Dream." And there are constant hints of a personal apocalypse. Hunter has often said that he never expected to live past thirty. He is now thirty-five, but those who watch him downing gargantuan torrents of alcohol and popping speed like jellybeans wonder whether he will make it to forty. Bob Semple says he fears "there will be a flaming demise one day, that Hunter will be the Jimi Hendrix of American journalism."

Hunter has downed his third double Margarita, and we are into a bottle of icy white wine when the lights go up to tell us it is two o'clock and all unconsumed liquor must be surrendered. Hunter sneaks the half-empty bottle onto the floor by his foot and we go on talking. But a few minutes later, as he tries to put the cork in, the bottle slips and the alert bartender hears it. He hustles over and demands the wine. Hunter demurs, saying he has paid for it and wants to take it home. "Give me that damn bottle," the burly bartender demands. "All right, you son of a bitch," shouts

Hunter. Leaping up from his chair, he brings the bottle down with incredible force on the unsuspecting head. It pops like a percussion cap, driving splinters of glass deep into the bartender's bald skull and spewing an eerie mixture of blood and wine all over the surrounding tables and flabbergasted patrons. Calmly, Hunter leans down, picks up a long, pointed shard of glass, rips the bartender's starched shirt front off, and with cool precision carves "THE AMERICAN DREAM" in bloody strokes on his chest.

A few minutes later, we are cruising down a deserted Pennsylvania Avenue in Hunter's Volvo. We pass the White House glowing unnaturally bright there in the dark. By the fence, four or five Quakers keep their endless vigil against the war. "Oh God," Hunter exclaims. "They're still there, those brave bastards." He drops me off at my hotel. We shake hands formally, silently. Then he whips the car into high gear and goes careening off down Pennsylvania Avenue, fishtailing along the white line into the night. And I remember the last pages of *Hell's Angels*, in which he describes what it is like to ride a monster bike along a California beach at night: "That's when the strange music starts, when you stretch your luck so far that fear becomes exhilaration and vibrates along your arms . . . You watch the white line and try to lean with it, howling through a turn to the right, then to the left and down the long hill to Pacifica, letting off now, watching for cops, but only until the next dark stretch and another few seconds on the edge . . . The Edge . . ."

November 1972

Several weeks after I wrote this, I got a letter from Hunter, chiding me about the penultimate paragraph. He wrote: "When I got on the McGovern press plane for the last week of the campaign I hadn't seen the piece, but most of the others had, and I was treated very strangely. Two Fleet Street types told [Tim] Crouse [of *Rolling Stone*] they felt very uncomfortable being on the same plane with me—as if

I might run amok on booze and speed at any moment and somehow blow a huge hole in the fuselage." Well, I don't want anyone to recoil from Hunter in fear or loathing. So let me confess that the paragraph in question was pure fantasy/-parody, my brief excursion into Hunter's own Gonzo Journalism. At the end of my day with him, I somehow felt compelled—for one moment—to describe not how he did act, but how he should have acted. I thought that would be clear to any careful reader. But, as Hunter has discovered, many readers swallow Gonzo whole—and I can only ask with him: My God, what made me write crazy stuff like that?

RICHARD SCHICKEL

Misunderstanding McLuhan

In 1965—My God, can it have been that many years ago?—
I wrote a piece on Marshall McLuhan for *Harper's*. It was
the first major article on him in a national magazine and it
preceded, by a few weeks, Tom Wolfe's more famous "What
if he's right?" piece in *New York,* then the *Herald Tribune's*
Sunday supplement. My piece wasn't exactly a scoop. Like
a lot of people hanging around literature and communications, I had been hearing vaguely about McLuhan for several
years and I remember attaching a clipping of a column about
him by Max Lerner—of all people—to my memo suggesting
the article. Indeed, it was only after getting a commitment
from *Harper's* that I settled down to read all of *Understanding Media,* McLuhan's *summa theologica.*
So I don't claim any remarkable prescience in this matter.
Like all journalists who try to make their living out of social
and cultural commentary, it's part of my job to be alert to
activities along what McLuhan himself used to call the DEW
line of intellectual life. In fact, what I'll be arguing in this
piece is that I wasn't alert enough to the full import of the
stirrings I was responding to, and neither was Wolfe or the
rest of the gang that rushed in along the trail we broke

toward this rich new Canadian gold strike.

Which is not to say that I think we were wrong, journalistically, to single McLuhan out from all the half-cracked academics of the world for extensive coverage or that he— or we—were entirely wrong about the importance of what he was saying. On the whole, I think the stir he caused was salutary. Writing in the *Columbia Journalism Review* (also in 1965), Dr. Ben Lieberman, a severe if not altogether brilliant critic of McLuhan, had to concede that he was "right to thrust out at the pipsqueak communication theories of the academicians and at the smug assumptions of most of the media leaders." Or, as Michael Arlen wrote in these pages a while back, "he snapped us out of John Crosbyism." Also Dwight Macdonaldism and Marya Mannesism, defined by Arlen as "that bookish, culture-conscious, giggly-Brahmin state of mind" that afflicted nearly all writing (and discussion) of television. Indeed, without McLuhan I doubt that Arlen would have been invited to write the marvelous television reviews he began contributing to *The New Yorker* in 1966 or that John Leonard's witty "Cyclops" pieces would have started running, a little after that, in *Life*. As I hope no one needs to be reminded, there was *some* truth even in McLuhan's most noisome catch phrases. The medium is surely the message—partly. We have, thanks to a growing (and tightening) communications network, become a global village. Sort of. Some media really are hot—i.e., more convenient to cram full of facts and information—than some others which might as well be called "cool" instead of Spot or Rover or something. There is a danger—as the giggly Brahmins keep demonstrating—in being too linear and sequential in our thinking. And surely print conditions us to exalt this mode over all others. And so on.

But I've come to bury McLuhan, not to praise him, however faintly, all over again. As I write, I have next to me two of the several anthologies of pieces about him that appeared as soon as the first wave of comment had broken. The striking thing about these collections is the repetitiveness of the articles they contain. One after the other synopsizes McLuhan's theory of a human "sensorium" unbalanced by excessive dependency on print, perhaps beginning to right itself as electronic communication forced a reorchestration of the senses, stressing the tribal—that is the "oral" and "tactile" modes of communication—rather than the more individualistic print mode. And nearly every piece—my own included —stressed the author's concern that McLuhan's subtleties and sweep might be lost through this inevitably reductive process in which we were indulging. All of us took pains to implicitly praise ourselves for making our way through the complexities of *The Gutenberg Galaxy* and *Understanding Media* in order to perform this service for our readers.

Looking back now, it seems to me there was less than meets the eye in McLuhan's two major works. I mean, the books *were* long and his arguments were indeed, as I said at the time, "at once repetitive and digressive." But as so many proved, they were not really at all difficult either to grasp or to summarize. What had happened was a fairly familiar phenomenon in the reviewing racket; we had spent a lot of time with these volumes of his—not merely because they were so long, but because they were so curiously organized. Or rather disorganized. I remember worrying away at them, making sure I dug out the logic of McLuhan's argument (such as it was) accurately, protecting my flanks, since at this point in time, no matter how you hedged, any article on McLuhan—even if you were striving for a certain neutrality of tone—would be construed by a scandalized literary community as a defense of the class enemy. Once you make this kind of commitment, in time and energy, one tends, almost inevitably, I think, to exaggerate not only the value of the work at hand but its difficulty.*

*Something similar has gone on recently with Thomas Pynchon's novel, *Gravity's Rainbow*, which demanded so much of reviewers that we almost had no option but to praise it. If it was bad, what were we doing spending three months reading it? I now think, certainly, that it was less good than I said it was in my review in *World*.

In short, those of us who gave the McLuhan bandwagon its initial shove were, among other things, demonstrating to the world that we were bright fellows. And unafraid, too, since our subject was, without doubt, mounting a radical and subversive attack on the literary culture to which, theoretically at least, we owed our primary allegiance. I say theoretically because, of course, journalists stand in ambiguous relationship to the literary and academic worlds. We are often invited to write for their magazines, participate in their forums, even teach in their institutions. But we are ever suspect of superficiality and commercialism, just as they are suspect, in our eyes, of a dangerous unworldliness (leading, of late, to excessive insistence on ideological correctness at the expense of real understanding about how the world works). All of which is a way of adding that most of us probably had a built-in bias favoring McLuhan, the provincial scholar, described by a former student in one of the many profiles about him as "a bit of a campus joke," now busily outraging the likes of Dwight Macdonald ("Impure nonsense, nonsense adulterated by sense") and Benjamin De-Mott ("The great gift offered is, ultimately, the release from consciousness itself"). He seemed to be our kind of guy—a swooping, sweeping generalizer, untroubled by any great need to offer definitive historical or observational proof for them, a veritable pack rat scuttling from one room to another in our culture bringing back disparate bright baubles which he claimed were related to one another, principally because he treasured them. Such a character may not fit very comfortably within any known academic tradition, but we, the journalists, knew the type very well; we were brothers under the skin. In the first fervor of enthusiasm he did indeed *"sound like* [emphasis added] the most important thinker since Newton, Darwin, Freud, Einstein and Pavlov," as Wolfe put it. And that sound was as music to our ears.

But of course we were being seduced, whether consciously or unconsciously I still cannot say. In any event, the self-styled media expert was demonstrating mastery of his subject in a highly practical way, manipulating the media to transform himself from campus joke to—as it turned out—an international joke; and we were his entirely willing dupes, prisoners not merely of our desire for a good story, our desire to shake things up, but, much more important, of a strange failure to ask the man certain basic questions, to pry away at a large group of evasions which would have piqued the blood lust of less fancy journalistic types—police reporters, for example.

For instance, McLuhan was less than forthcoming about the larger implications of his work. Implicitly, his argument posited a cultural catechism, one which would not merely destroy literary culture as we knew it, but politics, education, all known economic systems, *everything*. In an English television symposium one speaker quite correctly noted in McLuhan's work "an icy undertone which strikes terror." Not unreasonably, people wanted to know what, if anything, he thought we might do to stay upright, perhaps even surf along on the tidal wave he seemed to be predicting. At the end of my *Harper's* piece I noted that he had remained silent on this point but added, quite sincerely, that I thought it was "in his character for him to speak to it before he is finished." But he never has. Instead, we have had endless variations on this statement: "I am an investigator. I make probes. I have no point of view. I do not stay in one position. . . . I DON'T EXPLAIN—I EXPLORE." Now, that is very cute, and at first it was all right. There would be time enough later, when all the insights and epigrams were sorted out, to write a sequel (McLuhan kept telling interviewers that *The Gutenberg Galaxy* and *Understanding Media* were but the first parts of a trilogy) in which he made himself very clear about the exact dimensions of his Brave New World and what we might yet do to somewhat shape it more to our liking. One was especially encouraged by his repeated assertions that "I'm perfectly prepared to scrap any statement I ever made on any subject once I find that it isn't getting me into the problem."

This was, to put it mildly, a put-on. McLuhan was adopting the stance of the scientist, ready to drop or modify a theory whenever it was successfully challenged—ready, it seemed, to do so himself if one of his new "probes" invalidated an old one. It was very engaging, particularly in contrast to the literary world, where the letters columns of its journals are always full of communications from authors shoring up their defenses after some reviewer's attack, rarely conceding even a minor point. But as the years have worn on there has been no third book—not really. There has been a succession of nonbooks—*The Medium Is the Massage, War and Peace in the Global Village, From Cliché to Archetype*—designed to a fare-thee-well by art directors, to whom, of course, McLuhan was as a god, since to them print is just a design element. Mostly the books themselves were composed of quotations from McLuhan's previous works and from works of others he approved; or examples, drawn from all the media, which proved—to his satisfaction anyway—what he'd been saying all along.

What was going on in these later books was not scholarship, or even healthy popularization, but simple packaging, and almost from the beginning we should have probed more deeply into the process by which McLuhan was being merchandised. For example, Tom Wolfe's piece is an account of the scholar on the road in San Francisco and New York, bringing his theories to business and communications executives in person, and for a fee. Now, Wolfe had great good sport with these scenes: "the upward busting hierarch executives," sitting in fluorescent-lighted, air-conditioned conference rooms, "the day's first bloody mary squirting through their capillaries" while "this man with part of a plastic neckband showing at the edge of the collar, who just got through *grading papers* for godsake," tells them "in effect, politely, they all know just about exactly . . . nothing . . . about the real business they're in." Or: McLuhan at Lutèce, in New York, telling the shakers and makers, the people who've given their very lives to the proposition that a man should be able to eat in what they think is the city's best restaurant, anytime he feels like it, that the city itself is "obsolete." Delicious titillation along with the delicious food. "And all the gleaming teeth and glissando voices are still going *grack grack grack* in the same old way all around, all trying to get to the top of the city that will disappear."

Now, that's terrific stuff. It still makes me laugh to read it. But Wolfe was somewhat less than inquiring about the men picking up the tab that day—the late Howard Gossage, a San Francisco ad man, and Gerry Feigan, a surgeon turned psychiatrist, who as it turned out had pieces of McLuhan, the same way the mob used to have pieces of prizefighters. He was their heavyweight. And there were others in there, too —guys who knew not merely how to publish a book, but how to package it; the true message of a late McLuhan book was to be found on the colophon page, where the copyright notice might include three names, one of which might well be that of a corporation. There were more guys who knew how to profitably set up conferences at Paradise Island, where the execs could sit at the master's feet away from the hurly-burly of the home office; others who could publish a pricey in-sider's newsletter, a sort of Kiplinger report on media theory, so you could have the up-to-date line on the newest "exten-sion of man" a month before McLuhan blabbed to some itinerant journalist and the competition read about it in the newspapers.

Of course, all this was impossible. No individual could handle it all, and things like the special McLuhan issue of *Vogue,* supposedly edited by him, was in fact ghost-edited by academic friends. Indeed, around 1967–68 McLuhan was suffering from a brain tumor and until an operation took care of it, his behavior was reportedly erratic and he was incapa-ble of devoting himself to any project for long periods of time. According to at least one friend, he could barely keep his schedule straight, let alone determine whether he was getting his full monetary due from the many ventures under-taken in his name.

Be that as it may, the packagers were awfully clever. No word of McLuhan's illness seeped out until after it was over, and though common sense—and a look at the work that was going out under his name—should have told people that he was no longer functioning as a scholar, but as a celebrity, suffering a life and a career much closer to that of a movie star (or perhaps, more properly, a permanent talk-show guest), hardly anyone spoke of the matter in print.

Here one enters a dim realm. For it is written that it is not proper for journalists to inquire too deeply into the private lives, economic arrangements, modes of self-presentation, and so forth of serious thinkers. Good taste and long-established literary convention dictate that we may brighten a consideration of a man's ideas with a few homey details, but essentially we are supposed to stress thought, not "color." Generally I agree with that stricture. On the other hand, it is apparent that there is a relatively new phenomenon loose in the world, the multimedia author, whose life, or image, is his real work, with the books he writes being mere incidents in the larger celebrity drama that has first call on his creative energy. Mailer, of course, is the prime example of this phenomenon, but there are others—and they are not all named Jacqueline Susann. Buckminster Fuller is such a figure and so, too, were Timothy Leary, Father Daniel Berrigan and Daniel Ellsberg in recent years. But McLuhan was the first of these modern philosopher kings, orchestrating (or having orchestrated for him) the mixed-media barrage which established him as a household name—in certain households anyway.

Now, Tom Wolfe may have missed the distasteful implications of the Gossage-Feigan patronage of McLuhan, but it is greatly to his credit that throughout his pioneering piece he treated McLuhan as an unprecedented phenomenon in our culture, and it is discouraging that no one else really followed his lead. It is perhaps a measure of his own canniness that McLuhan, throughout the great debate on his work, so successfully restructured arguments to his own chosen grounds, that no one—until, as we shall shortly see, it was too late—challenged either the historical or "scientific" data on which his assumptions rested or the absurd contention that he was conducting a value-free "probe" of the media and their effect on us.

As you will remember there was plenty of moral indignation of the kind I've already quoted and there is no need, I think, to add more of these splutters here. Consider instead the spectacle of good minds falling down dead in front of McLuhan. For example, George P. Elliott, the novelist, noting a ridiculous misinterpretation of *Troilus and Cressida,* was nevertheless extremely gingerly in his handling of McLuhan generally: "It is not possible to give a rational summary of McLuhan's ideas . . . the attitude and tone of his writing are at least as important as the ideas themselves, and to systematize these ideas, even in outline, would be to falsify their nature and impact." Maybe so. But what the hell, why not give it a try, despite the inevitable scoff from McLuhan that "you are a print-formed mind who has been made obsolete by Hume and electricity." It is always possible that he could have been brought down by a really vigorous scholarly assault.

Frank Kermode did a little better. He saw that, among other things, McLuhan, the Catholic convert, was rewriting Biblical myth by substituting "the printing press for Genesis and the dissociation of sensibility for the fall," and he sensibly objected that contrary to McLuhan's interpretation of recent intellectual history, there is a social tradition defending the oral culture: "The very notion of 'prose style' implies a strong oral element, not only, for example, in Joyce, where it suits McLuhan's book, but also in Dr. Johnson. We typographic men have certainly paid our respects to oral culture." In other words, the apocalypse attributed to Gutenberg's invention may not have been so apocalyptic after all. Which means that the apolcalypse resulting from an electronic restructuring of our sensoria might not turn out to be as apocalyptic as McLuhan claimed either. But even the sharp-minded Kermode backs away from this important insight. McLuhan, he lamely concluded, "offers a fresh and coherent account of the state of the modern mind in terms of a congenial myth. In a truly literate society his book would start a long debate."

But of course it did not. A. Alvarez, like most of the other critics, had a good time with the irony that McLuhan had to announce the end of print culture by using print to do so. So did Raymond Williams and all sorts of people. Experts in film, among them Dwight Macdonald, were pleased to point out concrete examples of movies that were quite "cool" in their effect, while experts in television weighed in with the observation that there were plenty of "hot," high-definition TV shows that seemed to belie McLuhan's basic point about the medium. In due course, scholars began to scientifically test some of his notions. In 1970, for instance, Robert Lewis Shayon reported in *Saturday Review* on an experiment at the University of Pennsylvania which proved what should have been obvious, which is that content—a contemptuously dismissed nonfactor in McLuhan's equations—had a significant effect on subjects' "involvement" with a work. Boring content decreased interest in the allegedly automatically involving TV medium while interesting content, not surprisingly, increased involvement in the supposedly "hot" (that is noninvolving) movie medium. Indeed, the researchers discovered that on the whole the poor old, hot old movies involved their subjects far more consistently than TV did. Only a straw in the wind? Surely, but McLuhan's whole work was a house built of such straws, so he couldn't really complain.

Indeed, he is not much heard from any more, for he and his sponsors, in their manipulations, forgot to take into account the most primitive of all media rules: the Milton Berle syndrome, which holds that overexposure kills, that it is impossible for anyone to supply enough fresh new material to hold the attention of the large audience—or indeed any audience—for more than a few seasons. Or, to put it more boldly, he who lives by publicity (which is finally what multimedia campaigns come to), dies by it unless he rather carefully parcels out his appearances, in the manner of modern movie stars who do no more than one or two pictures a year.

There is, I think, a misfortune in all this, namely that the "long debate" Kermode called for never got underway. The whole thing simply petered out as the press turned to more up-to-date sensations. Indeed, if McLuhan's strategy had been merely a cynical one, one designed to promote himself into brief profitable notoriety, skim the cream off his celebrity and then subside whence he had come, in the academic backwaters, there to quietly enjoy his gains, it must be judged a success. For no one did successfully challenge him during his moment of ascendency. The scientists lacked the literary references to mount a full-scale attack on him while the literary gentlemen lacked the requisite scientific background to make a confident assault on him. In short, he had rigged the game so that he always had an escape hatch—out the door marked "science" if the attack came from one direction, out the one labeled "literature" if it came from the other side of the intellectual community.

I think, however, that he was a more serious figure than that, that the issues he raised, however crazily, are real issues and that we—that is, the entire intellectual community—ought to have pursued the matter further. Nothing so grand as an antithesis to McLuhan's thesis was required. Rather, the chord he set up reverberating needed simply to be resolved.

Indeed, someone did pursue the matter. That was Dr. Jonathan Miller, co-creator of the English satirical review *Beyond the Fringe,* now a director of movies, TV and things in London, but before all that, an M.D., and thus well-enough versed in scientific method to challenge McLuhan's scientific as well as his literary-historical bases. Kermode invited him to contribute the volume on McLuhan for the Viking Press "Modern Masters" series and Miller responded with a critical essay in the grand manner, a brisk wind that, if it offered no alternatives to McLuhan, at least cleared the air of the accumulated pollution that had surrounded his name and work.

Miller did what McLuhan was doing his best to discourage. He went back to McLuhan's personal history and to his literary criticism, published in the thirties and forties, demonstrating that a quite coherent system of values had been shaped in those early years and that those values are alive and operative in the later, more famous works. Miller noted, first of all, that having been born and bred in the agricultural provinces of western Canada, McLuhan must have acquired a near-instinctive taste for agrarian populism, which, of course, can be interpreted as a form of tribalism. The small farmer, one recalls, was cruelly exploited at the end of the last century and the beginning of this one by "linear and sequential" types—those super-rationalists who control the banking system and who in their day controlled the rates set by that most linear transportation form, the railroads, whose rates drove many a yeoman from his land and many of the survivors into a congenial, decentralized form of socialism, the cooperative movement. As a student at Cambridge, McLuhan came under the influence of an extremely sophisticated agrarian, F. R. Leavis, with his powerful belief that life was much richer in a predominantly agricultural society, when "speech was a popularly cultivated art, [and] people talked (so making Shakespeare possible) instead of reading or listening to the wireless." Here, one begins to see the beginnings of the line followed in *Understanding Media.*

So primitivism was a value. And so was Catholicism. Miller puts the matter in the kindliest possible way, noting that McLuhan's global nervous system is analogous to the "Noosphere" of another media-celebrity thinker, Teilhard de Chardin. Miller observed that as Catholics both men "give enormous and understandable priority to the fundamental spiritual unity of man. Any institution, natural or artificial, which gives *secular* thought world-wide expression would seem, on first principles at least, to be a congenial circumstance within which to establish a consensus of piety, too." McLuhan, in Miller's view, becomes a belated counter-reformationist, mounting a crusade "on behalf of the lost consensus, seeking aids to its recovery in the very culture that usurped it."

I don't have space to summarize all of Miller's successful assaults on the "science" McLuhan used mostly to snow us, but to take just one example, he devastates the notion that the sense ratio—that is, the importance that any individual or society assigns to the physical means by which it receives information—is in any way calculable, capable of being reduced to scientific quantification. One general point, however, is worth pondering: McLuhan's stay at Cambridge coincided with that university's ascendency in the sciences, and Miller argues powerfully that McLuhan's insistence that he is just a scientist making "probes" is a response to that ascendency, an attempt to disarm one group of potential opponents by turning their own weapons against them. Miller points out, however, that McLuhan misunderstood scientific method. He quotes Karl Popper, the distinguished historian of science: "The belief that we can start with pure observations alone, without anything in the nature of a theory, is absurd . . . Observation is always selective. It needs a chosen object, a definite task, an interest, a point of view, a problem."

Since McLuhan is anything but ignorant and anything but stupid, we may suppose, I think, that his posture as a disinterested observer was, like his failure to acknowledge both his agrarian and religious biases, a matter of strategy rather than oversight. One does not want to seem paranoid about it, but after reading Miller I am prepared to think that we were dealing with an extraordinarily clever, extraordinarily duplicitous exercise in propaganda, a veritable Watergate of the mind, orchestrated by a highly visible hidden persuader, developing an antirational (and therefore antidemocratic) ideology, which at its simplest level constituted not merely an assault on bookish culture, but on all culture, not out of simple perversity but out of a profound and dangerous conservatism—a conservatism carefully structured to seem "groovy."

Looking back now, it seems to me none of us behaved very well in the face of the McLuhan phenomenon. The popular journalists, me among them, were entirely too uncritical in our attempts to convey the essence of what he was saying, too in thrall of its seeming novelty to catch its true reactionary drift. The literary and scholarly community, on the one hand, was either too outraged to be persuasively coherent in its criticisms, or on the other, too worried about being "with it" to uphold its best and strictest standards in this case. Finally, I am dismayed that when Miller finally undertook the job we all shirked, the careful, reasonable, point-by-point assault on McLuhan, no one paid him any serious heed, his little book has sunk without a trace.

I am glad, of course, that McLuhan passed so quickly out of fashion, rendering Miller's work superfluous in the eyes of most critics and book-review editors. But I wonder . . . Dangerous ideas that are not fully—and generally—discredited, have a way of reappearing in new finery, new guises. I have the feeling that we may yet have cause to refer to Dr. Miller's little book, that those of us in communications may want to carry it around with us, as the vampire hunter keeps a supply of wolfbane handy. For the wicked count still lives, sulking in his northern redoubt, still available for consultation with his always anxious business and media friends, wounded perhaps, but still dangerous—particularly if the culture enters upon another antirational convulsion like that of the sixties.

August 1974

Sanford J. Ungar

The Voice of Middle America

"One thing more . . . (stridently) In Madison, Wisconsin, they've got a
female garbage collector. (staccato) And at the University of
California, they elected a boy as the homecoming queen. (pause, then
slowly) That's all right. (pause, more slowly) That's all right. (pause,
assertively) But I'm glad I lived when I lived. (pause, voice down)
Paul Harvey. (longer pause, voice sharply up) Good Day!"

—Conclusion of early-morning radio broadcast, November 19, 1973

Some think it's pure unprofessional cornball, the rat-a-tat-a-
tat routine of Paul Harvey. Others write it off as predictable
radio vaudeville with a right-wing twist. Many have not
heard him, or bothered to listen, since childhood, probably
in a small town, when he interrupted the hit music with an
alarming shout. They assume he is now a crusty old character, long past his prime, grinding out his line somewhere in
seedy obscurity. However, Paul Harvey is not only alive and
well but he also remains one of the best-known and perhaps
most influential personalities in the history of American radio.

At last count, 594 affiliates of the American Broadcasting
Company—large and small, from one end of the country to
the other—were using one or both of Harvey's two morning

broadcasts: a five-minute one at 7:30 A.M. central time that is generally carried live, and a fifteen-minute one sent out from Chicago at 10:30 A.M. central time but held until noon local time by most stations. Among the subscribers, for example, are fifteen stations in Alabama, thirty in California and eleven in Idaho. Thus there are bound to be millions listening six mornings a week when out booms, "Hello, America, this is Paul Harvey! Stand by for news!"

Paul Harvey's "news," neatly phrased and precisely articulated, wells up from deep within a well-developed, carefully codified and repeatedly tested philosophy of life. He has something to say about almost everything, and on important subjects—the issues that everyone is thinking, talking and worrying about—he has a great deal to say. Just ask him about the energy crisis (you don't have to ask, actually), and he'll tell you it is "the best thing that's happened to my country since the Wright Brothers. . . . The next ten years will be the most exciting, productive and fruitful. It's going to be exciting to be alive. . . . Why, we've been spoiled rotten by all this gas and oil. The time has come to harness the tides, the Gulf Stream, explore thermal energy, solar energy, even the windmill. . . . [A smile, almost a glaze, comes across his face as he shakes his head for emphasis.] Boy, this is gonna be a thrilling new horizon for us, really thrilling. . . . I feared it would take a depression to get us off dead center." The end result of a depression, he adds parenthetically and ominously, could be "anarchy."

Harvey is a crusader for the old values and virtues, for things the way they "used to be." In private conversation, he can be soft and relaxed and charming, but then, even with an audience of only one, if the talk turns to one of the hundreds of subjects on which he has strong feelings, he may nearly blast you out of the room with his voice. Although Harvey oozes self-confidence and control, a visitor fears occasionally that he will collapse on the spot in the midst of one of his marathon sentences rather than take a new breath. He likes to quote back his own well-turned phrases of the past

—such as "Mr. Nixon, I love you . . . but you are wrong," the battle cry with which he opposed his favorite president's dispatch of American troops into Cambodia in 1970. He is notorious for his softness toward some of the right-wing causes of the past quarter century; yet he can sound like the New Left when he pleads for restraint in the use of American power. He is a millionaire and a fundamentalist and a unique media event.

Simplicity is Paul Harvey's trademark and along with his extraordinary voice doubtless one of the secrets of his success. "He can take the most complicated news story and boil it down to a single sentence," says Dick Rosenbaum, former chief of ABC's Midwest radio bureau in Chicago. Sometimes that means heavy reliance on clichés, labels and shorthand. "Here's a Christmas present from the Supreme Court," Harvey shouted exuberantly during a mid-December morning broadcast. "Police can search anyone under arrest without a search warrant." End of story. Then there was the one about a man from Nebraska who had attended a European conference and learned that polyethylene, while in short supply domestically, was being shipped abroad and sold for nearly three times its price at home. The moral of the story: "Domestic price controls can create shortages." Interspersed among such news items and insights of the day are one- and two-liner minutiae from the AP and UPI tickers ("They're stealing trash in Texas"), obituaries, wedding anniversary announcements, predictions and advice like "toot your horn at anyone doing over fifty miles an hour."

The formula is phenomenally successful. In 1973 the standard rate for a sixty-second advertising spot on Harvey's broadcast was $2,000. But sponsors apparently find the high price worthwhile; Bankers Life and Casualty Company has been selling its insurance that way for years, and W. Clement Stone, President Nixon's biggest financial backer, used Harvey's voice to launch *Success Unlimited,* his little magazine intended to promote the philosophy of "positive mental attitude." (The magazine is itself now a financial success.) Harvey has, in fact, long been criticized for delivering commercials in his normally urgent and persuasive tone of voice. A careless listener might easily think them part of the news.

Although he is not particularly popular in the big cities (even WLS, his "home station" in Chicago, carries only the first five minutes of his second morning broadcast), Harvey saturates and delights the suburbs and the small towns, especially in what he likes to call "the unterrified provinces," whose delegate he fancies himself to be. "He's down-to-earth and earthy, I suppose," says Denny Pittman, of station KOVC in Valley City, North Dakota, in explaining why Harvey is "one of the top listened-to programs at our station. . . . This is true all across North Dakota. . . . He presents what people are interested in, a little bit of everything. . . . A lot of people call in and ask for his address; they have things they want to send him." Indeed, that's where Harvey gets a great deal of his material—in the mail from his admirers.

Harvey *has* been around for a long time, but that's partly because he started early. Paul Harvey Aurandt (the last name, of Pennsylvania Dutch origin, has long since been dropped as "difficult to pronounce and spell," but is now being revived by his only child, Paul, Jr., a budding concert pianist and, incidentally, a conscientious objector) was born in September 1918 in Tulsa, Oklahoma, the son of a policeman who was killed on Christmas Eve three years later. He began broadcasting on KVOO in Tulsa at the age of fourteen, continuing through the end of high school, and later dropped out of Tulsa University without a degree (he now has many honoraries) to hit the radio road. "In those days we were migratory. It was easy to get jobs," he recalls. After brief stints in Oklahoma City and Kansas, he went to work for KXOK in St. Louis. There he met and eventually married Lynne Cooper, a Phi Beta Kappa (something Harvey always mentions, saying that for him it was "a sneaky way to get an education") and a former schoolteacher who was doing programs at the same station.

Mrs. Harvey, whom he calls "Angel" and refers to frequently in his homespun broadcasts and writings, has played a major role in his rise to fortune and fame. "She wanted to be married to a network newscaster," he says. "She focused my ambitions." It was she who persuaded him, after some time in Hawaii, Kalamazoo, the Air Force and a regional branch of the Office of War Information, to settle in Chicago. Years later, after his syndicated newspaper column had taken hold, she persuaded him to go into television, too. "The radio program is my first love," he says. "I really kind of resented TV as an illegitimate stepchild thrust into the family, but Angel convinced me we were leaving that base uncovered." An the flyleaf of the book, *You Said It, Paul Harvey!*, edited by her, explains, "Angel is Paul Harvey's Executive Producer and most ardent fan. . . . Both as manager and wife, Angel is enthusiastic about her husband's work . . . Mrs. Harvey is President of Paulynne Productions, general business manager for Paul Harvey News, and hostess to many internationally known guests."

On arrival in Chicago in 1944, Harvey went to WENR, broadcasting the 10:00 P.M. news and a program called "Jobs for GI Joe." The injection of his personal opinions into the news caused some difficulty at the start, but he was an immediate success. One vacation he substituted on the network ("NBC Blue," which later became ABC) for commentator H. R. Baukhage ("Baukhage talking"): "Madison Avenue didn't like me, but the grass-roots station owners did, so they kept me on." From the beginning, he coined memorable phrases and put an unusual twist on the news. He had 25,000 requests in four days for transcripts of his radio obituary of President Franklin D. Roosevelt, which began, "A great tree has fallen. . . ."

Harvey's tree grew and grew, but not before he almost ended his career in 1951 by dramatically trying to prove that security was lax at the Argonne National Laboratory. Harvey felt the Illinois center for the development of nuclear reactors was being run "like a country club." So, accompanied by a security guard who had been fired and an off-duty naval intelligence officer, he climbed the laboratory's nine-foot-high fence one dark night. To his dismay, his overcoat snagged on the wire, and security turned out to be better than he thought. He was ordered to put up his hands and was arrested at 1:10 A.M. Newspaper reports at the time said that a gun had been found in Harvey's car, along with a radio script prepared in advance that told of his would-be successful penetration of the security shield. He was investigated by both the FBI and a federal grand jury, which did not indict him. "If our internal security has been improved by the fact that national attention was focused on this situation, I am extremely grateful," Harvey said after the decision.

Harvey's preoccupation with "internal security" made him a darling of the political right in the fifties. In August 1954, Senator Joseph McCarthy spent the night at the Harveys' home before speaking to an American Legion gathering in Chicago, and the same month Harvey told the Veterans of Foreign Wars in Philadelphia that the United States should continue full-scale "preparations for perpetual war." It was also during that period that Harvey got to know the late FBI director, J. Edgar Hoover, whom he greatly admired.

Middle America liked him. A 1970 study ranked one of his morning news broadcasts as the top-rated radio program in the nation. It is one of the factors that keeps many local stations, which might ordinarily switch from time to time, loyal to ABC, and, Rosenbaum concedes, is the "main reason" the network has a Midwest radio bureau—with a special private studio for Harvey—at all. The newspaper column, which Harvey boasts has correctly predicted the outcome of every presidential election since his first try in the Truman-Dewey race of 1948 ("The reason I've been able to do it, even when the surveys are wrong, is because I've stayed out in the country where the voters are"), runs three times a week in three hundred, mostly small newspapers. In Cincinnati, for example, it appears "exclusively" in the *Forest Hills Journal* and the *Community Journal.*

The television commentaries, which come in ninety-second and five-minute versions and are privately syndicated rather than sold through a network, are broadcast five days a week on more than one hundred stations; Harvey thinks they are responsible for a substantial percentage of the estimated 5,000 pieces of mail he gets every day. Listeners and viewers who write in asking for transcripts of his broadcasts are invited to purchase one of his four books—*You Said It, Paul Harvey!, Remember These Things, Autumn of Liberty* and *The Rest of the Story*—at $5.95 each. There are three talking records, *The Testing Time, The Uncommon Man,* and *Yesterday's Voices,* on the last of which "Paul Harvey narrates and ties together sermons and hymns by actual voices of the greatest Christian leaders of the past." Harvey gives an average of two or three lectures a week, often in out-of-the-way places, for which his standard fee is $5,000. He generally travels to the lecture engagements in his own Cessna 401. Although he has kept his pilot's license active, he now prefers to sleep or work en route and leave the flying duties to a pilot he keeps on full-time retainer.

The Harveys' annual gross income was estimated at half a million dollars in 1971, but is probably more today.* They own a cattle ranch in the Ozarks, a home twenty miles north of Scottsdale, Arizona ("I go out there and play cowboy") and property just outside Tucson, 1,000 acres of which they recently gave to the National Park Service, presumably for a handsome tax deduction. Harvey has been repeatedly selected by the Custom Tailors Guild of America as one of the nation's ten best-dressed men.

Harvey keeps an eccentric but efficient schedule, fending off most people he does not already know or have information about. He gets up at 4:00 every weekday morning and

---

*The figure is that of the *Wall Street Journal;* Mr. Harvey did not respond to a request that he update it. He initially cooperated with my research, as did Mrs. Harvey; but they later canceled plans for further meetings, pleading heavily over-committed schedules.

drives from a palatial stone home-and-headquarters in a western suburb to his ABC office overlooking the Chicago River by 4:40 A.M. (It is a disappointingly plain office, with just a few pieces of Indian pottery and, behind his desk, an enormous plaque representing the American Legion "Fourth Estate Award for Distinguished Public Service in the Field of Communications," presented to him in 1965 at the American Legion's 47th national convention in Portland, Oregon.) There he sorts and sifts material for his first morning broadcast and works on newspaper columns and television commentaries, drinking hot soup along the way.

He does little of his own reporting these days; his last actual legwork was apparently when he accompanied the Marines into Lebanon in 1958. But he still has a secret stringer in Washington ("I don't want to identify him; he doesn't introduce himself as working for me") and claims to have excellent sources in Congress, the military, the Internal Revenue Service and other agencies. His news judgment is based largely on what he thinks his loyal audience wants to hear; there is room for plenty of trivia, but not, to use his own example, for routine reports of congressional hearings or United Nations votes. At the same time, he says he is "bound by good taste . . . I use the standard of Aunt Betty [his sister-in-law] in St. Louis." On a morning when I visited the studio, Harvey said he had done "a lot of careful weighing" before including an item asserting that "the number-one hazard of being a department store Santa-for-hire . . . is water on the knee."

Harvey goes to a Chicago television studio every Monday to tape a week's worth of wisdom for that medium. There he is met by Angel, who flutters around him like a swallow and supervises the change of clothes that comes before each new spot. On one recent day, he used a wardrobe of sports coats that included several different bright colors and one collarless model. ("It was my idea six years ago, when he was syndicated, to put him in mod clothes," Angel confided. "We try to stay one step ahead.") His chest thrust forward and his eyes glued on the teleprompter, he delivers the television commentaries while sitting on top of a desk in a fake library setting (designed by Angel). Smooth though he is on radio, Harvey sometimes comes over very clumsily on TV, with poorly timed false smiles, forced laughs and marionettelike raised eyebrows. One week's dose is as varied as a single radio broadcast—from national affairs ("Well, there is a little less brightness this Christmas, but arntcha glad we're out of Vietnam?") to the need for fire prevention in the home and prayer in the locker room.

Not surprisingly, Harvey agrees with the bitter criticism leveled at the networks in recent years by former Vice President Agnew and other members of the Nixon administration. He was so infatuated with Agnew, in fact, that at one point he proposed switching jobs with the vice president for a day. (The network vetoed that idea.) "If there's a distortion of the news," Harvey claims, "it results from overcentralization. The epicenter is Manhattan Island . . . The hub of the wheel is off center. . . . It's probably true that civilization stopped at the Appalachians at one time, but no more . . . Despite the genuine sophistication [of those who live west of the Appalachians], the networks continue to feed the Kansans and Texans a steady diet of stuff that's predicated on the goofy morals and mores of Manhattan Island." These "morals," in his view, include "nutsy styles, jungle music and burlesque entertainment," and may result from New Yorkers' "feeling of closeness to London." The anti-New York theme is an old one for Harvey. In 1952, testifying before a House subcommittee investigating radio and television, he denounced the "purple humor" coming from the east and complained that successful comedians who were "rooted so deep in Broadway and the bawdy night life of Manhattan" were trying to impose "their distorted views on the rest of the forty-seven states."

Yet, for all Harvey's middle-Americanism, he clearly has a mind of his own. He was delighted by Nixon's victory over Hubert Humphrey in 1968. "It's going to feel real good again to be an American," he said in a television commentary entitled "The Nixon Smile." But he soon became disgusted when the Southeast Asian conflict continued and began to spread. He came to believe that "we should have said, 'We goofed, we meddled where we shouldn't have, we're leaving.' " But his most dramatic shift came on the occasion of American troops' entry into Cambodia, and that broadcast caused some gasps of outrage from Harvey's traditional constituency. "It was a shock to the old American Legionnaire types," he now recalls. "I had a lot of protests. . . . Some sent me white feathers in the mail." Harvey's decision was taken by several national publications as evidence of a genuine change in public opinion on the war, and he hammered away on the issue until the cease-fire was signed in early 1973, and beyond that.

Indeed, though Harvey is most often identified with the political right, he has been all over the lot. He suggested on the Dick Cavett television program in 1970 that if the world were threatened by nuclear war because of the Middle East conflict, all the people of Israel should be evacuated to a sparsely populated American state. In 1952 he won the first annual American Legion award for "militant Americanism" and in 1954 was selected by the Sumpter Guards of South Carolina as "the man who has contributed most toward preserving the American way of life." But in 1959 he was named "Man of the Year" by the editors of the prison newspaper at San Quentin. He has been critical of Nixon's handling of the Watergate scandals, but also believes that for the press "the exposé has turned into a vendetta."

For the future, he sees two ways that radio and television could evolve, "all homogenized network stuff" or "a spectrum" of people as free to express their opinions "with no restriction whatsoever," as he does now. But then he wonders aloud, "Will any network allow another Paul Harvey to develop?" A good question.

April 1974

J. ANTHONY LUKAS

High Rolling
in Las Vegas

What's he got in that damn thing? It's big enough to hold the natty bouncer at the Frontier or two of those Mexican jai alai players at the Grand or half the nude chorus line from the Stardust's "Lido de Paris '74." But the White House Plumbers, as we all know by now, were serious men dedicated to National Security and a Free Cuba. So what were Liddy, Hunt et al. after when they plotted to burglarize the gargantuan green Meilink safe that squats in the corner of Hank Greenspun's office next to a potted plant and underneath an autographed photo of Richard Nixon?

"Whatever it was, some sneaky son of a bitch wanted it pretty bad," Greenspun growls, as he sprawls back in his reclining black chair, hoists his big feet up on his desk and lights up another fragrant Antonio y Cleopatra.

"And the Watergate committee must have thought it was pretty big stuff, too. Sam Dash made a secret trip out here last year. Very hush-hush. He spent all night talking with me, left here at 3:00 A.M. Then the two of us had breakfast with Bob Maheu [Howard Hughes' former Nevada trail boss]. I wanted Maheu to tell Dash a story he told me once, a story that's never been told publicly before: that Hughes

once arranged to retain Mudge, Fudge, Pudge and Goulash
—you know that Nixon-Mitchell firm on Wall Street—to
represent him in the TWA fight. Maheu told me they put
down $75,000 out of a $250,000 fee and, in exchange, he said,
'We're going to have a hand in naming the next few Supreme
Court justices.' That gives you a little hint of the stakes those
boys were playing for."

As editor and publisher of the Las Vegas *Sun,* Greenspun
has seen a lot of high rolling. But even he wasn't prepared
in Spring 1972 when word got out that he'd been one of the
potential targets discussed by Gordon Liddy, John Mitchell,
Jeb Magruder and John Dean on February 4, 1972. According to Magruder, Liddy was instructed then to see "if there
would be potential . . . for an entry" into Greenspun's office.
As late as April or May 1972, Liddy told James McCord that
plans for the burglary were still on. Magruder says the project was later dropped, although Greenspun says that in
September 1972 he found evidence that someone had broken
into his office through a window and tried to get into the safe.

But what did he have in that damn thing? McCord says
the target was "blackmail-type information involving a
Democratic candidate for president." Greenspun insists the
only item in his files remotely filling that description is data
on a 1965 conviction of Senator Edmund Muskie and then-
Senator Eugene McCarthy for hunting ducks on a federal
reservation. He says he checked this out through his friend
Jack Anderson and found it genuine, but didn't use it because it was "trivial." Indeed, Greenspun thought so little of
the duck dope that he kept it not in the safe but in a cub-
byhole of his desk.

A more likely target for the Plumbers' plunge was a bun-
dle of memos from Hughes to Maheu that Greenspun concedes he does keep in the safe. During the four years Maheu
served as Hughes' Nevada Gauleiter, he never saw the Bash-
ful Billionaire face to face. Ensconced in his penthouse at the
Desert Inn, Hughes communicated with the world through
his squad of Mormon secretaries—and with Maheu and a

few other aides by notes scrawled on lined legal pads. In November 1970, when the two men parted amid Vegan pyrotechnics, Maheu took photocopies of several hundred memos with him—and about two hundred came into the hands of his friend, Hank Greenspun. In January 1972, during the furor over Clifford Irving's bogus autobiography of Hughes, Greenspun leaked some of those memos to colleagues in the press. Finally, on February 3, Wally Turner of *The New York Times* reported that Greenspun had the memos in his safe. The very next day the Plumbers began plotting to get into it.

Several motives have been suggested. The White House may have feared that the memos contained embarrassing references to Hughes's multifarious dealings with Nixon—including the curious passing of $100,000 through Bebe Rebozo when Hughes was having problems with the Justice Department's antitrust division and wanted favors from the Atomic Energy Commission. Senate investigators speculate that the Watergate burglary itself was designed to discover what Democratic national chairman Larry O'Brien—once a public relations man for Hughes—knew about these transactions and perhaps whether he too had copies of the memos.

Or Nixon may simply have been doing a favor for Hughes, who clearly wanted his memos back. Greenspun and Hughes, once allies, were now locked in a tangle of bitter legal disputes in which Hughes undoubtedly feared Greenspun would use some of the memos. This theory fits with Howard Hunt's testimony that Ralph Winte, the Hughes Tool Company security chief, promised the Plumbers support facilities, rooms, limousines and "a good time in Las Vegas at company expense" during the foray. And it would also fit with McCord's testimony that "the entry team was to go directly to an airport near Las Vegas where a Howard Hughes plane would be standing by to fly the team directly to a Central American country." Hughes was then in Nicaragua.

But a lot of other people besides Richard Nixon and Howard Hughes would like to see what Hank Greenspun has in that safe. It's a good bet he has some low-down on more than a few well-known public figures. For over the years Greenspun has accumulated an Enemies List which can rival the president's own. And when you get on Hank's list: Watch Out! Greenspun is the last of the Frontier Editors, a two-gun tough-guy who divides the world into Good Guys and Bad Guys, and when up against a Bad Guy is inclined to shoot first and ask questions later. Indeed, the *Sun* often seems less a newspaper than the journalistic equivalent of the Colt revolver, the gun that settled more scores than any other weapon on the American frontier and left countless bodies strewn across the saloon floor.

Greenspun's own prose—in his five-day-a-week front-page column, "Where I Stand"—can be lethal. He strafes his adversaries with staccato bursts like these: "filthy rabble rouser," "crawling and sniveling jackals," "whiskey-sodden despoiler of American journalism," "old buzzard bordering on the fringe of senility" and "vicious, disreputable, drunken, scurvy, lying, cowardly traitor."

In the fifties, Greenspun's prime antagonists were Senators Joseph McCarthy of Wisconsin and Pat McCarran of Nevada, the leading Red-baiters of that era. On the premise that you shall know a man by the enemies he makes, Greenspun rapidly became a darling of embattled liberals throughout the land. Supreme Court Justice William O. Douglas has described him as "one of our greatest Americans." Richard Donovan and Douglass Cater journeyed to Nevada for *The Reporter* magazine and called Greenspun "a sort of Robin Hood of the gambling community, attacking the wealthy and corrupt and taking up for the underdogs" (although they noted that the latter were "sometimes equally corrupt"). Lawrence Martin, then associate editor of the Denver *Post,* extolled Greenspun for his "utterly fearless physical and moral courage when he's fighting for what he believes." And no less a press critic than *The New Yorker*'s A. J. Liebling made a 1954 pilgrimage to Las Vegas where he savored, with a gourmet's delight, "the fine, free-rolling frontier invective that Greenspun . . . drapes over the objects of his scorn."

But over the years Greenspun has loosed that invective on liberals and conservatives alike. Indeed, his critics suggest, the only thing the objects of his scorn have in common is that each has stepped on Hank Greenspun's toes. Not surprisingly, most of his critics are unwilling to be quoted by name, for fear that he will bring his sharpshooting to bear on them. But when promised anonymity, newsmen who have known Greenspun describe him like this:

• "Hank isn't a liberal crusader. He's a very smart, very shrewd businessman who just happens to publish a newspaper in Las Vegas, Nevada."

• "His crusades rarely have anything to do with abstract principle. They almost always begin with personal grievance. They're a way of settling scores."

• "Hank uses his newspaper as a bludgeon to build and maintain power in Nevada."

Herman Milton Greenspun's combative spirit was nurtured not on the range but in the largely black slums of New Haven, Connecticut. There, he learned early to deal with anti-Semitism. Once, while delivering papers, he got a particularly raucous earful and ran home to his mother. According to Greenspun, his mother exclaimed, "You let him insult you and you didn't even insult him back? What's the matter with you? When you let people walk over you you might as well be dead." With which she marched back to the offender's doorstep and beat him up—teaching her son an-arm-for-an-ear lesson he never forgot.

Young Hymela, as he was known then, took a law degree at St. John's Law School in Brooklyn and then clerked in Congressman Vito Marcantonio's law firm. But he soon discovered that the law wasn't for him—partly, he says, because "it meant fighting for causes I couldn't support without making moral and emotional reservations." When Greenspun fights, he does so without reservation. Moreover, he found himself increasingly drawn to the Runyonesque world of

Broadway, which he got to know while working as a "runner" for a ticket agency—the world of the "lamisters," people on the lam, "petty crooks, pickpockets and hookers, who scuttled down our steps like medieval riffraff seeking sanctuary in the cathedral." So, after a wartime stint in the Army, he eagerly accepted a promoter's invitation to help build a race track in the brash gambling mecca then just beginning to rise out of the Nevada desert.

The track venture led nowhere. But Greenspun was infatuated by Vegas—a lamister's haven if ever there was one. So Hymela—now westernized to Hank—helped found *Las Vegas Life,* a magazine that covered the "more stimulating aspects of Las Vegas nightlife" (he wrote a column called "Gleanings from Glitter Gulch"). The new venture would have folded quickly were it not for a *hôtelier* who shelled out $250 for the back-cover ad issue after issue.

The benefactor was "Bugsy" Siegel, owner of the Flamingo Hotel and one of America's premier hoodlums. But Greenspun evidently suffered no qualms about accepting mob money. "It was legitimate business," he wrote later. "I felt there was no valid reason to turn it down." Nor did he see any reason to turn down Siegel's offer of a public relations job at the Flamingo while he was still running *Las Vegas Life.* "To date, no one had asked the chambermaids to carry machine guns or the chefs to stuff their chickens with illicit swag," he wrote. Greenspun flacked for Siegel until the gangster was killed in June 1947. Then he went to work as publicity director of the Desert Inn—in which he also owned a small interest—and stayed on even after control was purchased by "Moe" Dalitz and other members of the Cleveland mob.

Meanwhile, his fierce Zionist loyalties and native pugnacity led him into the wildest escapade of his life—running arms to Israel. Purchasing war-surplus machine guns and aircraft engines in Hawaii, he shipped them to California, then loaded them on a private yacht, and with a loaded Mauser at the owner's head, forced him to sail to Mexico.

Operating out of the Reforma Hotel in Mexico City, with funds supplied by the Haganah, he bribed and cajoled Mexican officials into letting a ship full of arms sail for Israel. The following year, he was indicted but acquitted of violating the Neutrality Act. A year later, he was indicted again on a similar charge. As part of a deal, he pleaded guilty and was fined $10,000, paid by "Friends of Israel." (In 1961 he received a full pardon from President Kennedy.)

Back in Las Vegas in 1949, he bought the *Free Press*, a thrice-weekly paper founded by the International Typographical Union in a dispute with the powerful Las Vegas *Review-Journal*. He renamed the paper the *Sun*, gradually converted it into a daily and began looking for ways to boost circulation.

Within a few years, he was locked in an epic struggle with McCarran, the immensely powerful senior senator from Nevada. Several motives probably converged to set off this scrap. Greenspun, in his 1966 autobiography, claims that his chief motive was to resist McCarran's political machine which was "bent on throttling all opposition, destroying democratic processes, dictating policy, and thriving on the proceeds." But principles like these probably played less of a role than some hard economic realities. To build his struggling newspaper in a showbiz city like Las Vegas, Greenspun needed plenty of alarums and excursions. As one colleague puts it: "Hank had to crusade. It was his only chance of competing with the *Review-Journal*. And let's face it, it's easier to crusade for Jesus Christ than it is for Judas Iscariot."

But when I asked Greenspun what had sicked him on McCarran, he gave me still a third answer, which may be closest of all to the truth. "It all came about one day as I was in the Senate gallery listening to a debate on McCarran's immigration bill. After Herbert Lehman spoke against it, McCarran sneered that Lehman represented 'a handful of cloak and suiters on Seventh Avenue.' I saw Lehman put his hands to his face as though he were going to cry, so I rushed to the cloakroom and told him, 'Senator, I'm just a small newspaper publisher from Nevada, but for what that man said to you just now, I'm going to hound him into his grave.' And I did, you know. McCarran died in September 1954 giving a speech in Hawthorne, Nevada. His last words were 'Greenspunism must be defeated.' "

McCarran had done his best to defeat Greenspunism—through an advertising boycott of the *Sun* by Las Vegas's hotel and casino owners. On the morning of March 24, 1952, they called one after another to cancel their ads—30 percent of the paper's advertising gone in thirty minutes. Greenspun dug up evidence to show that the boycott had begun with a call from McCarran to Marion Hicks of the Thunderbird, and he brought a $225,000 suit against the senator and fifty-six hotel and casino operators for conspiracy to drive him out of business. Ultimately the suit was settled for $80,500 and the casinos' promise to continue advertising in the paper. But for months the paper teetered on the edge of bankruptcy and Greenspun toured the country asking funds to keep it going and to fight for "freedom of the press."

Meanwhile, Greenspun took on McCarran's long-time Senate ally—Joe McCarthy. The motives here seem mixed, too. Undoubtedly, Greenspun despised McCarthy's demagoguery. Certainly he resented his alliance with McCarran. And he may have detected a hint of anti-Semitism on the senator's whiskey breath. But, typically, Greenspun did not launch his all-out crusade against McCarthy until the dispute became personal. This occurred on October 13, 1952, when McCarthy came to speak in Las Vegas and during his harangue called Greenspun an "ex-Communist." Greenspun concedes now that McCarthy meant "ex-convict" (a reference to his gun-running conviction), but at the time he was not inclined to overlook the slip. Instead, he leapt to the podium, and as the senator scuttled for the door, launched into his own harangue: "Liar! Liar! Come up here and defend this, you filthy rabble-rouser. Show me your proof."

But the anti-McCarthy crusade that ensued was grounded

as much in shrewd calculation as it was in personal pique.
McCarthy had clearly slandered Greenspun in the hearing of
thousands on a statewide radio hookup. Thus, Greenspun's
lawyers advised him, he could say virtually anything he
wanted about the senator because to sue him McCarthy
would have to return to Nevada where he could be slapped
with a monumental countersuit. Welcoming this opportunity
for a rousing (and circulation-building) crusade, Greenspun
served as a conduit for any dirt on McCarthy others could
supply. Some of it was dirty indeed—such as the repeated
charge that McCarthy was a homosexual (replete with dates,
partners and hotel rooms). A famous series of seven "Where
I Stand" columns began: "Is McCarthy a Secret Communist?" Greenspun was adopting McCarthy's own techniques
—"fighting the devil with fire," as he put it—but McCarthy
wisely refused to sue. Instead, he persuaded Postmaster General Arthur Summerfield to obtain an indictment for mailing
matter "tending to incite murder or assassination." The matter in question was a column that said, in part, "Senator Joe
McCarthy has to come to a violent end. Huey Long's death
will be serene and peaceful compared with the demise of the
sadistic bum from Wisconsin. Live by the sword and you die
by the sword!" Shrewdly defended by his friend, Washington
lawyer Edward Morgan, Greenspun was acquitted.

But ex-lawyer Greenspun couldn't stay clear of the courts.
By rough count he has been either a plaintiff or a defendant
nearly thirty times over the years. In 1954, for example, the
FBI raided Roxie's, a renowned whorehouse on the edge of
town. An hour later, Clark County Sheriff Glen Jones staged
his own raid on the thinly disguised motel. Greenspun's
column charged that Sheriff Jones had a financial interest in
the brothel, underlining the point with a picture of the law-
man on an old-fashioned bicycle with a caption that read,
"Sheriff Glen Jones pedaling a little on his own." Jones, up
for reelection, sued the *Sun* and Greenspun for a million
dollars. Greenspun then hired an undercover agent to imper-
sonate a hoodlum seeking to buy Roxie's. In the negotiations,

Roxie's owner told a hidden microphone "We had Jones on the payroll a long time." The sheriff dropped his suit and was later indicted.

A year later, a *Sun* editorial charged that George F. Franklin, a Las Vegas attorney, had been involved in some unsavory municipal deals. Franklin sued and Greenspun fired back with a front-page series charging Franklin with participation in a black-market baby ring. When the case came to trial, Greenspun alleged that the presiding judge had received two children through the same ring and asked him to disqualify himself. The judge refused; Greenspun lost his case and was ordered to pay Franklin a whopping $190,000. Then the judge, still steaming over Greenspun's charge, persuaded a justice of the peace to charge Greenspun with "blackmail." That case was later dismissed by the State Supreme Court and ultimately the libel judgment was overturned, too. But Greenspun and Franklin have been in and out of court ever since, costing the *Sun*'s publisher nearly $10,000.

And in November 1963 Greenspun suffered a far more devastating reverse—the *Sun*'s plant, only partially covered by insurance, burned to the ground. He quickly rebuilt a sleek new building, but he was heavily in debt when Howard Hughes began exploring a move to Las Vegas in 1966. Indeed, his financial condition may go a long way towards explaining the curious relationship that grew up between Hughes and Greenspun.

They had known each other casually during the forties and fifties, when Hughes would run up from Hollywood to do some night-clubbing and gambling. "He used to walk around the Flamingo in seersucker and sneakers when I was doing PR there," Greenspun recalls. "Once we hid him from a congressional committee. And from time to time he'd ask me to introduce him to girls in the show."

In the autumn of 1966, Hughes was growing dissatisfied with his quarters in Boston's Ritz-Carlton Hotel. He was particularly unhappy with Boston's aggressive newsmen,

who kept devising new techniques for breaking into his redoubt: they would turn on fire alarms for his floor and then
storm in behind the firemen. So he was particularly receptive
when Edward P. Morgan, the Washington lawyer who had
worked for both Hughes and Greenspun, sent him a memo
suggesting that he move to Las Vegas. Morgan relayed a
pledge from Greenspun that if Hughes came to Las Vegas he
would not be bothered by the press. When Hughes did arrive
in town later that fall—in the dead of night on a stretcher in
a private railroad train—Greenspun was alerted in advance
and ran a front-page editorial urging his colleagues in the
press to "give this man the privacy he wants."

It was a curious stance for a newsman to take towards one
of the world's most newsworthy individuals who was destined to become the most powerful figure in the state. But in
his relations with Hughes over the next four years, Greenspun was not so much a newsman as a fellow entrepreneur,
and at times an outright partner. Greenspun claims this
relationship grew up because he was fighting the "mob" in
those days and badly needed an ally in his effort to "clean
up Las Vegas." But to his critics, his motives seemed more
pecuniary.

Greenspun started with some small favors. He intervened
with Moe Dalitz to help buy the Desert Inn. The ubiquitous
Ed Morgan negotiated the sale and, according to the Washington Post, got a $150,000 finder's fee from Hughes—
$25,500 of which he gave to Greenspun. More significantly,
one of Hughes's secretaries called to say, "Mr. Greenspun,
the Man is very grateful to you."

Hughes soon had reason to be even more grateful. The
recluse was an addict of late-night TV movies. Greenspun
owned KLAS-TV, the CBS outlet in Las Vegas. Soon he was
getting phone calls directly from Hughes complaining about
the quality of the late movies ("He liked Westerns, real
cowboy stuff "). Hughes aides suggested that Greenspun em-
ploy someone to seek out films Hughes would like. Greenspun did. Then Hughes began calling him at 2:00 A.M., when

the station went off the air, asking why it couldn't stay on all night to show movies. Greenspun suggested that Hughes give him enough advertising to justify that. No response. Then, still badly in debt from the fire, he suggested that Hughes buy the station. Hughes, eager to get into Nevada communications, did just that—for $3.6 million.

But even this did not soothe Greenspun's financial qualms. Perhaps remembering the McCarran-inspired advertising boycott, Greenspun persuaded the Hughes Tool Company in 1967 to pay the *Sun* $500,000 on demand for fifteen years of hotel-casino advertising. No discount was given—the company would pay the prevailing ad rates at the times they ran. But, Hughes Tool officials say Greenspun continued to bill for current advertising instead of deducting it from the $500,-000. Greenspun concedes that he did not apply the advertising charges to the prepayment until early 1972.

But this was still penny-ante stuff compared to the really big transaction later that year: a $4 million loan from Hughes to Greenspun at 3 percent interest and eight years for repayment—what the *Wall Street Journal* calls "incredibly favorable terms . . . a loan General Motors couldn't have gotten at any bank."

As Greenspun describes it, the loan all began with a golf tournament. "When Hughes bought the Desert Inn, he decided to cancel the Tournament of Champions, a big PGA tournament that drew guys like Palmer and Nicklaus every year. He didn't want those huge crowds tramping all over the hotel he was living in. But when his decision came under attack, he got very sensitive. The other PGA-approved course in town was one I owned, the Paradise Valley Golf and Country Club. Hughes suddenly asked whether he could buy the club and put the tournament on there. I said he could. Then he wanted to buy up 2,600 acres around it. But he didn't want anybody to know he was the buyer. Would I buy it for him? I said I would. They loaned me the four million so I could pay off the existing indebtedness on my land and buy up options on the surrounding land for him.

Finally, in 1968, we were all set to sign the agreement. We went over to the lawyer's office to sign—and the Hughes people told me the Man wasn't going through with it. Why? Because my golf club was one of the first to be watered with effluent water from the sanitary district. And that meant—Germs! The Man is terrified of Germs. What he didn't know was that the Desert Inn golf course right outside his own window also uses effluent water."

Long, tangled negotiations ensued. Eventually, Greenspun says, Hughes agreed to buy the golf club for $2.6 million, but not the surrounding land. The old $4 million note, he says, was supplanted by a new one at the same rate of interest but with payments extended to the year 2000. As collateral for the new note, Greenspun put up the stock of his newspaper.

And some charge that he put up his newspaper for ransom, too. For, while all this was going on, Greenspun proved amenable to Hughes's suggestions on editorial policy. One of Hughes's memos urged Maheu to get Greenspun's support in the billionaire's efforts to end U.S. nuclear testing in Nevada (the fear of fallout from the underground explosions obviously could seriously hamper Hughes investments in the state's tourist industry): "I simply beg that you obtain, without one minute's delay, Hank Greenspun's all-out support . . . I am sure that he will make a real crusade out of this if we encourage him and if he knows that he has us to back him up." Greenspun did indeed make a crusade out of it and with such enthusiasm that, for one editorial, Hughes suggested that Greenspun should get the Nobel Peace Prize.

During those four years, Greenspun generally gave Hughes the privacy he had promised him. From time to time, he broke a big Hughes story—but apparently they were usually leaks from Maheu or others in the Hughes organization. Embarrassing yarns were usually squelched, and stories that might help the Hughes interests were given prominent play. In a *mea culpa* published in 1973, Greenspun wrote: "It is a little late but I must freely accept blame for helping create

[Hughes domination of the state]. I had prostituted my newspaper in Hughes' interest sufficiently, and would have no more of it."

As late as December 1969 Greenspun may have been working in close concert with Hughes. An indictment handed up by a federal grand jury in 1973—since dismissed by a judge because it was badly drawn—charged Hughes and four associates with stock manipulation, conspiracy and wire fraud in connection with the acquisition of Air West. Greenspun was not indicted, but he was named as a co-conspirator and the indictment alleged that he and others helped depress the market price of the airline's stock through concentrated sales of the stock in December 1969.

Greenspun says he got off the Hughes bandwagon in 1970 because he "decided that the Hughes influence presented a threat to the orderly development of the area." In fact, it appears the rupture occurred in November 1970 when Hughes abruptly dismissed Maheu and left for the Bahamas. Maheu had been Greenspun's closest ally in the Hughes organization—the man through whom he had negotiated most of his deals—and he naturally sided with him in the fierce struggle that developed between Maheu and the faction headed by Chester Davis.

Greenspun insists that he was not all that friendly with Maheu, that his intervention in the struggle was a matter of principle. "The order came down to destroy Bob Maheu. Nobody is going to destroy anybody in the state of Nevada as long as I am breathing." But he also says that when Davis came in to take over the Hughes interests he warned that he was going to "bury" Greenspun. "He found me a very reluctant corpse," the editor remarks with a chuckle.

When Greenspun continued to flail away at Hughes almost daily, Davis took the first step to bury him. He filed the original $4 million note—which Greenspun insists was rescinded but Davis says is still valid. He also put a lien on the land and the *Sun* that Greenspun had put up as collateral, then threatened to sell them. Greenspun responded with a

$142 million law suit against the Hughes Tool Company ($42 million in compensatory damages for land development deals he said had fallen through and $100 million in punitive damages.)

Following the suit, Greenspun says, Chester Davis told him, "You are going to have some IRS (Internal Revenue Service) trouble." I said, "You just take care of your IRS problems and I'll take care of mine." But, sure enough, in the summer of 1973, the IRS hit Greenspun with a $1.6 million notice of deficiency. The claim was based on the difference between the 3 percent interest rate that Hughes charged Greenspun and 6 percent, which the IRS said was the going rate. The IRS claimed that the difference should be counted as additional taxable income from 1967 until the year 2000.

Greenspun broke this story in an unusually prominent "Where I Stand" column on page one of the *Sun* on July 8, 1973. "It appears that a 'contract' has been let on the good publisher of this newspaper and the IRS has been chosen to make the 'hit,'" he wrote. "It appears that I may have some enemies who have some influence with this agency of the government." But Greenspun warned: "We have just begun to fight back." He announced that the paper was launching an investigation of the IRS by "one of the *Sun*'s top investigative reporters." And, anticipating his critics, he wrote: "I have no hesitation in spreading my personal involvements with the Internal Revenue Service, or any other agency of government, over the front page of this newspaper, because if the IRS is wrong in this matter, it could be wrong in all matters . . . The Internal Revenue Service has stabbed many a little taxpayer in the back without recourse. At least now the cry can go up."

And spread across page one it was—in twenty-one articles by staffer Lou Dolinar and free-lancer Jim Phelan. The series was a credible job, filled with juicy tidbits of IRS bumbling and favoritism and written in a lively style ("What do black-jack dealers and radical college newspaper editors have in common? They've both been victimized by the IRS"). But it did not seem worthy of the Pulitzer Prize—for which Greenspun nominated it—nor of the J. Arthur Rank gong which the editor sounded in his opening and subsequent editorials. Finally, one wonders: if the little man is stabbed in the back by government agencies every day, why didn't the *Sun* take up his cause until its publisher was personally wounded?

But then the *Sun* rises only for Hank Greenspun. From dawn to dusk, and through the dark hours, too, it responds only to his whims, his loyalties, his feuds, his interests. This is personal journalism practiced literally with a vengeance. When I was ushered into his office one day, he was grumbling "Goddamned cop!" It seems a local police lieutenant with the unlikely name of Walter Zawrotny had been bold enough to appear on TV news the night before to criticize Greenspun for breaking a story on something called "the Terry Romeo slaying." Zawrotny said the story had impeded the police investigation. Greenspun said our first interview would have to be cut short so he could pound out a response. That day, page one carried a headline, SUN PUBLISHER DENIES ZA-WROTNY ACCUSATION. And the next day the hapless Zawrotny got it again in a "Where I Stand" column that read, in part: "A time for silence and a time to speak . . . We have always maintained good relations with all agencies of law enforcement . . . But when the reputation of the newspaper is on the line we'll battle the world and all the little minds in it."

When A. J. Liebling met Greenspun in 1954, he described him as "a big, strong-looking man of forty-three, with black hair, a square, undershot jaw, and two rows of square white and gold teeth frequently exposed in a menacing grin." Twenty years later, that is still a pretty good description. At sixty-three, he has graying hair now, and his squashed-in boxer's nose emphasizes his aura of an aging, but still agile boxer (he was once known as "Dempsey" because of his uncanny resemblance to the ex-champion).

But Greenspun *has* changed since Liebling knew him. For

one thing, he has become a wealthy man. Nobody knows for sure how wealthy. A millionaire certainly. Probably more. Besides the *Sun* (which now claims a circulation of 46,000), he also owns the Colorado Springs (Colorado) *Sun,* an outdoor advertising company, and the potentially lucrative cable TV license for Las Vegas (the city is an ideal site for pay TV). He is generally not ostentatious about money, although he does own a Rolls Royce.

But those who have followed his career closely say the new wealth and status in the community have taken their toll. His style is still flamboyant. But now those pyrotechnics are enlisted less often on behalf of the downtrodden and more frequently on behalf of the powers that be in Nevada. In the words of one of his former reporters, "Hank's gone uptown."

His working relationship with Hughes is the best example, but there are others. Greenspun campaigned for Sheriff Ralph Lamb on the front page of his newspaper and ever since they have been as close as handcuffs. He played a major role in putting Governor Mike O'Callaghan into office and enjoys considerable influence in the state house. And he is still a strong supporter of President Nixon, whose Plumbers planned to burglarize his safe.

Greenspun has been a nominal Republican ever since he joined the F. H. LaGuardia Republican Club in New York in the thirties. "I'm a Republican in the Little Flower's image," he says. But in practice he has supported as many Democrats as Republicans, and Richard Nixon's domestic record, notably Watergate, distresses him. "Basically, I'm an anarchist. Nixon's against almost everything I stand for and yet I still support him. I've been going around the country these days giving speeches for him. There's one simple explanation: Israel."

Greenspun's Zionist passions have never flagged. Pictures of him with Ben-Gurion and Golda Meir decorate his office walls and he makes frequent forays to Israel, the latest during the war of the fall of 1973, when he rushed to the front and filed dispatches datelined: "With the Israeli forces in Syria."

And Greenspun considers Richard Nixon the best current guarantee of Israel's survival. "In Portland, he put his arm around me after a press conference and said, 'Hank, as long as I am president, Israel will not lack for arms.' And he had me to lunch to further reassure me. No matter whom we have as president—Grant, McKinley, Harding—the country has survived, but if anything happens to Israel that means the end of freedom for all small nations."

But less defensible than averting his eyes from scandal in Washington is his failure to go after corruption at home. Greenspun makes much of a few glancing scraps with the mob in the fifties, but of late he has barely bothered to cover the flashy hotels and gambling casinos along the Strip where most of Las Vegas' "action" is. The "mob" is still very much in evidence. The Teamsters, with outstanding loans to a score of hotels, play a curious role. But the *Sun* doesn't even have a reporter assigned full-time to the Strip.

The explanation for this is not hard to find: the hotels, casinos and other tourist-oriented businesses in Las Vegas provide a major part of the *Sun*'s advertising revenue. Every Friday, the paper runs a foldout section called "Las Vegas Entertainment Scene" packed with lucrative ads for nightclub and lounge acts. So, not surprisingly, the "stories" that fill out the section are almost indistinguishable from the ads. (e.g., "Liberace, whose dazzling nightclub productions have made his name solely synonymous with the title, 'Mr. Showmanship,' will present what promises to be his most entertaining effort yet when he opens an extended run Saturday night in the main showroom of the Las Vegas Hilton Hotel.")

Although Las Vegas has more live entertainment than any city in the country except New York, neither the *Sun* nor the *Review-Journal* prints anything that could be called criticism. Even the *Sun*'s two entertainment columnists—Joe Delaney and Ralph Pearl—fire off a fusillade of puffballs. Pearl, a law school buddy of Greenspun's, has fallen out with his editor of late and claims that this blandness is enforced from on high. "He wanted to sell newspapers while I wanted to write fearlessly, the hotel advertisers be damned," he has said. Without passing judgment on this self-serving version, there have been some spats between the two. The most renowned occurrred some years ago when Pearl wrote that Betty Grable had been seen "bending an elbow" around the local bars. Greenspun, leaping to the defense of the "lovely, gracious lady," publicly reprimanded his own columnist.

And Greenspun has been even more accommodating to another habitué of Las Vegas nightspots, one who is not known for graciousness. When Frank Sinatra got into a fight with a pit boss at Caesar's Palace a few years ago, a reporter named A. D. Hopkins was assigned to write the story for the *Sun.* He recalls: "As I was finishing up I was summoned to Greenspun's office. Two guys in dark glasses were there. Hank asked me to read my story. Hank and the guys in dark glasses exchanged a few cryptic words and then Hank dictated another story to me. It didn't bear too much resemblance to the one I'd written. You could say it was sympathetic to Sinatra." (Greenspun concedes he may have "corrected" Hopkins's piece because he had "better sources," but calls Hopkins's version of the incident "a little dramatic.")

When Sinatra returned to Las Vegas in January 1974 for his first gig in three years, the *Sun* ran a page-one story that began, "Old Blue Eyes, Francis Albert Sinatra, Sr., came back in magnificent style, still the all-time champion in the Caesar's Palace Circus Maximus." And Greenspun, in his column, crooned: "It's magic, it's fantastic, it's genius."

When he wants to be, the Fighting Frontier Editor can be a real pussycat.

May 1974

J. Anthony Lukas
Taking Our Cue from Joe

When we resolved to name our Counter-Convention after A. J. Liebling, we assumed his name would ring defiantly in newsrooms throughout the land. We were wrong. For many of our younger colleagues, it appears, Liebling has long since passed into ill-deserved obscurity along with his friends, Whitey Bimstein, Maxwell C. Bimberg and Colonel John R. Stingo. "Why is the title in German?" one reader wanted to know. A Midwestern editor and a journalism school dean both wrote letters for more information addressed "Dear Mr. Liebling." So perhaps the time has come to reintroduce Abbott Joseph Liebling (1904–1963), *The New Yorker*'s press critic, gourmand, boxing writer, war correspondent, labor reporter, medievalist, Francophile, chronicler of Broadway and resident epicure.

Trying to explain Joe Liebling, the mind gropes for an adequate metaphor. For few could wield a metaphor or simile like Liebling. *The New York Times,* he once wrote, "is in many respects a sound newspaper within the translucent mass of which one may occasionally discern the outlines of commendable purposes, fixed like strawberries in a great mold of jello, and of good men struggling feebly, like minnows within a giant jellyfish." The press chorus for decontrol of meat prices in 1946 he likened to the Great Goumba, Swahili for "the inordinate longing and craving of exhausted nature for meat." Writing of Ezzard Charles's strange reluctance to hit Rocky Marciano, he said "Charles's intuitive resentment of violence had set in like ice on a pond." And woe be to him who handed Liebling a ready-made metaphor, for he would surely get it slapped back in his face like a wet mackerel, as Anthony Sampson found out when Liebling reviewed his *Anatomy of Britain* like this: "In cutting his lecture to fit his time, the anatomist has performed a record number of excisions, including most of the viscera. It is as if he offered for demonstration a body lacking the left lung, the sternum, the pancreas, the other endocrine glands, the second and third vertebrae and—just for the hell of it—the aorta, the right kidney, both intestines, and the medulla oblongata, assorted frenula and both wishbones."

When my metaphor search was ended, I could do no better than critic Joseph Epstein who, in a retrospective review last year, called Liebling "the Minnesota Fats of American prose." But the comparison appealed to us for somewhat different reasons. Epstein likened Liebling to the corpulent pool hall wizard, played by Jackie Gleason in "The Hustler," in order to show that he was that intriguing type, the nimble fat man. "Like Minnesota Fats with a cue ball," Epstein wrote, "so Liebling with an English sentence—there was nothing he couldn't make it do." What came to my mind, though, was the movie's last scene in which Paul Newman, as "Fast Eddie," has just beaten Gleason in their climactic match. Newman refuses to split the take with George C. Scott, his promoter-backer "Gordon," who has been getting 75 percent of his winnings. Gordon warns Fast Eddie that if he doesn't fork over he will never play again in any respectable pool hall in America. Although he knows Gordon can enforce that threat, Fast Eddie turns away with a contemptuous sneer on his lip and, looking down at Minnesota Fats, says, "Fat Man, you shoot a great game of pool."

"So do you, Fast Eddie," says Minnesota Fats.

That was Joe Liebling. He was above all a craftsman who

loved and respected other men who did their work well—
whether it was making a perfect bank shot, mixing a brilliant
bouillabaisse, landing a great left jab or turning a polished
phrase. But he could not abide men like Gordon who lived off
others' work, particularly if they did it while pretending to
be the working man's friend. Thus, the keynote of Liebling's
writing about the press was his contempt for the publisher
who owned the pool hall but could dismiss a splendid craftsman with a wave of his pinky and two weeks' severance pay.

He had his particular *bêtes noires* among publishers. Chief
among them was Roy Howard, who owned the *World-Telegram,* where Liebling put in his last years as a newspaperman (1931–35). Howard was cutting costs sharply then, and
Liebling recalled that his salary was cut 20 percent in eight
months, skidding to $60.75 per week. On this pittance, he
had to live himself and try to get adequate care for his first
wife, who spent most of those years in mental institutions.
"This took the carefree, juvenile jollity out of journalism for
me definitively," he wrote. "It taught me that society is
divided, not into newspaper people and nonnewspaper people, but into people with money and people without it. I did
not belong to a joyous, improvident professional group including me and Roy Howard, but to a section of society
including me and any floorwalker at Macy's. Mr. Howard,
even though he asked to be called Roy, belonged in a section
that included him and the gent who owned Macy's. This
clarified my thinking about publishers, their common interests and motivations." In 1941 Liebling got his revenge in an
unusually long, four-part profile detailing Howard's use of
his columns to defend his own tax loopholes, his personal
extravagance but frugality where his employees were concerned, his feud with Heywood Broun and his "ideological
affinity" with Westbrook Pegler.

Then there was Frank Munsey, the chain-store grocer who
acquired seventeen papers but merged and killed them off
until at his death he owned only two; William Randolph
Hearst, for whom Liebling worked just long enough to be
told by a Hearst executive "the public is interested in just

three things: blood, money and the female organ of sexual intercourse"; and Henry Luce, on whom he planned to write a long exposé (the notes for which still lie in his widow's filing cabinet, marked by a colleague, "Liebling's Time Bomb— Keep It Safe").

Liebling recognized, of course, that publishers varied somewhat in character and disposition. "The pattern of a newspaperman's life," he once wrote, "is like the plot of *Black Beauty.* Sometimes he finds a kind master who gives him a dry stall and an occasional bran mash in the form of a Christmas bonus, sometimes he falls into the hands of a mean owner who drives him in spite of spavins and expects him to live on potato peelings." The New York *World,* whose Sunday section he joined in 1930, was his one dry stall; but it sprang a bad leak the next year and sank beneath him, destined to remain from then on the one glorious exception to Liebling's every journalistic rule.

But, ultimately, his dislike for publishers was generic: he couldn't abide the breed. He drew a sharp line between the news side and the business side (which he called the "lopside") of journalism. Publishers were businessmen who inherited their papers as they did grocery stores. "Try to imagine the future of medicine, law or pedagogy," he wrote, "if their absolute control were vested in the legal heirs of men who had bought practices in 1890. . . ."

Liebling simply didn't believe you could run a newspaper the way you ran a shoe factory. "Will everyone stand up please who publishes or works on a newspaper where the top reporter makes as much money as the top advertising salesman," he once asked. And he reserved his most scathing scorn for publishers in one-paper towns, or towns in which one publisher owned both the morning and evening papers. Such situations, he said, amounted to "a privately owned public utility that is Constitutionally exempt from public regulation." Much of what he had to say on this subject was, of course, prophetic. Since his death, the contraction and concentration of the press has proceeded apace, now combining under single ownership not only A.M. and P.M. papers but increasingly television and radio stations.

But other parts of Liebling's running vendetta with the publishers are no longer very convincing. On some of the best American papers at least—*The New York Times,* the Los Angeles *Times,* the Washington *Post* and *Newsday* come to mind—the problems do not lie so much with the publishers. Money in sufficient quantity is being pumped into these enterprises. The problems on these papers—and there are many —more often stem from a failure of imagination or nerve among the editors. Yet Liebling never quite plumbed the editorial mind as he did the publishing mind. "Joe's views on the press were really rather simple ones," says Gardner Botsford, his longtime editor at *The New Yorker.* "He was no philosopher."

But he had other talents as a press critic. First, he was a dedicated and incredibly alert reader. Jean Stafford Liebling, his third wife, recalls his mornings: "He'd finish breakfast by nine and sit there in the living room reading the papers, all of them, until noon. When he finished a paper he'd tear it up like a puppy dog and leave the scraps all over the carpet." But every morning he'd save a scrap or two and often it would be something nobody else had noticed. Those scraps were the germs of his "Wayward Press" pieces. That *New Yorker* column, inaugurated by Robert Benchley in 1927 and largely written by Liebling from 1945 until his death, was the first regular press criticism to appear in any American medium. And with all its faults it is still the best.

Perhaps the greatest virtue of Liebling's press pieces was their specificity. He liked to take one story and analyze how the papers had covered it. A classic example was his 1947 piece on the "Lady in Mink" case. A woman on welfare was discovered living at city expense in a New York hotel, although she was reported to have $60,000 in assets and a mink coat. The *Times* went wild over the story, splashing it across the top of page one under a three-column headline. But Liebling took the story apart line by line. He showed, among other things, that the woman had not $60,000 but between $36,000 and $56,000; that she had had it five years before but there was no indication how much she had left when she went on welfare; and that the famous mink coat was six to eight years old, had a torn lining and was worth about $300. By playing the story as it did, he concluded, the *Times* was saying that "the poor are poor because of their sins and whatever they get is too good for them," a principle he distilled into a pithy phrase: "the undeserving poor."

If Liebling was consistently antagonistic toward publishers and indifferent toward editors, he was generally sympathetic toward reporters. "I am a chronic, incurable, recidivist reporter," he once wrote. Even when he was tracing his colleagues' wayward ways, he could not suppress an indulgent smirk. For what outraged Liebling far more than error or stupidity was pomposity and pretension, traits he regularly found in the publishers' offices but rarely in the city room. "There is a healthy American newspaper tradition of not taking yourself seriously," he wrote. "It is the story you must take that way." So long as a reporter remained a reporter, practicing his craft as best he knew how, Liebling was with him. It was when he began fancying himself something else that he risked the fat man's scorn.

With few exceptions, Liebling had no use for columnists, news analysts, interpretive reporters and their ilk. He saw all these fancy titles as mere excuses to avoid the hard work of chasing down a story on the street. In 1953 he had a world of fun with the "constructive reporting" which followed Stalin's death; witness this beauty in the *World-Telegram*. "Washington, March 4.—Gen. James A. Van Fleet replied, "I don't know," when asked today whether the death of Russia's ailing Premier Stalin might lead to a weakening of Communist morale in Korea." And he once wrote: "There are three kinds of writers of news in our generation. In inverse order of worldly consideration, they are: 1. The reporter, who writes what he sees; 2. The interpretive reporter, who writes what he sees and what he construes to be its meaning; 3. The expert, who writes what he construes to be the meaning of what he hasn't seen."

So great was his distrust of the experts that, at times,

Liebling could be almost antiintellectual. He was fond of speculating on "what the boys on the quarterlies would say." Essentially pragmatic, his writings on politics often betrayed an almost Orwellian distrust of ideology. Although decidedly "left of center" all his life, he was never drawn into organized Left politics, even during the thirties when so many newspapermen, writers and artists flirted with the Communist party. "If Joe had an ideology it was labor," says Jean Stafford Liebling. "He was a big labor man." Gardner Botsford recalls: "In his labor reporting, he almost always went overboard in his sympathy for the unions. He was so completely in their camp that I don't think he even recognized the grafting or self-interest or gangster domination when it was there. I tried to restore some semblance of balance with the editing."

Roger Angell, who was a young *New Yorker* writer when Liebling was in his prime, calls him an "old-fashioned newsroom liberal," and that is probably as good a description as any. What outraged Liebling was a rich guy pushing a poor guy around. Curiously enough, he had a blind spot on the race issue. Although the civil rights movement was underway long before his death, he rarely touched on it. When he wrote about the South—notably in two excellent pieces on the press coverage of a secret police force in Mississippi—he barely mentioned segregation. Jean Liebling suspects his lack of interest in race may be related to his apathy toward his own Jewishness. "Even Hitler didn't make him an intensely self-conscious Jew," she says.

Or perhaps it was because he was such a thoroughgoing New Yorker and took the heterogeneity of Broadway and the Garment District for granted. With the striking exception of New Orleans—for which he harbored both a Francophile's and a gourmet's lust—Liebling never really had much use for America west of the Catskills. Some of the most stinging invective of his career was ladled into his short book on Chicago, *The Second City*. When he told Harold Ross, then *The New Yorker*'s editor, that he wanted to do some reporting on America's heartland, Ross said "You wouldn't like it, Liebling, you wouldn't like it." And he didn't.

But it wasn't, as with so many New Yorkers, a snob's disdain for the rest of the country. Nor was it merely Menckenesque raillery at the prejudiced "booboisie" (although, at times, Liebling's tone could be very much like Mencken's). It was just that the florid, bizarre, rococo characters he enjoyed writing about—like Bimstein, Bimberg and Stingo—flourished best here in New York. He was anything but a snob. In fact, he was one of very few writers able to describe hustlers, touts, con men, pimps, and telephone booth Indians (Broadway operators who use phone booths as their offices) without the slightest trace of condescension. Another was Joe Mitchell, Liebling's closest friend on *The New Yorker,* who expressed their feeling in an author's note to his *McSorley's Wonderful Saloon:* "The people in a number of the stories are the kind that many writers have recently got in the habit of referring to as 'the little people.' I regard this phrase as patronizing and repulsive. There are no little people in this book. They are as big as you are, whoever you are."

But what draws me most to Liebling is the fun he so obviously got from his work. Journalism is all I've ever wanted to do because it's the only work I really enjoy. On a good story, Liebling positively radiated satisfaction, as only a fat man can. Botsford recalls him sitting at his typewriter "jiggling with joy" at something he had just written. Sometimes when he was thoroughly enjoying himself he would get carried away and ornament the facts a bit. Jean Liebling recalls meeting Colonel John R. Stingo, the baroque centerpiece of Liebling's "The Honest Rainmaker," and finding him "a stunning old bore." She concludes that "Joe must have invented—no, embellished him." Roger Angell once stayed in the Louvois Hotel, the Paris hostelry about which Liebling waxed rhapsodic. "I was aghast," Angell recalls. "It was like an enormous Dixie Hotel." But the embellishments are half the fun.

It wasn't all fun. There was a dark side too, which only those closest to him saw. His first wife's mental problems were an enormous drain on him. His second wife was, by all reports, a virago who made his life miserable. At times, Liebling would retreat into deep and gloomy silences. At other times, he betrayed an incredible lack of confidence for a writer who could boast of 485 published manuscripts. He was an eccentric and he knew it. Once he told Jean Liebling, *"The New Yorker* gang is so crazy they think I'm normal."

Liebling's interests and his published works covered such a vast spectrum of human endeavors that it is not surprising to find little unanimity about his best work. Joseph Epstein likes *The Earl of Louisiana,* his profile of Earl Long. Jean Liebling prefers *The Second City.* Gardner Botsford leans to his war reporting, Roger Angell to his boxing stuff. Most critics feel Liebling was best when he was thoroughly enjoying himself—writing about food, sports or Paris—and least effective when grinding an axe or exposing a felony. But, as a lifelong reporter, I am drawn most to his acerbic press criticism, like this jibe at the "inside" man:

> There are in every newspaper office the congenital, aboriginal, intramurals. They are to be distinguished from the frustrates because they have never even wanted to see the world outside. They come to newspapers like monks to cloisters or worms to apples. They are the dedicated. All of them are fated to be editors except the ones that get killed off by the lunches they eat at their desks until even the most drastic purgatives lose all effect upon them. The survivors of gastric disorders rise to minor executive jobs and then major ones, and the reign of these non-writers makes our newspapers read like the food in *The New York Times* cafeteria tastes.

Fat man, you shoot a great game of pool.

May 1972

INSTITUTIONS

CHARLOTTE CURTIS

An Adventure
in "the Big Cave"

The journalistic weakness for reducing complicated controversies to oversimplified struggles between the Good Guys
and the Bad Guys has seldom had a better workout than in
the Great Harper's Flap. According to the now almost myth-
ologized script, Willie Morris and his talented staff resigned
during that fateful week in March 1971 because the bright
young editor had created the "hottest" publication in America only to be harassed and ultimately knifed by publisher
William S. Blair, who after all came from wicked Madison
Avenue, who constantly meddled in editorial policy and who
finally nailed Morris not just for lavishing too much money
on his writers but for devoting most of the March 1971 issue
to Norman Mailer's four-lettered *The Prisoner of Sex*. As
Morris put it in his bitter aphorism of resignation, "It all
boiled down to the money men and the literary men. And,
as always, the money men won."

The story may read better that way, but what actually
happened was more than somewhat different. More accurately, it is an unhappy tale of an almost willful failure to
communicate and often astonishing inexperience—of a confused publisher who had never published a national maga-

zine, of a headstrong editor who had never edited one, and not least, of a well-meaning owner, John Cowles, Jr., who had never owned one. And perhaps saddest of all, it is the story of a brilliant young Southern writer who felt driven to run with New York's literary pack and lost his way in an alien city he so aptly described as "the Big Cave."

Perhaps the best place to start is in 1968, the year young Cowles succeeded his father as chief of *Harper's* parent firm, the Minneapolis Star and Tribune Company. That was the year *Harper's* purchased the defunct *Reporter* magazine's paid-up subscribers and Blair became publisher. Morris had been editor for more than a year. At thirty-three, he was already being hailed as the brightest publishing star in a generation. He was the Yazoo kid, all slicked-down blond hair, pale blue eyes, apple cheeks and bitten fingernails. "Only a family Bible and a grandmother away from Reconstruction," he liked to say.

The New York literary set, used to pomposity in blue jeans and poetry in peasant dresses, found it hard to match the special intellect of Morris's work (particularly his much-praised 1967 autobiographical book, *North Toward Home*) with the shy, disarmingly wide-eyed Southerner in the prim blue suit, white shirt and slim tie.

Yet before long, the former Rhodes Scholar was being described as "a young Turner Catledge," after the politically astute Mississippi-born managing editor of the *Times.* Anyone who cared for details, however, might wonder at the comparison. Catledge was a seasoned political infighter, a meticulous mender of fences and a strategist of the first order. Morris was more the gutsy, crusading writer whose personal stamp, imposed emotionally as well as intellectually on the facts, often turned his work into memorable journalism. Whether as editor of the University of Texas's student newspaper, when he battled the school regents with scorching attacks on the oil interests, or as writer-editor of the muckraking weekly *Texas Observer,* when he infiltrated the

John Birch Society, Morris worked through the written word.

Yet the Catledge comparison stood. After all, John Fischer had invited other promising young writer-editors to join him at *Harper's* in the sixties, dangling the editor's job before them, and Morris, wide-eyed or not, had managed to walk off with the prize. There was never any suggestion that Morris, with Cowles's blessing, actually pushed Fischer out the door in 1967, only that he maneuvered effectively with Cowles, and that it worked. Or so it seemed. From then on, it was assumed that besides being a sort of literary genius, Willie Morris was a shrewd politician, a man with survival power, which he was not.

When Bill Blair arrived at the magazine's 2 Park Avenue headquarters, he had been president of Harper-Atlantic Sales, Inc., the advertising sales company jointly owned by *Harper's* and its rival, the *Atlantic*. A Scotsman, he came to the United States in 1940 to study economics at Princeton's graduate school. He served with the Canadian Army during World War II. He was vice-president and research director of Ogilvy, Benson & Mather, Inc., in 1957 before moving to Harper-Atlantic to establish a research and promotion department. He is considered one of the best research men in New York. Upon his arrival, Blair had his office expensively refurnished and added a bar. There were literary cocktail parties to celebrate each month's closing. He hired an art director and spent what the editors called "lavish sums" on color, layout, binding and promotion.

The new publisher was named president of the magazine. Morris was executive vice-president. Blair was, in Cowles's words, "the boss"; Morris was "the number-two man." Explains Cowles: "I took great pains to talk with Willie about Bill before he became publisher. I said if Willie thought Blair was wrong or Bill thought Willie was wrong that I was available to decide matters of dispute. I was not putting Bill over Willie and leaving Willie no recourse. Willie could come to me anytime." Morris exercised that option only once—in February of 1971. "Blair thought he was going to have the predominant influence in running the magazine," Morris says. "He'd written a book or something. He thought he was literary. He was disabused in about three weeks. He found he was facing professionals. He shut up. He sure as hell did. He was afraid of us. There were all these proposals, but he never made the decisions. We did."

The "we," of course, were Morris and his editors. Robert Kotlowitz, a former editor of *Show* and a *Harper's* editor in Fischer days, became managing editor. The two, later joined by Midge Decter, wife of Norman Podhoretz, editor of *Commentary,* ran the editorial department. And there were the contributing editors, none of whom actually edited, but who worked as contract writers: David Halberstam, who quit *The New York Times* to join Morris; John Corry, also from the *Times;* Larry L. King, the Texas journalist; Marshall Frady, another Southerner, and John Hollander, who was poetry editor.

Some days in 1968 were better than others, and for a while there was at least something of a cease-fire. Blair, aware Morris was seriously upset by his impending divorce from Celia, the childhood sweetheart he had married on a trip home from Oxford University, offered Morris a home at his apartment and Morris accepted. He lived with the Blairs for six weeks. Asked repeatedly to explain exactly how Blair harassed him, Morris said such things as, "Blair was always after me about money," or "The editorial budget was cut last year," or "The feeling of joy went out of the magazine," or "Blair wanted to get rid of Kotlowitz and Midge Decter. He didn't think they were any good," or "He wants to get rid of the contributing editors."

Blair doesn't deny repeated discussions and even arguments about money, nor that the editorial budget, like budgets all over New York, was cut in the 1970 recession. But he insists he didn't needle Morris. "He couldn't have," said a staff member who had access to both offices. "They really didn't see each other very much." In late 1970, Blair did propose eliminating either Kotlowitz's or Miss Decter's job as an economy measure, but it was never an order and had nothing to do with their talents.

Blair also questioned the necessity of having so many contributing editors on the grounds that they weren't producing enough and because simultaneously the magazine was buying so many free-lance articles. Yet Cowles himself set the spending pattern. In 1967 Morris coaxed his friend William Styron into letting *Harper's* publish 45,000 words of *The Confessions of Nat Turner*. He suggested offering Styron $7,500. Cowles said $10,000 would sound better when the word got around. Later, Mailer got $10,000 for *Armies of the Night*, $10,000 for covering the Democratic National Convention and a record $12,500 for *The Prisoner of Sex*. Rates ran anywhere from $500 for 3,000 words on up; $3,500 for 10,000 words wasn't unusual. At the same time, the contributing editors were collecting annual salaries that ranged up to $20,000 for Corry and Halberstam. Blair particularly criticized the latter, who he claimed produced far less than the six articles his last contract called for. This infuriated Halberstam, who maintained that he should get extra credit for long pieces, such as his profile of Robert S. McNamara.

Occasionally Blair attacked a specific article openly, but he never interfered. Morris was never ordered to change a word of copy, cut or kill a story, run an article he didn't want, favor an advertiser or pitch a story to circulation. Yet in the late spring of 1969, Morris insisted to King, one of his oldest friends, that Blair was trying to do the writers in. "I said in what way?" King recalls. "He said Blair was critical of the magazine's contents. A general dissatisfaction. Nothing specific. Willie's not a man of specifics. It was always general. They'd been to some meeting. Willie was upset. From then on it was downhill. Willie would periodically tell me about his lack of rapport with Blair. He would say, 'I'm going to quit,' and I'd say, 'No, bite the bullet,' and all that. After that, he was always threatening to quit. I didn't take it seriously."

It was at about this time that the "great experiment" began. Blair and Morris went to Glendalough, the Cowles family's northern Minnesota retreat, for the express purpose of facing the economic realities. Blair, armed with statistics and projections, warned Cowles and his business associates that the magazine was headed for what could become fatal financial difficulties. The question was whether Cowles was willing to underwrite additional losses, and if so, to what extent. After a great deal of discussion, Cowles decided to continue to gamble on Morris's style of editing. He not only backed Morris but agreed that *Harper's* should continue to overspend on both the editorial department and promotion to see if by the end of 1970 it had substantially changed the various measures of the magazine's acceptability to the public. These measures included newsstand sales, conversion rates, renewal rates, letters to the editor, and a general sense of excitement. It was never the intention that these indicators should change by the end of 1970 to the point where the magazine would become profitable. Instead, the goal was to see whether enough change came about to cause any hope for the future. The magazine was saved for the time being. The spending spree was on again. Morris was still free to do with the editorial content exactly what he wished.

What he did, and it was a continuation of what he'd been doing all along, was to search out gifted writers for special projects and give his able team of journalists their heads. King says Morris improved his copy 30 to 40 percent. Halberstam says he was the only editor who ever really understood him. Bill Moyers, whose *Listening to America* ran 45,000 words in the December issue, says Morris constantly fed his ego, made him want to write and then treated the finished copy in a cool, professional way.

As an editor, Morris was a night owl who rarely returned telephone calls and loathed administrative work. It has been strongly suggested that Miss Decter and Kotlowitz did the hard work, but perhaps out of loyalty they deny it. Morris's style was to appear in the office in the afternoon, and then work into the night. His blue suit and short hair soon gave way to turtleneck shirts and shaggy locks. He spent a lot of time along the literary party circuit, drinking heavily and talking with other writers. In the late evenings, he presided over a table at Elaine's, periodically commissioning articles he sometimes forgot he had ever discussed. Some of these articles, including Jack Richardson's clinical report on the whores of his life, were published. Some weren't. According to several writers who were neither contributing editors nor lustrous names like Mailer, Morris often said yes to an idea when in fact he had no intention of publishing their work.

Morris also increasingly irritated his contributing editors. He would, for example, allocate space in an issue for one writer, then deliver it to another. And in general he promised more than he delivered, let problems slide and refused to contend with what he did not want to see. For instance, neither Kotlowitz, Miss Decter nor the contributing editors had any real knowledge of the financial difficulties despite their closeness to Morris. "He couldn't give you a simple no," Halberstam says. "He'd hide, prevaricate—anything so he wouldn't have to say no. He didn't want to hurt anybody's feelings. He hated to give bad news and it made things very complicated." Says another editor: "Willie's response to any of Blair's ideas, whether it had to do with changing the concept of the magazine or the fiscal problems, was to say, 'I'll kill that son of a bitch,' and then do nothing." Blair's way apparently was just as ineffective. "He'd say, 'We've got to do something'," says the same editor, "and nothing happened. He never suggested anything concrete."

The result of Morris's editing, often the art of accident rather than any serious planning, was a lively, controversial, uneven and at times downright brilliant magazine. But what appeared to be either a team effort or the reflection of the editor's view of the world was in fact dependent for its

editorial success not just on the periodic tours de force of
such luminaries as Styron, Moyers and Mailer, but upon the
special interests and performances of the individual contributing editors. Nobody had to write about anything that
didn't interest him. That made the writers happy, but inevitably the issue boiled down to the relationship between
editorial content and circulation.

Cowles had bought the *Reporter*'s subscribers against the
time when *Harper's* could produce its own. However, not
only did the purchased readers fail to stick (certainly no fault
of Morris's), but new readers did not sign up in sufficient
numbers. Particularly disappointing was the younger audience. Surveys showed that the bright new magazine, with its
"now" covers and its controversial articles, bored its younger
readers. Morris's reaction to the first survey that indicated
this—a Minneapolis Star and Tribune Company poll of two
hundred *Harper's* subscribers in 1967—was to drop it in a
drawer and forget it. He was equally unenthusiastic about a
more extensive Oliver Quayle study in 1970. When Quayle
reported his bearish findings at an administrative meeting
that year, Miss Decter considered it a move against the
editorial department. She waited for Morris to object. But he
remained silent. He has since said that "you can't edit by
polls," which is doubtless true; but it is equally true that a
magazine can't publish at a continuing loss without eventually coming to grips with the problem.

Morris's refusal to deal with the circulation problems and
nearly everything else having to do with the business side
lasted until shortly after January 19, 1971. On that date, Blair
sent him a confidential memo saying that the overspending
experiment had failed. The memo, reminding Morris of the
forthcoming quarterly budget meeting in Minneapolis, described the extent of the circulation problems, the rising costs
and the future prospects for advertising. The only good sign,
Blair wrote, was "the amount of 'talk'—but this appears to
be mainly in a limited circle of communicators, mostly in
New York and to some extent in other cities." Blair urged

some serious thinking about limiting circulation to reduce costs and about cost-cutting in general.

He also suggested the possibility "in theory at least—to convert *Harper's* into a special-interest magazine . . . which reaches a definable group of people in the population, in the same way as *Golf Digest* reaches golfers or *Skiing* reaches skiers. To do so would require an effort of both editorial and promotion. It is not easy to see what kind of definable audience might be *Harper's* specialty; the only possibility that comes to mind is to recall the fact that traditionally our appeal has always been very high to people who are active in civic and political affairs. Possibly *Harper's* could be made into the magazine of the activists and sold on this basis to a range of advertisers—particularly those with corporate messages. To do so would require a conscious and deliberate shift in editorial policy so that we had more articles dealing with political process at all levels and less dealing with personal relationships." Later, Morris would use "Eastern communicators" and "He wanted to turn it into ski magazine" when he described his "fight" with Blair to the press. Morris would also ignore this passage from Blair's memo: "I don't think there is much point at this time in trying to allocate blame or responsibility for what has happened. We all share in the responsibility, and in addition we were hit by a disastrous economic period."

In any event, Blair's memo went unanswered and another month passed. On February 11, 1971, Blair sent Morris another memo, this one outlining the necessity for severe cutbacks throughout the magazine. He proposed to cut out virtually all promotion expenses, let the assistant publisher go and sublet half the office space. He asked for drastic changes in the contributing editor setup and the elimination of some secretaries. And it was here that he suggested "it should be possible to get this magazine out with one Editor-in-Chief (yourself), one responsible senior editor (either Midge or Bob) and one junior editor." On February 17, Morris replied. His memo agreed to some of the reductions, stood up for the money paid the contributing editors and their productivity, defended the editorial quality of the magazine, proposed that as an economy measure his salary of $37,500 and Blair's of $54,000 be reduced by a third and appealed to Cowles's sense of obligation to keep up the traditions of the magazine.

On Monday, February 27, two days before the now-famous budget meeting in Minneapolis, Morris called Cowles to tell him he wanted to talk and that he was arriving that night. Cowles didn't get the call, but his secretary, who said Morris called from the airport, took the message. Cowles waited for him to appear. Monday night came and went without word from Morris, and so did Tuesday morning. Cowles kept Tuesday lunch open for him, but he didn't show. Then, at about 2:00 P.M. Tuesday, Morris arrived—shortly before a regularly scheduled *Star and Tribune* staff meeting. The owner gave the editor just fifteen minutes in which to talk. Morris handed Cowles the memo he had written Blair, and Cowles promised to read it and think about it. Cowles invited Morris to join him at the staff meeting. Morris said he would, but left and did not reappear either Tuesday afternoon or evening. But he was there at 9:00 A.M. on Wednesday, when the budget meeting began.

The meeting, like previous ones including the "experiment" launching, dealt strictly with money. Morris says he was "hit with a twenty-one-page memo," which is true. It was Blair's working paper, incorporating the substance of his previous memos to Morris as well as criticism of the editorial performance as it related to circulation and his suggestions for cost-cutting in all departments. Blair called it his "game plan" for saving the magazine. Cowles asked Morris whether he had any alternatives to propose. Morris said no, but objected to suggested cuts in the editorial budget. Decisions on editorial matters were postponed. The rest of Blair's proposals, involving a six-month budget, were accepted. "It was terrible," Morris recalls. "One of those zombies spoke up and said, 'No wonder it's such a failure. Who are you editing this magazine for, a bunch of hippies?' Then the Mailer thing. Nobody liked it." Cowles remembers it somewhat differently. "One of our Minneapolis men may indeed have kidded or needled Willie about the Mailer piece, but it was not a formal part of the meeting. As a matter of policy, I'd not have regarded that a proper part of the meeting. If Bill and I had thoughts about editing, we'd have taken that up with Willie privately."

Morris was the only editorial person at the meeting. He views the entire three and a half hours as an attack on editorial content. He says, "It was more a mood than anything else. The atmosphere was very, very cold. They were extremely hostile to the magazine. It brought it all to a head for me. I felt the game was up. I didn't want to work with those people. To have followed Blair's plan would have involved acts of humiliation. The literary qualities were severely threatened. They decided to go on with the poll-taking. I didn't think the magazine had much future."

When the meeting ended, Morris begged off a previously arranged lunch with Cowles, Blair and some *Star and Tribune* news executives. On the plane back to New York, he decided to quit.

The following Monday he told Kotlowitz and Miss Decter his plan and showed them his letter of resignation. He had resigned for them, too. They tried to persuade him to reconsider, suggesting they work together until summer and then, if the situation hadn't improved, resign together. Morris refused, but removed their names from his letter. "I came into the office that Monday and Midge and Bob were sitting there looking as if their dog had died," recalls Larry King. "They told me what happened. Then Willie walked in and we went to Greenstreet's and he showed me the letter. I said, 'You know this is an irrevocable act,' and he said, 'I don't give a damn.' He handed me Blair's memos to read. The memos alarmed me. I didn't realize Blair was going so strongly against Willie. I asked him to sleep on the letter. He wouldn't.'' The resignation was typed that afternoon, reread by King and airmailed special delivery to Cowles that night.

On Tuesday afternoon, when King and Morris returned from lunch, Blair's secretary came up to them. "I'm sorry you're leaving," she said.

Morris looked surprised. "My God, they've accepted my resignation," he said.

"Didn't you think they would?" asked King.

"No," said Morris, and left the building.

What Morris failed to explain to almost anybody was that on Monday afternoon, after lunching with King, Blair came to his office to work out alternatives to the editorial budget proposals and decide whether Miss Decter or Kotlowitz was to be fired. "I was very angry," Morris says. "I told him here you are making sixty thousand dollars a year and for that we could have all the editors. I told him I was going to resign." And so Blair, armed with Morris's plans and still uncertain just what Cowles would do or how his own job might be affected, put in a call to Cowles. "Bill said Willie had told him he was planning to resign or was going to write me a resignation letter," Cowles recalls. "I said, 'Well, gosh, let's keep everything cool and calm until I see what Willie writes. Maybe he'll change his mind." Cowles received the letter on Tuesday. He decided it was "unequivocal." He says he wasn't able to reach Morris, although Morris's secretary says Cowles didn't call or leave a message all that day. Instead, he called Blair and read him the letter. It was only then that Blair, who'd obviously confided in his secretary, realized the resignation had been accepted. They then talked about how to announce it. Cowles wanted a letter "that would do the least harm to Willie." He might also have added the magazine. He and Blair worked on a statement. "I tried to pay tribute to Willie without being dishonest and without being critical," he says.

By this time, everybody at *Harper's* was in an uproar. The editors were furious with Blair for spreading the news of the resignation before it was confirmed. They were equally angry with Cowles for failing to reach Morris. Nor did it help matters when Blair airily announced: "John's on jury duty this week and that's why he's been unable to call." And they were unhappy with Morris because he acted unilaterally without consulting them. On Wednesday, King insisted Blair persuade Cowles to call Morris, which he finally did. But when the Cowles call came, Morris was nowhere to be found. King arranged for Cowles to call again, and the two finally talked. The conversation lasted for perhaps twenty minutes, with Morris expressing surprise that his resignation had been accepted and Cowles saying he felt he'd been left no alternative. Cowles asked if he'd seen the draft of his and Blair's statement. Morris said he had, and that it disturbed him. He thought people might think he was fired. Cowles suggested he work with James C. Crimmins, the associate publisher, on a new statement, and call him back when he finished.

Morris says that he asked Cowles if he would sell the magazine, that Cowles was surprised and said he'd have to think about it, and that he eventually did call back and say no. Cowles confirms that Morris asked to buy the magazine, says his first response was "Well, I'll consider anything," and then adds, "But I said no." He denies there was a second call. Morris, who was having a dinner party that night, went away from the telephone telling friends, "That son of a bitch wanted to get rid of me." King, Moyers, Halberstam and Bill Bradley, the New York Knicks star, were among the guests, and so was Muller. At Morris's urging King told everyone what had happened. The party ended in the early morning with a broken chair. On Thursday, when Cowles didn't hear from Morris about the resignation release, he called Morris at home and at the magazine. He says he couldn't reach him. So, as he put it, "we finally let fly with our press release." Morris countered with his statement, indicating "severe disagreements with the business management over the purpose, the existence and the survival of *Harper's* Magazine as a vital institution in American life."

When the *Times* asked Blair about the resignation, he said that it was "all a surprise to me," but that *Harper's* circulation was down 25,000 copies a month to a total of 300,000 copies. The figures were incorrect. The total, and it's public information, should have been 325,000 copies. Blair now denies ever having given out the original figures, but they ran that way in succeeding stories throughout most of the press. Nor did Blair call the *Times* to change them. The editors and even some *Harper's* business people think Blair gave out the lower figures on purpose. They tended to make Morris's editorial performance more dismal than it actually was. He later sent the correct figures to advertisers.

In Minneapolis, Cowles denied the magazine's content was a factor in the dispute, said he hadn't finished Mailer's *Prisoner of Sex,* but that he thought it was "superb so far." If he ever did criticize the piece, it was to intimates who are not telling. The question then was what the editors would do. Miss Decter was the first to resign. She has never given any explanation other than, "I owed Willie a debt and he collected it. It had nothing to do with love of the literary over the money." By the following Sunday, the other six editors, announcing they would act as a unit, had succeeded in getting Cowles to agree to a meeting. Morris was still telling people his resignation might not be accepted. By this time, Blair was saying that an editor should be "held responsible for the economic consequences of what he does."

The denouement by now is well known. Cowles met with the editors. He accepted the responsibility for Morris's performance as editor and the disappointing circulation and financial performances, chided "some editors" for acting as if he should subsidize *Harper's* regardless of its losses and for not making the magazine sufficiently interesting to enough readers to pay its way, and ended by asking them to work for Blair. Their response was hardly enthusiastic. Yet instead of refusing to work for Blair or demanding Morris's reinstatement, they asked that Kotlowitz be named editor and Cowles turned them down. Said Halberstam, "It was as though we were talking in English and Cowles was listening

in Chinese." Within twenty-four hours, the editors had resigned.

June 1971

In the weeks after the debacle, a score or more names
figured in the speculation over who *Harper's* new editor
would be, among them Lewish Lapham, the only contributing editor who did not resign; Otto Friedrich, the last managing editor of *The Saturday Evening Post;* Irving Louis Horo-
witz, editor of *Trans-action;* Bill D. Moyers, who was
publisher of *Newsday* just before taking his wandering assignment from Morris; and columnists Tom Wicker and
Anthony Lewis of the *Times.* In the meantime, John Fischer
returned to run the magazine, issuing a memo that was to
forecast its future.

Fischer called for "a drastic and prompt change in
editorial direction," which he found "necessary if the magazine is to survive. *Harper's* must not be identified in the
minds of potential readers as a 'literary' magazine. No literary magazine has existed during my lifetime either in this
country or in England without a continuing subsidy. *Harper's* has no source of permanent subsidy; it soon must return
to paying its own way, as it has in the past." To do this,
Fischer wrote, "we shall have to devote less space to books,
writers, fiction, and literary criticism [and] a higher propor-
tion . . . to science, medicine, business, the changing cultural
scene and all other aspects of American life." What *Harper's*
needed most, Fischer wrote, was articles about the future.
"We don't need pieces about dead people. We don't need
criticism of Henry James, or Proust, or William Dean Ho-
wells. We don't need articles about defeated politicians. We
don't need nostalgic reminiscences of childhood. We need
material about people who are on the way up, not on the way
down."

Three months later in June, the job finally went to Robert
B. Shnayerson, a *Time* magazine senior editor who'd written

law and education before editing essays and cover stories. A year later, Russell Bernard, a partner in a venture capital firm that jointly with the Minneapolis Star and Tribune Company had established a company to publish *Country Music* magazine, became publisher. Lewis Lapman became managing editor.

Once Upon a Time in the West

One afternoon in late 1972, Nicolas H. Charney, editor-in-chief and chairman of the board of Saturday Review Industries, invited his staff to a slide show. The topic was not the charms of San Francisco, though most present were certainly new to the area. "Nick decided we should learn something about the look and feel of magazines," one senior editor recalls, "so he produced a sixth-grade audio-visual show. Don Wright, the art director, was at the back of the conference room running the projector. Nick was on a folding metal chair providing the voice-over."

Charney went on for nearly three hours, discoursing on good graphics and bad graphics, contrasting "old" magazines with new. *Look* had died because it was not with-it graphically, Charney told the audience, which included several former *Look* staffers. Other examples of yesterday's magazines were ordered up: *Harper's, Atlantic* and *The New Yorker,* which would last perhaps another five years. The *Newsweek* alumni in the room, all imported at high salaries, were surprised to see a *Newsweek* cover flash on the screen. "Is that supposed to be there?" Charney inquired. Then came examples of "new magazines," those with hot graphics:

New York, Psychology Today, Ms. and *Clear Creek.* Somebody observed that *Clear Creek* had folded.

Charney next discussed the distinction between "linear" publications, those that use primarily words, and nonlinear ones, which make heavy use of graphics. A magazine must be able to pass a "flip test" on a newsstand, said Charney, explaining that the back of the book is key, because many flippers flip from back to front. "Never mind if we have anything to say," an editor remembers thinking. "Can we stand up under the rigorous demands of flippership?" Executive editor Ron Kriss, just hired from *Time,* was shredding a napkin, absolutely silent.

It had been less than a year since Nick Charney descended on New York flashing charts and projections over lunches at Lutèce, offering five- and six-hundred dollar weekly salaries *and* the good life in San Francisco. Charney and his partner, John Veronis, had sold *Psychology Today* and acquired *Saturday Review.* Norman Cousins was out; Charney was remaking the turgid weekly into four flashy monthlies— *SR/Education, SR/Society, SR/Science and SR/Arts.* And Charney was hiring. For editors who had reached the heights of corporate publishing while still in their thirties, here was a heady opportunity: a chance to drop out without dropping out, to launch a fresh national magazine without having to bootstrap it, long-term contracts, moving expenses, and for the higher echelons, stock options. "We were told," one émigré recalls, "don't worry about advertising, we're going to do it from house industries. You just put out the best magazine you know how."

SR's newly transplanted editorial staff of seventy-five had scarcely unpacked in San Francisco in October 1972 when the first of several financial tremors struck. Only after Charney and Veronis had gone back to the original investors for an additional five million dollars did word filter down that the magazine had nearly folded while the staff was out apartment-hunting. At one point, *SR* was over a million dollars in debt to the printer, who was refusing to publish until the debt was paid. On November 9, 1972, a memo assured the staff that the cash crisis was over, and urged everybody to "help us save money, large and small, where each of you can. We want to be sure that our resources go into people and editorial content, and not into avoidable delays, wastes, frills, and expenditures not central to our purpose."

The authors of these sobering words had just dropped several hundred thousand dollars moving the editorial offices from New York to San Francisco, and were well into a second million converting first a firehouse, then a warehouse, into a suitable funky-mod headquarters for the new *Saturday Review.* The memo went on to explain, in case there were any doubts, that "Profit is an important, not a nasty, word. We are a very special business, a business with a high public calling, and one about which we feel strongly. But we are a business."

Quite so. The editor-in-chief and chairman of the board of Saturday Review Industries habitually referred to his quad-rumvirate of magazines as "the business," pronounced in three measured syllables, *biz-i-ness,* as if it might be a family dry-goods store. At thirty-one, Nick Charney was still the *Wunderkind,* breezily confident in the mystique of California living and his computers to solve all ills, volunteering charts, eager to share the secret of how he does it. In an interview before the four magazines collapsed, Charney, with no particular prompting, sketched a graph to demonstrate precisely how *SR*'s pretax profit would have increased to nearly $10 million by 1976, presto. "We have tried to take the unpredictability out of starting magazines," said Charney. "We are a group of young bright individuals. We've got one foot into tomorrow."

Like the fellow down the hall in the dorm who made a small fortune on the laundry concession and wants to borrow a hundred dollars so he can move on to charter flights, Charney looks to the future. Charney's boyish insecurity sometimes leads him to lean on weak or incompatible advisers and to dress up his talk and life style with financial hyperbole. He is part owner of a ranch in Bolinas and is still trying to unload a $750,000 white elephant complete with grottos and artificial boulders left over from his days in Del Mar. "Nick is basically a promoter, and a brilliant one," says an associate. "But he doesn't know anything about managing a magazine."

Charney and Veronis's formula for remaking *Saturday Review* was an embellishment on several currently fashionable publishing axioms. First, this is the age of the specialty magazine. Second, monthlies produce a higher per-copy revenue than weeklies. Third, the subscriber should be a major source of direct income, not just a customer to attract advertisers. The new *SR* was to combine all three axioms (and others) into a neat equation: the general-interest 11¢ weekly reborn as four specialized 50¢-and-up monthlies. The cost, Charney explained, was a mere fraction of the expense for starting such a venture from scratch, because they were building on an established magazine and a base of 650,000 subscribers. *Psychology Today,* with its slick graphics and aggressive marketing, was a rough model. With *Psychology Today* and its merchandising spin-off, Communications/ Research/Machines (CRM), Charney and Veronis had shown it was possible to use a magazine as a vehicle to sell not only advertising, but mailing lists and a whole array of ancillary products, like lab kits, filmstrips, games, travel packages and textbooks. As Veronis put it to Robert Stein for an article in *New York* early in 1972, "We don't consider the reader as a twelve-dollar-a-year subscriber to a magazine, but as a potential hundred-dollar-a-year customer in the magazine's field of interest for books, records, games, posters, video casettes, conferences, school courses and other products and services." Partner Charney insisted, however, that these spin-offs were never uppermost in his thoughts. The game plan was to put out four specialty magazines.

In short, Charney and Veronis were publishing a marketing formula. All that remained was to fill in some editorial content to accompany it. "This is the age of the specialty magazine, all right," says Alfred Meyer, former managing editor of *SR/Science.* "But successful speciality magazines usually bubble up because of some real interest. They are difficult to impose from above." As long as the financial equation seemed to be working, Charney and Veronis let their newly acquired editors edit. The honeymoon ended with the emergency $5 million capital infusion in October 1972.

Actually, most of the money was used up almost as soon as it came in: over a million to pay the printer, most of the rest on a massive, eighteen-million-piece mailing. Less than a million dollars was set aside to operate the magazines until this summer, when Charney and Veronis hoped the renewal cycle would revive the cash flow. By February 1973, *SR* was out of cash again.

The autumn bail-out by investors Louis Marx, Jr., of the toy fortune, investment banker Daniel Lufkin, and the Rock Island Corporation left Charney and Veronis with badly watered *SR* stock, amounting to less than 10 percent of the total, and no early prospect of going public, as they originally planned. It also left a self-fulfilling cycle of bad trade publicity, a jittery advertising department, and some very nervous investors, who promptly inserted Frederick Wyle as chairman of a new "executive committee" to monitor the operation. Charney, whose own control clearly had been diminished, insisted that Wyle was just what the doctor ordered. "Fred is a very down-to-earth, numbers-oriented guy. He is providing us with a kind of in-house skepticism, a general executive ability that the business badly needed. In the Defense Department, Fred ran Europe for Bob McNamara." (Charney once explained to a staff meeting: "When you're starting a magazine, you need a man of genius. You know, an expert in cost accounting.")

With Wyle looking after financial matters, Charney began to turn his attention to "shaping up the editorial side of the business." The editorial staff also felt increasing pressures from Wyle, the investors, and the ad department, which was run in New York by John Veronis' brother, Peter. Ad men, investors, advisers, everybody seemed to be ordering or vetoing articles. An investor was impressed by one of California Senator John Tunney's speeches. An article was duly commissioned. A special *SR/Science* supplement on mechanized agriculture was overruled. No advertising angle. A similar story turned up in *SR/Society*. John Veronis asked for and got a profile of Jay Rockefeller. Fred Wyle thought a long-term publishing plan would be a useful idea. Dutifully, each of the four editorial staffs worked up lengthy generalizations on the mission of their magazine, the intended audience, as well as story ideas for the coming year. Something concrete to show investors and advertisers. Harried editors got on the phone to writers, pumping them for story outlines; several free-lancers were promised commissions that never materialized, but turned up nonetheless in the publishing plan. No sooner were the plans drafted than the ad department complained that the format was changing too fast and spooking Madison Avenue.

One day in September 1972, during the height of the first cash crisis, Nicholas Charney was leading Ed Scarfe, an investor from the Rock Island group, on a tour of *SR*'s offices. On a production board, the visitor glanced at some galleys left over from the October 1972 "premier" issue, which had closed earlier in the week. The article, a profile of then White House Science Advisor Edward David by *SR/Science*'s Washington editor Daniel Greenberg, began: "Being President Nixon's Science Advisor is like being bartender to a teetotaler . . ." Scarfe, a big Republican contributor, scowled, "If that's the kind of crap you print, forget it." Charney ordered the lead changed on the spot. As it ran in the October 1972 *SR/Science,* Greenberg's story began: "The job of science advisor to the President figures large in fictional sagas of crisis and government, but in the reign of Richard M. Nixon, that is not quite the case." The editors were promised it wouldn't happen again.

It did, of course, again and again, as the magazines became

"people-oriented, not policy-oriented." The architect of this new course was Peter Drucker, futurologist, management consultant and philosopher of free enterprise. (He was alternately known at *SR* as "Charney's guru" and "Mother Drucker.") Shortly after the move west, editors began pilgrimages to Claremont to sit at Drucker's feet. His grand design for *SR* was spelled out in a cranky forty-page position paper, and subsequently at a stormy meeting in San Francisco with the editors.

Drucker's paper was particularly harsh on *SR/Society,* which he said was trying to be "just another journal of opinion." *SR/Society,* Drucker wrote, in "predictable" and "grim," as well as "anti-people." Drucker urged pieces such as: Is heroin really addictive? The early escape to the suburbs in the nineteenth century. The disenchantment with big government spending. In addition, he wrote, "I would love . . . to see in *SR/Society* a piece that tells the reader how beautiful much of the Interstate Highway system is." Drucker also put down *SR/Society* as "the magazine of the dashed hopes of the Kennedy liberals, who now look for a scapegoat." Not surprisingly, the criticism appalled *SR/Society*'s managing editor, William Honan, whose credits include a biography of Ted Kennedy.

Honan is reluctant to discuss the contretemps. But a colleague provided [MORE] with his reply to Drucker. In it, he agreed that *SR*'s focus needed to be on "people," denied that he was publishing an opinion magazine and concluded by listing the eleven "ideological" pieces published in five issues of *SR/Society,* rating four of them liberal, four conservative and three as balanced. More to the point, Honan observed:

> If an editor is forced to think in ideological terms, he will begin to "play it safe," and my dear colleagues, there is no quicker way to plunge our magazines into dullness than by creating an environment, whether deliberately or otherwise, in which editors "play it safe" because they suspect or believe that management is en-

gaging in Witch Hunts or because management permits
slurs against the integrity and good judgment of its
editors . . . There is only one way for management to
deal with an editor, any editor, in order to get the best
out of him: *trust him.* It comes to that. Trust him. If
management cannot do that, there is another solution:
severance pay.

Charney declined the offer, but Honan gave notice as soon
as *The New York Times,* from which he had been plucked,
offered him an expanded version of his old travel bailiwick.
Before he came back east, however, Honan suffered the additional indignity of having to publish a special supplement
entitled "Can Business Save Us?" that starred none other
than Peter Drucker.

Drucker's probusiness essay was carefully paired with a
con article by New York Deputy Mayor Edward Hamilton.
But this editorial balance hardly negated the fact that the
supplement grew primarily out of advertising demands. Indeed, all managing editors in the *SR* family were asked to
come up with a special issue each that could be keyed to ad
sales. The *SR/Society* editors resisted the order at first, but
finally compromised on the sixteen-page "supplement." One
of the sixteen pages was headed KUDOS FOR CONSCIENCE,
and congratulated several companies for "corporate responsibility," to wit: "On May 1 of this year, Quaker Oats will
introduce a learning program for young children on its Life
cereal boxes. The back and side panels of 12 million packages
will be used to print a series of six lessons designed to increase the learning power of children." (Actually, such puf-
fery was a throwback to the old *Saturday Review,* in which
Norman Cousins constantly plugged the splendid efforts of
advertising and public relations.) Drucker may think that
business can save us, but it didn't save the supplement. Neither it nor an *SR/Arts* supplement on stereos raised enough
ad revenue to pay for the paper they were printed on. (Travel

supplements, on the other hand, did well.)

The great hope for the new, "people-oriented" *SR* was a how-to-do-it section in the back of the book that the editors called "departments." Introduced in February 1973, after several months' delay, they were in display and content a deliberate copy of *New York* magazine, one of Charney's great success models. *SR* editors were persuaded that the feature gave the magazine a utilitarian as well as an intellectual appeal. But with *New York* providing highly focused local consumer intelligence (leanest pastrami, cleanest steam baths) and *Harper's* "Wraparound" preempting the cosmic version of the genre, *SR* had staked out a huge, amorphous middle ground.

SR was offering the sort of all-purpose, better-living tips Kiplinger's magazine served up back in 1958. *SR/Society,* for example, divided how-to-do-it into five departments: Politics and Government, Business and Economics, Lifestyles, The Law, and Communications. The assumption appeared to be that the reader, high suburban demographics and all, lived in an igloo until he subscribed to *SR*. (A piece trumpeting the economies of second-hand appliances advised: "The forsale classified ads in your local newspaper are a good place to begin.") Other samples were genuinely informative, but the vein was heavily overworked.

With the decision to people-orient the back of the book, Charney, Wyle and Drucker moved to play down *SR/*Up Front, which had been producing much of the magazine' better writing and thinking. Originally, *SR/*Up Front was intended to help glue together a family identity for the four otherwise distinct magazines. But the concept flew head-on into the marketing plan to promote four separate monthlies. Up Front's material was seen as too general for a specialized reader, nor did it provide any useful advertising tie-ins. Moreover, charged Drucker, it was "antibusiness." He attacked the section as "poorly written . . . with animosity and spite . . . as grim as nineteenth century teetotalers' tracts, and apparently written by the same kind of people." In December 1972, Up Front was finally killed as a distinct weekly feature.

The death of Up Front along with the ensuing tug of war among ad men, investors, Charney and the managing editors left executive editor Ron Kriss with almost no role beyond writing editorials and memos. Unlike Charney, whose enthusiasm (at least on the surface) seemed boundless, Kriss was glum, resigned and looking for a job, as were many other *SR* editors. "You can manufacture perfectly good shoes like this," says one of the editors who was bailing out, "but you can't put out a magazine."

True enough. And the unhappiest irony was that despite the corporate taffy-pull, the men and women who came west with Charney did manage to put out a magazine that sometimes contained first-rate material. *SR* published the first excerpt from the provocative Christopher Jencks thesis on education and inequality; it printed Bruce Porter's lengthy investigation of asbestos poisoning in Manville, New Jersey; Ernest Dunbar's moving account of a fallen upper-class black family, and a delightful profile of the man who writes Ripley's "Believe It or Not." *SR* also examined archaeological commerce long before the Hoving/krater affair surfaced in New York; and the magazine turned over much of one issue to an incisive appreciation of Vladimir Nabokov.

But the solid writing always ran side by side with the fluff. The new *SR* never quite lost the reek of packaging. And for all the charts and formulas, *SR* was not the scientific publishing operation it professed to be. "These are not evil guys," travel editor Ken Pierce commented weeks before the collapse. "I've seen Nick wheel and deal, make commitments, and change his mind. Mercury is the prevailing element of company policy. They're both very western, very open; they're not really corporate types at all."

And that, of course, was the rub. Despite the computer-era trappings, the financial bungling was legion. *SR*'s rate base was raised prematurely; the eighteen-million-piece promo-tional mailing in December 1972 was an all-or-nothing gamble; the move west was a foolish extravagance. But ultimately, *SR* died because the public didn't buy it, and the public wouldn't buy it because, as several frustrated editors remarked, it never found its editorial soul. Even Charney's one authentic success, *Psychology Today*—for all its slickness—grew out of an editorial conception, not a set of marketing axioms.

Similarly, editing a national magazine from San Francisco, away from "incestuous New York," was a reasonable idea. But then why do it with transplanted New Yorkers? In part, *SR*'s identity crisis persisted because the staff never recovered from psychic jet lag. "The move was a great idea," one editor told me. "But it was much more disorienting than most of us expected. After all, journalism runs on contacts." After six months on Pacific Street, most of the staff was still looking wistfully eastward. Copies of *The New York Times* had been hard to come by in San Francisco because the first thirty-five were reserved for the distributor's best customer, *Saturday Review. SR*'s monthly long distance phone bills, strictly budgeted at $13,000, were regularly exceeding $20,000.

On April 24, 1973, Fred Wyle called the staff together and announced that the board had filed for bankruptcy. Charney and Veronis, in fact, had run up a net loss of $16 million, including the $5 million they paid for *SR*. Their huge December mailing netted a return of about 45,000 subscribers per magazine, just over 1 percent; each new subscriber cost *SR* nearly $25. Circulation had been projected at an average of 675,000 per magazine. The reality was under 900,000 all told, half of them Cousins's faithful weekly subscribers, who were continuing to write letters inquiring after John Ciardi. Still, Charney had been prepared to mortgage everything to keep going until the renewal cycle began in July. This time, the investors said no. Before bankruptcy was declared, word went out to twenty publishing concerns—including *Time, The New York Times* and McGraw-Hill—

that *SR* was for sale. Nobody was interested.

Looking to the future, Charney put out a characteristic press release declaring that *SR* was "merging" with Norman Cousins's *World.* The staff was told that Cousins had raised nearly $3 million to pay off creditors. But Cousins says he's not spending a nickel on Charney's back debt. "We have to take it clean, or not at all," he says. After a bankruptcy plan is accepted and the creditors disposed of, Cousins hopes to take over the name and the list. *SR*'s investors would get stock in the new venture. Thanks to the kind of bankruptcy (Chapter II) *SR* declared, the creditors included the staff. All but a handful were fired on two days' notice. The long-term contracts, moving expenses, and even back expense accounts were lumped with nearly $4 million of other company debts to be settled at so many cents on the dollar. The investors made the staff "a gift" of one week's severance pay.

After Fred Wyle's announcement that everyone was fired, Charney stepped forward with four cases of champagne. "Those of you who want to can go home and sulk," Charney said. "We thought we should go out in style." Several gamely accepted the offer; some went home to sulk; others rushed to the bank to exchange their last checks for cash.

May 1973

Eventually, Cousins got his magazine back—and for a bargain $530,000. It is once again doing its mid-cult business as usual, albeit now under the title of *Saturday Review/- World.* As for Charney and Veronis, they persuaded several hundred small backers to invest close to $1 million in a new venture called *Book Digest,* which hopes to have a circulation of 400,000 by the spring of 1975. The C. & V. pitch to investors went something like this: "You can benefit from a unique education; no other magazine publishers know as much about what not to do." When all the tuition bills were finally tallied, the education cost $29 million—$17 million in direct loss plus $12 million in creditor claims—the most expensive collapse in magazine history.

A. KENT MACDOUGALL

Up Against the Wall Street Journal

In December 1971, after informing managing editor Frederick Taylor that I had decided to resign from the *Wall Street Journal,* I returned to my desk in the newsroom, rolled a half-sheet into my typewriter and dashed off a message. It was in the style of the round-up memos that editors in New York send nearly every day to all fifteen bureaus except St. Louis, which has all it can do to cover the dying shoe industry. It read:

ALL CITIES (EXCEPT ST L)

ON JANUARY 7, AFTER 10 YEARS AND 3 MONTHS OF DJ [DOW JONES] PEONAGE, I WILL BE FREE AT LAST, FREE AT LAST, GREAT GAWD ALMIGHTY, FREE AT LAST.

RGDS

MACDOUGALL NY

Within minutes, two veteran bureau chiefs phoned Taylor demanding to know why he was permitting the use of the wire to preach insurrection to the field hands. The normally good-natured Taylor, who had not seen the memo, although by this time it had drawn dozens of staffers to the newsroom bulletin board, bolted from his office. He stormed the length of the newsroom, shouldered aside the tax columnist who was waiting to shake my hand, and as a score of colleagues looked on incredulously, stood over me shaking with rage. In a voice on the verge of breaking, he demanded to know how I could show such disloyalty by accusing Dow Jones, the *Journal*'s parent company, of "peonage." I explained that the memo was my way of saying goodbye to my friends and with a smile suggested that he was taking the whole matter too seriously. Taylor wheeled and marched angrily back to his office.

Now I had to be fired. Late that Friday afternoon, Taylor summoned me to his office and summarily announced that while he would keep me on the payroll another four weeks, he didn't want me on the premises another day. I was now being given the same bum's rush that previous managing editors had accorded at least three other reporters after they had the audacity to resign, one to go to the Washington *Post,* the two others to *The New York Times.* The first *Times* reporter had been on the *Journal* sixteen years and was told upon giving four weeks' notice, "You don't have to stay another fifteen minutes!" He didn't. But I wanted to go in my own good time and on my own terms. So, unprepared as I was for Taylor's edict, I talked him out of it. Forcing me out, I told him, would hurt morale etc. etc. He took the weekend to calm down and on Monday he evened the score by mailing his own memo to the bureau chiefs. In it, he said he regretted my departure even more than my method of announcing it, and warned that further use of the wires for personal messages "will be dealt with severely."

In retrospect, my cable caper doubtless reflects a certain overexuberance in declaring my independence from 9:30–to–5:30 office confinement to begin, on the eve of my fortieth birthday, a new life of teaching, writing and traveling. But my memo equally epitomizes the mixture of affection and resentment I share with nearly everyone who has spent any time at the *Journal.* Resentment that management does so little to encourage reporters to make a career at the *Journal.* Affection for a product that is almost always intelligent. Resentment that it is so seldom inspiring. Affection for a publication that regularly uses its news columns to discredit many of the establishment's worst abuses. Resentment that the newspaper's editorials even more regularly defend the establishment. Affection for a publication that, despite the limitations of its business-oriented coverage and an institutional monotone as gray as its make-up, is a great place to practice journalism at close to its highest level.

In my ten years at the *Journal* (nine of them covering the publishing beat), I never heard of any reporter being asked to write a puff piece for an advertiser, take it easy on a news source or angle a story beyond what the facts warranted. In a poll for *Time* magazine, Louis Harris found the *Journal* to be the nation's "most trusted" periodical. Even radicals give it grudging respect (the *Guardian* has called the *Journal* one of "the two best sources for information" on American capitalists, the other being the society pages of the *Times*). As one outsider unable to fix a story complained, the *Journal* is "rotten with integrity from top to bottom." Yet for all its deserved reputation as a tough-minded chronicle of American business, the *Journal* seldom questions the fundamental premises of the business community it covers. It may be the best newspaper in the country at exposing rotten apples in the barrel, but the shape of the barrel itself is almost never an issue.

That, of course, may be inevitable for an enterprise whose very name is a symbol of the System and whose own pursuit of profit has been so successful. The *Wall Street Journal* is far and away the nation's most profitable daily. It netted an estimated $16 million in 1969, its best year. The newspaper accounts for an estimated 75 percent of Dow Jones' total profits, and year after year Dow Jones sports the highest profit margin of any periodical publishing company with publicly traded stock. Dow Jones accomplishes this in classic capitalist tradition: by keeping revenue high and costs low. For example, the *Journal* keeps advertising revenue high not by packing in ads—the *Journal* publishes only on weekdays and never prints an edition of more than 48 pages (and sometimes as few as 12)—but by charging "class" ad rates. A full-page ad in the *Journal* costs $20,957—more than double the *Times*'s charge. The *Journal* justifies the high rates by the affluence of its audience, though cynics sometimes add that lack of head-on competition has something to do with it, too. In any event, it is humbling for a reporter to learn that a two-inch ad in the *Journal* costs only $5 less than the $335 weekly scale for a five-year journeyman reporter.

That salary is below what the far less profitable *Times* and Washington *Post* pay reporters after comparable service. Moreover, the *Journal* tolerates none of the deadwood that accumulates at many major dailies. Young reporters who aren't catching on fast enough and veteran reporters who have slowed down too much are routinely given two or three months to find another job. Such sackings never encounter union opposition. The Newspaper Guild has been shut out at the *Journal;* in its place is a largely ineffectual company union representing white-collar employees. Blue-collar employees belong to AFL-CIO craft unions that have put up little resistance to streamlined operations at the paper's technologically advanced printing plants. One reason is that the *Journal* has moved six of its nine printing plants out of big cities to suburbs and outlying towns, escaping the largest and most militant union locals. In seven of the plants, typesetting machines run automatically on a diet of perforated paper tape generated in Chicopee, Massachusetts. The two other plants get along without a composing room; each receives facsimile pages via microwave from another plant. (Advanced as the *Journal*'s technology is, *Pravda* outdoes it by printing in forty-two different locations across the Soviet Union; the sixteen farthest from Moscow are sent photographs of pages by cable or even satellite.)

The *Journal*'s network of nine printing plants and four

regional advertising editions has facilitated its rapid growth, but hardly accounts for it. The main propellant has been the prolonged postwar boom in the economy and the stock market. In the last twenty years, the number of Americans owning stock has increased fivefold. Information-hungry investors and businessmen have snatched up most reasonably well-edited, broad-scope business publications. *Business Week*'s circulation has tripled since 1952 and *Forbes* has quadrupled. But the *Journal*'s circulation has quintupled, jumping from 234,000 in 1952 to 1.3 million. In the *Journal*'s case, trust has been crucial to its success. The paper has become essential reading because—unlike most business publications, which tend simply to celebrate corporate success—it provides businessmen with unadulterated information they can count on.

Among dailies, the *Journal* is in a unique position to be pure. Its nationwide distribution, with nearly as many readers in California as New York, frees the *Journal* from dependency on readers or advertisers in any one area. It can afford to offend a city or a state, as it has with downbeat stories on Seattle and Hawaii. More important, the *Journal* doesn't depend on any department store or other big advertiser for financial security. Offend an advertiser and his pullout will hardly tell at the till. Not that the advertising department goes out of its way to offend its customers. On the contrary, in the recession year of 1970, when financial advertising fell off badly and dragged Dow Jones profits down with it, Donald Macdonald, vice-president for advertising, decided that this was the time to win points with the securities industry, then suffering a bad press because of back office paperwork problems, brokerage house failures and disregard of small investors. His scheme was to offer the New York Stock Exchange and four other securities organizations free space to tell "their story" to *Journal* readers.

Dow Jones President William Kerby, an ex-editor who should have known better, went along with Macdonald's giveway, as did others in the high command. But when three financial reporters learned of the offer from sources on Wall Street, they protested directly to Kerby. They argued that the offer implied the *Journal* wasn't adequately covering the securities industry—an implication they resented—and that other industries soon would want free ads to answer their critics. A couple of months later, at the *Journal*'s annual conference of editors and bureau chiefs, banking editor Charles Stabler eloquently renewed his attack, and Kerby conceded that the offer might not have been such a great idea after all. It wasn't withdrawn, however, for another six weeks, and then only after the company's general counsel advised Kerby and Macdonald that the offer could be deemed discriminatory toward competitive organizations not offered equal largesse.

This episode hardly had receded in memory when *Journal* newsmen were angered by what they divined—rightly or wrongly—to be an offense as serious as it was rare: publisher interference in the news operations. The flap arose over the paper's coverage of proposed increases in second-class postal rates. *Time, Newsweek* and some other publications have yielded to the temptation to use news stories to complain about proposed increases in postal rates, but no *Journal* reporter expected the *Journal* to. When the new rates were announced in 1971, the *Journal* used the back page, considered the most prominent display space after the front page, for an impact story. That was legitimate enough. But then six weeks later it ran an even longer impact story, also on the back page. This one included three paragraphs on Dow Jones, quoting the late Buren McCormack, executive vice president, bemoaning the prospect of a $10 million annual increase in the *Journal*'s postal costs. A week later when executive editor Edward Cony was in Washington having drinks with the paper's Capital staff, reporter Wayne Green raised the question of the two back-pagers. "I understand the eighth floor ordered up both those postal-rate stories," Green said. Cony turned white, then raged: "Anyone who thinks management orders stories from special interests shouldn't be working for this newspaper!" Whatever the facts—Cony concedes only that management "may have suggested" the second story—his overreaction, like Taylor's in my case, typifies management's persistent confusion of dissent with disloyalty.

Journal staffers tend to be as solid, stolid and straight as the publication they work for. Most occupants of the *Journal*'s new newsroom at 22 Cortlandt Street (the newspaper has never been on Wall Street) blend into the carpeted, partitioned, clatter-free insurance-office decor so well they could easily be settling collision claims. Reporters work earnestly in individual cubicles. Feet on desks are uncommon, bull sessions rare, spitballs unknown, wall decorations forbidden. Reporters stay in their own little worlds, worrying about their page-one production. Office parties are so tame that even Tom Wolfe would have difficulty making one seem lively, much less worth parodying. Yet, despite the heavy atmosphere, the *Journal* is in many ways an exceedingly pleasant place to work. The intrigue and empire-building that poison the air at publications where competition for good assignments and space is fierce are refreshingly absent at the *Journal*. Pay may not be high, but in pursuit of a major piece, the *Journal* reporter can travel freely and run up huge long-distance telephone tolls. He can take two weeks to two months—and even more—to research and write a single leader, the page-one features for which the paper is noted. If it is an investigative piece, the reporter will find the paper's libel lawyers permissive. If people mentioned in the story complain, he will find that editors will go out of their way to support him. On the other hand, friends and professionals whose opinions he most values won't compliment him because they don't buy the *Journal,* and the only readers who seem to write letters are gold bugs, gun nuts, right-wingers and fools—and they are usually complaining or missing the point of the story altogether.

As for in-house complaints, no subject evokes them like the transgressions of the six rewritemen in New York (there's a seventh in Washington) who do nothing but rewrite page-one leaders and other feature stories, sometimes giving them maddeningly coy leads. Cutsey leads ("Hi there, housewives. Bored with scrubbing floors and wiping runny noses?"). Hypothetical leads ("Just for the sake of conversation, let's say you want to export hormone-fed chickens to Italy and taxicabs to Greece"). Absurd leads ("An analogy between cement silos and service stations? Absurd! Perhaps not so absurd as it might seem"). Leads with made-up characters ("Mrs. Amanda Gotrocks, swathed in furs and diamonds, is walking Cuddles, a 250-pound Great Dane"). Leads in which a rewriteman has quoted a friend (example mercifully omitted). This numbing practice dates back to the late Bernard Kilgore, who stamped his Hoosier personality on the *Journal* as its long-time president. For Barney, every story had to be simplified and sugar-coated to make it comprehensible and palatable to the auto dealer in Elkhart. By and large, the formula for feature articles that Kilgore decreed in 1941 remains unchanged today. The quality of the rewrite staff, though, has improved markedly in recent years, and for all its meddling it often rescues reporters from their own lazy reporting and clumsy writing.

If the rewrite wringer doesn't get a reporter, the managing editor may. Fred Taylor acts as a one-man Legion of Decency, censoring anything that may offend prudish readers and attract letters he will have to answer. He excised "crotch" from a story on panty hose, substituted "(blank)" for "crap," "ass" and "goddammit" in a profile of the profane president of White Consolidated Industries, and deleted a description of the operation from a piece on vasectomy. "I winced reading that description," he explains, "and I could see guys with their morning coffee all over America reading the paper in intense pain. So I just left them to wonder whether the procedure was in the ear or the foot."

Like news-magazine group journalism, the *Journal* editing process tends to homogenize the product by imposing the standards of a handful of editors and rewritemen in New

York on 150 reporters and bureau chiefs from Los Angeles to London. About the only reporter with a distinctive style whose stories escape homogenization is Peter Kann. The Southeast Asian correspondent and 1972 Pulitzer Prize winner breaks all the rules of leader writing. Leaders are supposed to stick to the significant. Kann's stories are replete with less-than-momentous vignettes about dead elephants, camel races and Philippine gambling casinos. Leaders must be dense (the goal is two facts to every line). Kann's leaders are fluffy. A leader states its theme and then hammers it home. Kann's leaders are so leisurely they sometimes don't get to the point until the jump. Leaders are impersonal, Kann's are usually personal and sometimes first-person, as in his two-part diary from Dacca under siege. Leaders are usually neutral, presenting all sides and then letting the reader decide. Kann is partisan. His sympathies for the Bangladesh cause showed through, as have his misgivings about the Vietnam war, most clearly when he ridiculed a hawkish congressman's VIP tour. Kann gets away with his rulebreaking because he is, as he puts it, "far from bureau chiefs and editors, and far from subjects that anyone in New York knows a great deal about. The stateside reporters, or most of them, are providing the meat and potatoes. I'm kind of providing the dessert for our readers. And, kind of like a pastry cook, I'm permitted (perhaps even expected) to experiment more and to provide some style along with the substance."

Kann's presence at the *Journal* as kind of the house freak is central to the frustration that afflicts so much of the staff and ultimately forces so many good journalists to leave. Readers buy the paper not for pastry but for meat and potatoes—to learn what's happening to interest rates, steel prices and pork belly futures. So for every Kann, there are a hundred reporters spooning out the daily ration of business stew. Most find such reporting dreary at best, but as Bill Kerby observed in a speech, "People don't read the *Wall Street Journal* because one or another of two-hundred-odd newsmen may have his or her name signed to it. They read it because they want to find out what happened." Inevitably, the needs of the institution come first, and just as inevitably the spirit of the individual is eventually stifled, a truth that hardly applies to the *Journal* alone.

Given these circumstances, it is not surprising that the *Journal's* business coverage is wildly uneven. Some industries—auto, steel and airlines, for instance—are well covered. Others, such as construction, packaging and farming, are underreported. Shipping is left to the *Journal of Commerce.* Some industries get short shrift because reporters assigned to them are inexperienced, unsophisticated or unenthusiastic about business reporting—or all three. Few reporters keep a beat long enough to build up much expertise; eleven reporters have passed through the food and liquor beat in ten years, for example. Hiring a specialist to fill a beat is rare. When the banking beat fell vacant several years ago, veteran *Journal* reporter Charlie Stabler was thrown into the breach. "I didn't know anything about banks then, and I still don't feel I understand even half of what's going on," he says. Indeed, Wall Street money men look not to the *Journal* but to the *American Banker* and the *Bond Buyer* to tell them what's going on in the money markets. And that's probably inevitable. Because it covers all industry, the *Journal* can't devote as much space to any one industry as a trade journal can. Also, the *Journal* is edited for the layman rather than the specialist. Every time Stabler writes a story about short-term interest rates, he has to sprinkle it with seven to ten definitions of terms that Wall Streeters know by heart but many Main Streeters don't understand.

The *Journal* has also tried to help shoe clerks figure out when to get in and out of the market—not always with happy results. Early in 1971 three page-one stories reported predictions that the market would turn up; after each piece the market turned down. So unerringly was the *Journal* in error that even its sister publication, *Barron's,* couldn't resist twitting it in print. Though a fourth bullish article in late 1971 finally was borne out by subsequent events, page-one editor

Michael Gartner has clamped a ban on further stock-market-dope stories. "How many times do you have to be burned before you learn? We've become a counterindicator."

The *Journal*'s front page, six columns of gray relieved only by one small chart each day, is the most predictable-looking in American journalism. But the three feature stories that appear there each day are equally *un*predictable. Page-one editors, whose limited enthusiasm for business stories matches that of the reporters, consistently run surprising stories, such as a profile of a stripteaser and an article on life in a Scottish monastery. The monastery story appeared several years ago and immediately became legendary by triggering complaints from on high that too many leaders were becoming frivolous. Thus began a counterrevolution of sorts, away from imaginative leaders and back to trendy business articles, known around the newsroom as DBIs (dull but important).

One type of story that increasingly fills one of the three page-one slots deals with crime in the suites. In recent months, the *Journal* has exposed oil-drilling promoter Jack Burke for going through $30 million raised from investors with the help of Los Angeles publisher Otis Chandler, Occidental Petroleum for paying off $200,000 to gain drilling concessions in Libya, and Kaiser Industries officials for profiting from the illegal purchase and sale of Canadian coal-mining stock. The Kaiser story was dumped in the *Journal*'s lap by a disgruntled ex-employee who walked in off the street. But most such stories result from old-fashioned digging. "I don't get any leaks," says Jerry Landauer, the *Journal*'s investigative reporter in Washington. Landauer has exposed a free-spending member of the House Banking Committee who was in hock for more than $100,000 to banks, another congressman who used his congressional office to champion the cause of a legal client before a government agency, and the chairman of the House Post Office Committee, who pocketed $11,000 from a dinner thrown for him by postal union leaders, lobbyists and big-volume mailers.

In 1966 a story reporting payoffs from gambling casino operators and land developers to leaders of the ruling party of the Bahamas resulted in the party being voted out of office. Stanley Penn, one of the two reporters who won a Pulitzer for the Bahamas story, is the paper's senior investigative reporter. Besides Penn, there's at least one reporter in each of the *Journal*'s dozen domestic bureaus who has investigated corporate chicanery from time to time. Despite this pool of talent, the *Journal* has been left behind on most of the biggest business scandals in recent years. It was on top of Tino De Angelis' $200 million salad-oil swindle and Westec Corporation's smelly collapse. But that's about all. The *Journal* got beat badly on Billy Sol Estes's liquid fertilizer swindle in the early sixties. It gave Bernard Cornfeld's manipulations at Investors Overseas Service only piecemeal and occasionally misleading coverage. It was caught by surprise by the Penn Central debacle, though it recouped nicely with excellent follow-up stories. And it was scooped on International Telephone & Telegraph's brazen favor-seeking in Washington, while it practically overlooked ITT's political interference in Chile.

And astonishingly, the *Journal* all but ignored Howard Hughes and his "autobiography." Though some editors contend that Clifford Irving's escapade wasn't a business story, the involvement of the nation's least-seen and most-publicized businessman, the humiliation of Time Inc. and McGraw-Hill and the story's fascination for both general and business readers would indicate otherwise. *The New York Times* smothered the story with a task force of top reporters; the *Journal* didn't assign a single man full time. The Hughes noncoverage illustrates the *Journal*'s reluctance to react quickly and decisively to a breaking story that isn't a must because of its direct impact on the economy or the stock market. With its network of bureaus, the *Journal* is in an excellent position to do both spot and enterprise team reporting. But editors seldom mobilize reporters for a task force effort, and without direction and encouragement from above, individual reporters hesitate to start on a story they can't handle alone.

Given their head, many of these reporters would eagerly provide some first-rate crusading work. But crusading is a dirty word at the *Wall Street Journal.* The paper seldom gets riled by any amount of evil, suffering and stupidity in the world. Unjust wars, unnecessary famines, environmental rape, even unwise government regulation of business don't seem to anger the cool (some would say cynical) men who run the paper. The editorial writers comment on the earth's ills as though they didn't live on it. With morticianlike dispassion, they minister to the nearly departed without a tear. Passion is out of fashion at the *Journal.* "I'm suspicious of the mentality of crusaders," says Robert Bartley, who edits the editorial page. "And I'm not all that much for change anyway. I see no serious, major defects in the System, even though individuals screw up and some policies are wrong." It's hardly surprising that a System that provides Dow Jones with lush profits and key employees with more than comfortable livings would appear basically defect-free. Even a bloated federal budget and massive government intervention in the economy doesn't upset the *Journal* much any more. It doesn't like farm subsidies, high tariffs or wage-price controls, but it has long since dropped opposition to government regulations that stabilize industries, rationalize market conditions and police the worst abuses.

Those who think *Journal* editorial writers are still living in the nineteenth century haven't been looking lately; they are less polemicists for lost causes these days than pragmatists pushing what they think is the possible in this best of all possible worlds. "A lot of my friends think I am a right-wing ideologue," says Bob Bartley. "They're wrong. I'm conservative and pro-Establishment. But I'm not a *National Review* type. The *National Review* opposed Nixon's trip to China. I didn't. Right-wing ideologues think there is a creed that would solve all our problems—if only the United States were more anti-Communist, more laissez-faire, etc. I feel that things are so complex, society is so complicated, that we have to learn to live with problems rather than solve them. I am less doctrinaire, more willing to accept unpleasant realities."

One of the "unpleasant realities" Bartley accepted was the carnage in Indochina. Despite some questioning, Bartley backed Nixon's Vietnamization program and the stepped-up bombardment of North Vietnam. Not since early 1968 had the *Journal* seriously questioned the wisdom of U.S. intervention in Vietnam. At that time the Tet offensive prompted the paper to run a widely publicized editorial advising the public to "be prepared for the bitter taste of a defeat beyond America's power to prevent," and declaring, "The Administration is duty-bound to recognize that no battle and no war is worth any price, no matter how ruinous." The editorial carefully avoided passing moral judgment on the American role in Vietnam, but was simply a realistic appraisal that "the whole Vietnam effort may be doomed."

The editorial has always been credited to Bartley's predecessor, the late Joseph Evans. But Vermont Royster, who was then editor of the *Journal* and now is a columnist, says he wrote the Tet editorial and Evans only rewrote it. None of Evans's associates remembers Royster having any part at all in the editorial. Whatever the authorship, one thing is certain: no editorial since then has sounded the same note. It is almost as if the *Journal* was surprised and shocked that many people saw the Tet editorial as a clear sign that Wall Street had turned against the war, and reluctant to be cast as a spokesman for Wall Street and uncomfortable at being in opposition to a Republican administration, pulled in its horns.

Even when their reasoning defies logic, *Journal* editorials affect an air of sweet reasonableness. This calm tone contrasts sharply to the vituperation in the *Journal*'s sister publication, *Barron's,* which has used editorials to red-bait, in discredited McCarthyite style, the Pacifica Foundation and Consumers Union, and attack child-labor laws in an editorial with a title as quaint as its thesis: SUFFER THE LITTLE CHIL-

DREN. *Barron's* editorials probably come closer to Dow Jones President Kerby's own views. For all that, he was a crack newsman and remains a genial gentleman, Kerby fired a reporter, James Garst, for taking the Fifth Amendment in 1954 and has no regrets about it to this day. And back in 1935, Kerby deserted the *Journal* for more than a year to write anti–New Deal pamphlets and press releases for the right-wing Liberty League. Though his *Journal* job paid $50 a week and the League $115, Kerby maintains, "I was not a prostitute; I had no quarrel with the league's ideology."

Kerby seems to have no basic quarrel with U.S. policy in Indochina, but he has said publicly that he regrets the *Journal* didn't get the Pentagon Papers. The sad fact is that the *Journal* wasn't even in the running for them. Says Washington bureau chief Alan Otten: "No one in the Washington bureau knew Ellsberg, and we didn't make an attempt to get the papers. We wouldn't have known what to do with them anyhow. We probably would have boiled them down to one leader." Kerby claims that the *Journal* is "the most powerful publication in the world." But as Otten says, "It would be silly to contend that we consistently have as much clout in Washington as the *Times* or the *Post*. On the bus I take, I see the *Times* coming in and the *Journal* going home. The *Journal* is required reading . . . but not urgent reading." One reason, of course, may be that the *Journal's* Washington coverage, though invariably competent, is understandably selective and usually conventional. Otten himself is widely respected for his savvy about two-party politics, yet he was so convinced that I. F. Stone was an uninfluential nobody that he tried (unsuccessfully) to kill a page-one profile of the maverick journalist a few years ago. "I still don't think Stone was worth profiling," says Otten.

There is a good deal of *New York Times* envy at the *Wall Street Journal* and the unmatched power, prestige and pay uptown account for the largely one-way traffic between the two papers. At least eighteen former *Journal* reporters now work for the *Times.* No former *Times* reporter works for the

Journal, although several former news assistants and copy editors do. Among the eighteen defectors at the *Times* are Robert Bedingfield, an assistant financial editor; R. W. Apple, chief political writer, and David Jones, who in 1972 was named national editor. John O'Connor went from obscurity at the *Journal* to instant celebrity as the *Times*'s television critic. His paper provides him with three TV sets at home and a fourth in the office. When James MacGregor took over the TV beat at the *Journal* he was refused even a 17-inch portable.

Journal management doesn't like to provide reporters with titles and trappings, such as news assistants to do routine legwork and secretaries to answer the phone, because it doesn't want to make life too comfortable. The system at the *Journal* is geared to spewing out senior reporters at thirty-five or forty. It is not simply that management wants to get two junior reporters for the price of a single senior; just as important is that a senior man's departure often opens up a choice beat for a younger man. The *Times* goes out of its way to promote its reporters' and columnists' reputations, using house ads with their pictures. In contrast, it takes a Pulitzer Prize award to rate a *Journal* reporter a mention in a *Journal* ad. The *Times* encourages staffers to trade on their status as *Times*men by lecturing and appearing on TV. The *Journal* bars staffers from going on TV if they are to express opinions of their own rather than ask questions of others. The *Times* sends a staffer off to Harvard on a Nieman Fellowship nearly every fall. The *Journal* banned such leaves from 1943, when the only *Journal* staffer ever to take a Nieman failed to return, to 1969, when it allowed me to participate in a similar program at Stanford.

Journal editors and executives acknowledge that the *Times* is a great newspaper, but shake their heads at *Times* management for tolerating what they regard as high-priced and slow-moving prima donnas and for knuckling under to union demands for ruinous wage hikes. In short, the *Journal* is a profit-making corporation first and a newspaper second while the *Times,* to its credit, is just the opposite.

The *Journal* retains vestiges of paternalism common to family-owned businesses, which the *Journal* was until twelve years ago when Dow Jones first sold stock to the public. For example, the paper kept Vermont Royster on the payroll at his regular salary for nine months after he retired as its $100,000-a-year editor. And it created an undemanding job for a managing editor who had to be relieved of that pressure post after six months because his long liquid lunches rendered him dysfunctional in the afternoon. The Dow Jones company union, whose ace in the hole is management's fear that its humiliation and collapse would open the way for the Newspaper Guild, has negotiated wage scales that are good by most standards but inferior to those in New York and Washington. The *Journal,* which in 1956 became the first daily to pay beginning reporters $100 a week, now pays $195 —$18 a week less than the *Times* pays beginning news assistants. The *Journal*'s top minimum of $335 after five years compares with $361 after two years at the *Times.* Half a dozen *Journal* reporters, most of them in Washington, earn more than $500 a week, but senior Washington reporters figure they make $50 to $75 less a week than counterparts at the *Times* and *Post.* They resent this, along with severe limitations on overtime pay and Dow Jones's refusal to institute a stock purchase plan for employees. When managing editor Taylor visited the Washington bureau in the spring of 1972 the reporters aired their grievances, Taylor was unsympathetic, and the confrontation turned ugly. Says Taylor: "They tore me apart." Says a reporter: "I have come to the conclusion reluctantly that management basically doesn't care; they would just as soon see senior guys go and replace them with cheap talent." At least management no longer rubs reporters' noses in their second-rank salaries. It has stopped running subscription ads headlined I WAS GOING BROKE ON $9,000 A YEAR, SO I SENT $7 TO THE WALL STREET JOURNAL. Recalls one reporter: "How do you think that made me feel when I was making $6,400 a year?"

At any salary, covering business year after year wears down all but the most hardy souls and least imaginative minds. Rewriting company handouts and attending annual stockholder meetings soon becomes mechanical as well as boring. A reporter can't do justice even to the rare lively annual meeting because he has to rush out periodically to phone bulletins to the Dow Jones News Service, the financial wire that all *Journal* reporters must service before they service the paper. Delay in feeding the "ticker" bulletins may result in a scoop for its arch competitor, the Reuters financial wire, and rate the reporter a rebuke. Besides being a legman for a wire service, the *Journal* newsman is a daily reporter for the inside of the paper and a news-magazine writer for the front page. He switches back and forth from the most routine and dreary journalism to the most demanding and fulfilling, a schizophrenic role unlike that on any other newspaper.

Like most other major publishing institutions, the *Wall Street Journal* has passed out of the era of personal stewardship. Barney Kilgore was the innovator credited with broadening and deepening the *Journal*'s coverage and converting the paper from a struggling financial trade journal into the prosperous general business daily it is today. From 1945, when he was made president, until his retirement in 1966, Kilgore served ex officio as editor of editors. He suggested stories, thoroughly critiqued each day's edition, and fired off salvos of wrist-slapping and back-patting memos to editors, bureau chiefs and even reporters. Besides serving as a one-man quality control panel, Kilgore contributed infectious enthusiasm for the *Journal* and intense drive to improve it. But he could be arbitrary as well as inspiring, most notably in 1960 when he clamped a ban on double bylines, claiming they were "pretentious." The ban hadn't been in effect more than a week or two before it deprived reporter Ray Schrick of half the credit for a Pulitzer Prize-winning story. The story, which Schrick initiated, exposed officers and directors of Georgia-Pacific Corporation who were engaged in dubious sideline transactions with the lumber company. Schrick's collaborator, Ed Cony, who got the byline and the Pulitzer, graciously offered Schrick half the prize money, but Schrick turned it down, explaining it was the prize he really prized.

William Kerby, who succeeded Kilgore as president six years ago, is of a different mold. Though a former editor himself, as are several others in the high command, he is content to keep hands off the editorial product and mind the business operation. Kerby will be sixty-five in July 1973 and is expected to step out of day-to-day operations and become part-time chairman of the board. His heir certain as president is forty-six-year-old executive vice-president Warren Phillips. Whether Phillips will carry the disengagement process another step remains to be seen. The son of a Jewish slip manufacturer from Queens, Phillips seems the logical choice to follow the Protestants, most from the Midwest, who have run Dow Jones for generations. Phillips is bright (he graduated from high school two weeks before turning fifteen), able (his news judgment as managing editor in 1957–65 was highly respected), and generous (he willingly takes the rap for some of his fellow executives' unpopular decisions).

It would be tempting for such an adroit team player to tread lightly as president, to settle only for refinements and eschew innovation as dangerous tinkering with an enormously successful product. But only by making the paper more penetrating and vital will Phillips help achieve its considerable promise. This need not conflict with the *Journal's* commercial viability. On the contrary, there are thousands of government officials, academicians, intellectuals and other nonbusiness readers who ought to be looking to the *Journal* for intelligent insights into the labyrinth of American business.

As a beginning, Phillips should purge the paper of many of the business stories that tell what is happening on the surface—sales rising, companies merging, managements changing—and replace them with stories that tell how businessmen really do business—how they make decisions, set prices, create markets for products that are too often unneeded and unsafe; how competitors exchange production, price and other supposedly confidential information; how they administer prices, curtail output and stifle genuine product improvements. The *Journal* covers the spectacular business scandals when they erupt, and its investigative reporters uncover less spectacular ones, but the paper ignores the day-in, day-out systematic corruption that is built into the American way of doing business, the corporate corruption that is far greater and more pernicious than big-city police corruption. Ralph Nader and his associates have described how some businesses really do business. The *Wall Street Journal* rarely has. For all that many consider it the "Bible of Business," the *Journal* publishes more in-depth stories on medicine than on merchandising, more leaders on athletics than on agriculture, more on personalities than on petroleum.

The solution is not to cut back on nonbusiness coverage but to improve business coverage. The *Journal* should study individual corporations and industries as deeply and deftly as it studied a South Bronx slum several years ago. Two reporters turned out four prize-winning leaders on life on Kelly Street. Given enough time, four reporters could turn out an even more memorable series on ITT, or Chase Manhattan, or Metropolitan Life. Taking on the biggest corporations, many of them practically countries unto themselves, is a lot tougher than going after the small fry that are the target of most investigative stories, but the results are much more likely to win new readers and keep old ones. Nothing fascinates businessmen more than reading stories that embarrass other businessmen; it is only when the rake reaches their own muck that they squawk. Articles should avoid a crusading, muckraking tone; the paper's standard calm, matter-of-fact, balanced presentation is eminently serviceable. The *Journal*'s strongest suit, of course is meticulous, unhurried reporting. Nearly all the paper's embarrassing failures have been hastily written dope stories long on speculation and short on reporting.

The *Journal* encourages overproduction by keeping count of each reporter's page-one output and giving the most prolific writers most of the raises and promotions. The effect of rewarding quantity over quality is to encourage reporters to bat out fast-forgotten formula leaders, when what is most needed are memorable nonformula pieces. These, of course, take far longer to conceive, report and write. Instead of encouraging reporters to produce more, management ought to limit each reporter to no more than half a dozen major feature stories a year. Besides improving the quality of stories, this would reduce a swollen inventory (as many as eighty stories have been backed up waiting for space on page one) and delay in publishing stories. Reporters worry constantly that page one is holding their stories too long (two months is the average wait between submission and publication for a piece without a specific time peg) and that their stories will be overtaken by events or upstaged by another publication.

As minimal steps to improve staff morale—ergo, the *Journal*—management should make pay scales at least competitive with the Washington *Post* and *The New York Times,* end once and for all the penny-wise, pound-foolish practice that requires all *Journal* reporters, senior as well as junior, to do double duty for the Dow Jones ticker, stop making reporters put phony datelines on spot news stories and relax the silly restrictions on free-lance writing and television appearances. The next time a reporter reworks a story the *Journal* already has run and sells it to *New York* magazine, management should not tell him, as it told reporter William Burrows, that *New York* is a competitive publication and off-limits to *Journal* reporters and—hold on!—another such sale will result in dismissal.

In September 1972 the *Journal* proudly announced that it had signed up a four-man board of contributors "intended to present a broad range of viewpoints on current topics." This quartet typifies the *Journal*'s constricted notion of "range," including as it does establishment heavies Walter Heller, Irving Kristol, Paul McCracken and Arthur Schlesinger, Jr. Unlike the *Times* Op-Ed page, the *Journal*'s editorial page remains largely inhospitable to all but the most "respectable" views, left or right. What the *Journal* needs is someone like Philip Geyelin. And the paper had him. But like so many others, he left. In his case, to give the Washington *Post* perhaps the best editorial page in the nation, one where a sense of humanism and reform prevails.

Whatever Warren Phillips' virtues as a newsman—and he has many—it is unlikely that when he rises to command in 1973 he will move the paper in that direction. A few years ago Phillips complained that some reporters were taking "glee in needling the establishment" and that too many page-one stories reflected an "antibusiness bias." Today he boasts that the problem no longer exists. One reason is the break-up of a group of activist reporters who hit management with six petitions in twelve months in 1969–70. Among other things, they protested two editorials (one blaming poor telephone service on minority hiring, the other suggesting that the young had gone to Woodstock to wallow in the mud) and asked management to go on record against government efforts to subpoena reporters' notes. The most controversial petition (signed by fifty-five staff members) asked management to observe Vietnam Moratorium Day by stopping the Dow Jones ticker for one minute. Management rejected this and the other demands and reprimanded reporters who had participated in a Wall Street peace demonstration holding aloft banners identifying them as *"Wall Street Journal*ists." Predictably, the militants are gone now—Ronald Kessler to the Washington *Post,* Alan Adelson to write a book, and Stanford Sesser to teach. Other activists stayed, but pulled in their horns. Management breathed easier, failing to understand that in stifling such activity and discouraging iconoclasm in the *Journal*'s pages it had severely damaged the early warning system that stories critical of business provide the paper's readers.

One of the astonishing facts about the *Wall Street Journal* is that Jane Cook and Jessie Cox, stepgranddaughters of early owner Clarence Barron, own (together with a family trust) 47 percent of Dow Jones stock. At current prices, it's worth $300 million, and each year these elderly sisters receive $7.1 million in dividends. They leave the operation of the *Journal* to the managers, but even so it is hard to be optimistic about change in an atmosphere so quintessentially Wall Street. But perhaps there is some hope. Bringing a sense of innovation and humanity to the *Journal* would cost Dow Jones relatively little. All of the changes I have suggested would add only a percentage point or two to the news operation budget, which even now amounts to less than 10 percent of the newspaper's overhead. Maybe someone in command will recognize what a small price that would be to pay for restoring morale and energizing the *Journal,* which for so long has been on the verge of being the best newspaper in the country.

October 1972

Warren Phillips succeeded William Kerby as president in 1973. His only visible innovation has been to reduce the size of the *Journal* page by nearly 10 percent to save newsprint and postage costs; the newsstand price has gone up 33 percent, to 20 cents. The editorial page is letting in a little light by printing more letters from readers. But editorials continue to deny discomforting realities, to mock reformers and to praise reactionaries. While deriding Chile's Salvador Allende as "a buffoon, a libertine and worst of all an amateur," the *Journal* stuck by Richard Nixon almost to the end, calling for his resignation only on the day he announced it, and then only to spare him "certain" impeachment and conviction. Ralph Nader told a group of advertisers in mid-1974 that aside from its "Pleistocene" editorial page, the *Journal* is "the most effective muckraking daily paper in the country."

That certainly is so, but it is more by default than by design. The *Journal* still goes after stories of stock swindles that harm a few wealthy investors with more zeal than it pursues systematic corporate corruption that victimizes millions of workers and consumers. For all its sharp eye on the rotten apples, the *Journal* still can't quite get the feel of the barrel.

CHRIS WELLES

Soft Times for Wall Street

Businessmen who opened *The New York Times* to the financial section on the morning of November 11, 1971, were greeted by a three-column photograph atop the page of Paul A. Salomone, the new president of the New York division of Gimbels. What had Salomone done to merit such prominence on the first business page of the nation's most influential newspaper? GIMBELS WILL PUT STRESS ON ITS 'BETTER-TASTE' ITEMS revealed the headline. Salomone, the story below further explained, had announced a trading-up program which "should catapult us into a higher plateau of better merchandise." At the New York City store, this would involve expansion of "town-and-country" wear, including leathers, suedes and knits, and the "at-home" fashions, including robes and "pajama groups."

If the article seems of less than monumental significance, it is nevertheless representative of the *Times*'s coverage of the world of business and finance. The same newspaper that invited government censure and legal challenge by publishing the Pentagon Papers, that as of 1974 had won 40 Pulitzer Prizes for its international, national, and metropolitan reporting, that regards as routine the creation of a four-man task force to produce the most authoritative and complete account of the Attica tragedy to appear in any newspaper or magazine—this same newspaper regularly publishes a business and financial section of astonishing mediocrity. Day after day, it is seldom more than a bland, tedious, disorganized and turgidly written rehash of the previous day's handouts and spot news events, mere surfaces and façades bereft of even the most rudimentary analysis, explanation, color or perspective.

Feckless financial coverage, of course, is by no means unique to the *Times.* Indeed, it is endemic to the press as a whole. Though a few business publications, notably the *Wall Street Journal* and *Fortune,* often scrutinize business with commendable tough-mindedness, most of the nation's newspapers and magazines seem possessed by acute schizophrenia. Editors whose adrenal glands pump furiously at the prospect of exposing a state senator with his hand in the till for a few hundred dollars steadfastly shrink from an investigation of a possible price-fixing conspiracy among several large corporations with a cost to consumers in the millions. Magazines that will spend months gathering evidence for an exposé of a major Mafia leader seem to have little interest in the equally odious machinations of a high corporate executive.

One obvious reason for this neglect is economic. State senators and Mafia leaders do not buy advertising space (at least not directly). But an equally important reason is the still-persistent belief that business is inherently dull and obscure, that it is nothing but an arcane world of indecipherable charts and incomprehensible jargon that few people care about and even fewer understand. Though the behavior of a few large corporations has a much greater effect on the average family than, say, pornography or the results of most political elections, the effect is more diffuse and less sensational, and therefore, in the view of many editors, less deserving of coverage. Then, too, there is the matter of sheer sloth. Reporting is almost always easier in nonbusiness areas. The

Justice Department and the FBI are usually eager to supply Mafia investigators from the press with nonattributable background, leads, and wiretap and other surveillance data. Politicians are usually willing to provide derogatory information on their opponents. Members of federal agencies know well how an adroit leak can effect policy changes. For all the plaudits the *Times* deserves for publishing them, the Pentagon Papers were still essentially a press release from Daniel Ellsberg. Getting behind the handouts in business and finance, however, is much more difficult. Business is a relatively closed society where the common interest in a healthy market environment is generally stronger than competitive differences over precise market shares. Most companies do not feel accountable to anyone but their stockholders (even then the accountability is usually perfunctory) and prefer to release little more than routine flackery and the barest minimum of financial information required by the Securities and Exchange Commission.

If any publication ought to be able to overcome these problems, it should be one with the sophistication, power and financial resources of the *Times*. Instead, in the opinion of almost all the many financial journalists (including a surprising number of *Times* business reporters) whom I interviewed in researching this article, it seems to be decidedly sensitive to them. The degree to which press releases, unembellished spot news and public relations trivia dominate the business section can be seen by an analysis of its Monday-Saturday coverage during August and September of 1971. During the fifty-two days, the section ran 590 articles on its first page. Some 362 were simple accounts of the previous day's events. Twenty-three were what might be called features, usually of less than overpowering importance: new tiny radio receivers floor brokers at the New York Stock Exchange use for communication; the promotion of birdwatching in this country by Japanese interested in boosting binocular sales; the first export of amusement-park equipment to the Soviet Union. Twenty-three other articles were columns: the weekly roundup of new patents from Washington and occasional "personal finance" columns, such as how a revision in New York state law makes financing of boat purchases more difficult. Many of the personal finance columns were little more than rewrites of reports from tax services and similar groups. Eleven stories were interviews, also usually less than compelling: Calvert Doorman, portfolio supervisor of Tri-Continental Corporation, said he was optimistic about the stock market; an Italian politician said U.S. trade strategy was hurting Italian business. Only seventy-one stories could be categorized as principally analytical or interpretive. Of these, eighteen were the routine articles on the outlook for the credit markets, steel industry, and overseas monetary and Eurobond markets normally published on Monday. Twenty-six pieces were written by reporters outside the business department, five by Leonard Silk, a member of the *Times* editorial board, who contributes a lively and thoughtful weekly economic analysis, and most of the remainder by *Times* Washington and overseas correspondents.

Of the five hundred and ninety articles, only twenty-seven —less than 5 percent—were analytical pieces written by the business section's New York staff of twenty-seven writers and editors. During the two months, only two stories were published that might be considered investigative reporting. Both were surveys, one a country-by-country roundup based on overseas dispatches on the reaction to Nixon's trade policies and the other an analysis of the likely effect of Nixon's proposed 10 percent tax credit on business investments. The latter story, which concluded that the credit would probably not create jobs, as the administration had contended, but would merely boost profits, as labor critics had charged, was perhaps the sole reportorial effort with any degree of lasting importance published by the *Times* business section during the two-month period.

The *Times* business pages have always devoted an especially large amount of space and prominence to corporate earnings and dividend news. On October 27, 1971, for example, when many firms were releasing third-quarter results, this news accounted for ten of the fifteen stories featured. Bylines of *Times* reporters appeared on seven of the ten stories. Yet the only explanations offered in any of these stories as to why earnings were up or down, or why dividends were being cut or omitted, were those of the company itself. Often no explanation was given at all. The opinions of the dozens of investment analysts with close knowledge of these companies or the views of their major competitors, which the seven *Times* reporters might have quickly sampled with a few phone calls in the course of a day, remained unreported.

Not all earnings and dividend news are of sufficient import to require intensive analysis. But even reporting of major events in this area usually lacks elaboration. Typical was a lead article October 2, 1971, on A&P, the country's largest food chain, which had announced the worst sales and earnings in a decade. The story quoted the company's press release explanation that the decline was due to "accelerated competition" and "sharp increases" in costs. Why did competition accelerate? Why did costs sharply increase? Was A&P's explanation the real one? Were other less obvious and possibly more embarrassing reasons actually responsible for the decline? What was the long-term significance of the results to investors and others with an interest in the company? These questions were never answered.

The tendency of the business section to leave vital questions unanswered goes well beyond the reporting of earnings news, of course. Important executive changes, even elections of new presidents at large corporations, are reported like weddings on the society pages, the reasons for which it is unnecessary and impolite to pursue. Other omissions are much more serious. For example, the controversy over what many critics, including congressmen and economists, feel is the growing trend toward monopolization of the energy business by the major oil companies has gone largely uncovered. Over the past several years, the large oil firms, which already control the nation's natural gas reserves and production facilities, have acquired sizable interests in the country's coal, uranium, oil shale and geothermal steam resources. The threat to consumers, claim the critics, is the erosion of competition among the various fuels, and the likelihood of unreasonably high prices for all fuels should the oil companies gain a complete hegemony. There is considerable evidence that the current "shortage" of natural gas has been in part artificially induced by oil companies to force the Federal Power Commission to permit higher gas prices and stop gas from burning into oil markets.

This controversy has been the subject of numerous congressional hearings, government reports and other studies over the past two years. Investigations by the Justice Department and the Federal Trade Commission are underway. The Washington *Post,* the *Wall Street Journal, The National Observer* ("Fears Rise of a Stranglehold on Fuel Supplies"), *Business Week* ("Oil is Taking Over the Energy Business"), and even *Playboy* have published stories. Yet *The New York Times* has yet to examine the issue, and so far as I can determine, has only mentioned it once—in a story on synthetic fuels from coal and oil shale. There was nothing about it in a long, three-part series in the *Times* in July 1971 called the "Nation's Energy Crisis," which was written by John Noble Wilford, a member of the national news staff. The business page has, on the other hand, often found space for such stories as an announcement by the National Petroleum Council, a group of oil industry executives, that it intended to study the energy situation.

Even when the *Times* does cover criticisms of business practices, the reporter is usually content merely to set down the charges and replies, leaving it up to the reader to puzzle out the facts. A glaring illustration of this kind of journalism followed the release in June 1971 of the 547-page report on the First National City Bank, the country's second largest, by a sixteen-man task force sponsored by Ralph Nader. The paper covered the study's major charges and reported the bank's response to them in a lengthy, page-one article by

Eileen Shanahan, a member of the *Times* Washington Bureau. Yet neither Erich Heinemann, the *Times*'s knowledgeable banking reporter, nor anyone else at the *Times* (or the *Wall Street Journal,* for that matter) bothered to explore the many issues raised by the report (such as the allegation that Citibank systematically drains money from New York's poorer sections) to provide its readers with an insight or two into where the truth might lie. Heinemann complained that the Nader office didn't send him a copy of the report until a month after its release, by which time it had become "stale." Following up on it, he added, would have "accorded it a credibility it didn't deserve." The explanation hardly seems adequate for the report's wholesale dismissal by a paper which covers in detail the most minuscule fluctuations in the major banks' prime rate policies.

An even more surprising omission concerns Wall Street, to which the business page has always devoted a great deal of space. Though the *Times* Wall Street reporter, Terry Robards, a former writer with the *Herald Tribune* and *Fortune,* is among the more capable members of the business department, he seems to have occasionally fallen prey to the loss of perspective which often comes with dependence on official sources. One of Robards's top sources has been Bernard J. Lasker, former chairman of the New York Stock Exchange. While Lasker leaked to Robards several exclusives on the efforts of the exchange to aid failing brokerage houses during the street's recent financial crisis, Robards wrote a number of effusive reports on Lasker's heroism in staving off mass disaster. Much less well reported were widely held contentions, especially at the SEC, that the exchange bore much of the responsibility for permitting the crisis to develop, that it failed to take timely remedial actions, and that it deliberately misled the public and the SEC on the situation's severity.

Though he has covered bits and pieces of it on a day-to-day basis, neither Robards nor anyone else at the *Times* has made a detailed investigative study of the growing challenges to the New York Stock Exchange's status as the nation's main securities market, and of the strong likelihood of a revolutionary restructuring of the securities markets, including possible dismantling of the Big Board itself. Significantly, Lasker and other high-level exchange officials, as well as other members of the Street establishment, have been working diligently to deny the importance of the threats to the Big Board and to resist any changes in the status quo.

Nowhere is the line between news and public relations more blurred than in the business section's extensive coverage of the retailing and garment industries, which occupies the full time of no less than three reporters, Isadore Barmash, Leonard Sloane and Herbert Koshetz. The traditional reply of the *Times,* when asked about this, has been that retailing is one of New York's biggest industries, though Wall Street, which Robards must cover by himself, is certainly much more important to the city. A much more significant factor, of course, is that retailers are by far the *Times*'s largest advertisers. The overall thrust of retailing and Seventh Avenue coverage is strongly, enthusiastically positive. Forward-looking developments gain quick attention. In September 1971 Barmash went all the way down to Allentown, Pennsylvania, for a four-column story on Fair-tex Mills, Inc., a small maker of knitted fabrics whose claim to newsworthiness was that after the Catasauqua Creek had overflowed and almost wiped the company out, Fair-tex rose from the mud, relocated on higher ground and is now expanding its plant for the fourth time.

Unpleasant developments get quieter treatment. When in July 1971 Gimbels announced its sharply lower earnings for the first half of 1971 and a big loss for the second quarter, the *Times* mercifully buried the news eight pages behind the business section's first page, and devoted most of the brief item to the company's optimistic hopes for its new stores. Though the *Times* gave much space to Gimbels New York President Paul Salomone's trading-up plans, it never investigated, as did *Women's Wear Daily*, the severe losses and administrative foul-ups which led to the ouster in October 1971 of his predecessor, Bernard Zients.

During the summer of 1971 the Federal Trade Commission announced a major unfair competition test action against three large department stores in a surburban shopping center outside Washington whose leases enabled them to exercise broad controls over the entire center, including price-fixing, prevention of discounting, monitoring of other stores' operating procedures, approval of other stores' leases and admittance of new tenants. According to *Women's Wear Daily*, which put the story on its front page two consecutive days, three other shopping centers were also under investigation, and FTC officials felt that if they won the Virginia case, similar leasing arrangements through the country would have to be dropped. The story was also reported in the *Wall Street Journal* and carried by the wire services. Though the *Times* regularly provides readers with extensive reports whenever Bloomingdale's, Gimbels, Alexander's or some other retail chain opens or announces a new suburban store (see the *Times* of August 19, September 9, and October 16, 1971), it failed to record the FTC action anywhere in the paper. It would not seem that the problem was tightness of space in the business section. On July 22, the day after the FTC move was announced, the business page ran a long feature with a three column head on a bill-collecting organization in Buenos Aires called "The Gentlemen," whose representatives dress in top hats, white ties and tails.

In October 1971, when the FTC issued a specific proposed complaint against Gimbels for twenty-four shopping center leases, which *Women's Wear Daily* front-paged the day the announcement was made, the *Times* finally ran a brief report in the business section. But it failed to follow up with any analysis or investigation into the importance of the event to the industry or to consumers.

Even Seventh Avenue, though, is not so obligingly serviced by the *Times* business section as the advertising industry, which has, in effect, its very own column by Philip H. Dougherty. Dougherty has achieved wide readership on Madison Avenue with his cutesy prose and wrist-slapping twits. Surrounded by high-priced premium ad space purchased by those trying to reach the advertising community, mainly magazines, the column is said to be one of the most profitable single features at the *Times*. A typical recent excerpt:

> COOL SCOOP
> Barnett, Zlotnick, Inc., has just
> picked up its fourth account and it's a
> sweet one—Costa Ice Cream,
> Woodbridge, N.J.
> Put that in your cone and see if it
> melts.

A major share of the blame for the business section's deficiencies, in the opinion of several *Times* reporters, lies with John G. Forrest, a career *Times*man who edited the section during the forties and fifties. Though a hard-drinking newsman from the old school, Forrest exercised little control over the department. Many of the competent reporters quit or transferred to other sections of the paper, leaving business coverage to tired, aging writers who felt no story was worth more than 700 words and an hour at the typewriter, and who much preferred to spend the afternoons at Gough's, a bar on Forty-Third Street across from the *Times* building. Forrest's long tenure in the department was due in part to his close friendship with former publisher Arthur Hays Sulzberger and assistant managing editor Theodore Bernstein. He was finally retired in 1963 and replaced by Thomas E. Mullaney. A personable, if somewhat aloof, man, Mullaney had joined the *Times* in 1942 as a copy boy in the financial department and later became the section's steel industry reporter, and then Forrest's assistant.

Mullaney's efforts to assert authority over his domain have

been about as successful as the *Times* Western edition, over which he presided as news editor from its beginning in 1962 until shortly before it folded in 1964. The biggest problem is personnel. "In order to turn this section into the kind of financial page the world has a right to expect from the *Times,*" says one reporter on the paper, "you'd have to fire about 85 percent of the people." The Newspaper Guild vigorously fights such purges, of course, but they can be brought off. And no one knows this better than the paper's managing editor, A. M. Rosenthal. He chopped away so much deadwood in the city room when he became metropolitan editor in the mid-sixties that more than once his regime was described as a reign of terror. "You have to realize," says another *Times* reporter, "that the paper is Mullaney's whole life. He doesn't want to rock the boat organizationally by really going to the mat with the Guild or, for that matter, digging behind the press releases. Tom is also a thoroughly compassionate man. What we need is a son of a bitch."

Mullaney has displayed even less leadership in editorial matters. His principal policy seems to be laissez faire. Though the section, according to assistant managing editor Seymour Topping, is "aimed primarily at businessmen," it fails to provide even the kind of detailed analyses of corporate developments featured by most business publications. Mullaney seems to permit press conferences and news releases to dominate the section not because he has determined that this particular news is of the greatest interest to readers but merely because it is the most readily accessible. Certain areas of news, such as banking, railroads, government economic policy and international monetary affairs, are stressed simply because of the abilities of the reporters covering those beats—Erich Heinemann and Robert Bedingfield of the business staff, Edwin Dale and Eileen Shanahan in Washington, and John Lee and Clyde Farnsworth in Europe. Morale, says one reporter, is "terrible," and most of the department's reporters have sunk into such indolence that many freely admit they see their primary job as reporting simply what an industry says it is doing, leaving to others—they are vague as to just who—to report the views of critics or probe into what industry is really doing. "We really don't know what we're supposed to be doing, who we're supposed to be talking to, what our priorities are on any given day," says one of the section's more prolific reporters, "There is simply no exercise of editorial control at all. The only time we look good is by accident."

Even more serious has been Mullaney's archaic view of business journalism, his failure to recognize the growing importance of external influences such as federal agencies and consumer groups on business and finance, and the increasing importance of the once insular world of business to society in general. Because Mullaney has allowed his department to languish in traditionally narrow channels, the kind of business coverage displayed by most well-edited business publications has had to come on an ad hoc, uncoordinated basis from *Times* reporters on the metropolitan and national staffs and in the Washington bureau. Yet their generally competent and thorough stories—on regulations agency actions, the activities of consumer organizations or the environment —seldom appear on the business pages. "You almost get the feeling," says a top editor at a business publication, "that they are deliberately trying to keep the business page bland and safe so that businessmen won't get upset. Everything that's dirty and nasty, that reflects what's really going on, ends up somewhere else in the paper."

In fairness, there has been an attempt to improve the Sunday business pages. This has been most notable in investigative pieces by Michael C. Jensen, a recent recruit from *American Metal Market,* on such subjects as the growing criticism of ITT and the troubles of the Copeland family that rules the du Pont empire. Most of the Sunday changes, though, have been cosmetic: dressing up the section with new typography and magazine-style layouts. The profiles of businessmen remain as worshipful as ever. One, headlined FIGHTING BATTERY MAKER and set off by a series of heroic sketched portraits, concerned Harry J. Noznesky, president of General Battery Corp. It began: "Harry J. Noznesky is not one to back out of a fight." Whom was Noznesky fighting? The Federal Trade Commission, which was spoiling his plans for a merger with TRW, Inc., by attacking the move as anticompetitive. The same sacred cows of weekday coverage are respected on Sunday. In August 1971, for instance, the Sunday section ran a "U.S. Business Roundup" describing in detail how revolving credit plans at banks and department stores were coming under legal challenge across the country. Several paragraphs each were devoted to developments in Wisconsin, Indiana, Connecticut, Minnesota and South Dakota. But the story ignored completely the fact that class actions against revolving credit plans are pending in New York against Abraham & Straus, Bloomingdale's, Macy's, Gimbels, Fortunoff's, Martin's, Barney's, Korvette's, W. & J. Sloane and the Chase Manhattan Bank.

Mullaney's response to criticisms is generally defensive. Too little interpretation and analysis? "I would have to dispute that." Unwillingness to undertake big investigations? "If we want the space we can get it. But you have to remember, I don't have a staff the size of the city desk." Too much deadwood? "We're constantly trying to upgrade our staff. But I think our staff now is a hell of a good one." Low morale? Criticism of his leadership? "I'm not running a popularity contest. Every paper has grumbling. I think it's healthy."

Dissatisfaction with the *Times* business coverage certainly cannot be a surprise to the paper's management. In a widely quoted article on the *Times* a few years ago in *The Public Interest,* Irving Kristol, professor of urban values at New York University, wrote: "It is not too much to say that if the entire financial section were to vanish tomorrow, no one on Wall Street would particularly notice the event." Yet assistant managing editor, Seymour Topping, who oversees the business section, denies the asserted deficiencies with almost as much vehemence as Mullaney. He admits that the business section has been in the past a "stepchild" and "too separated from the rest of the paper," but contends he and managing editor Rosenthal are working hard to "integrate it more fully with the other departments." Though he concedes a "much broader involvement" of people in business affairs, he explains the disjointed coverage in different parts of the paper under different editors as due to the paper's "configuration." When asked about one reporter who, as a member of the business staff puts it, "poured out his spleen" to Rosenthal and Topping over lunch only to be greeted with seemingly indifferent shrugs, Topping denied any knowledge of the incident. "We haven't had any complaints or suggestions from reporters in the department," he maintains. "But if people do have ideas to contribute, we have an open door. We're hungry for ideas."

Reporters in the department are dubious. One tells of a day in 1970 when Dolly Madison Industries filed a petition for bankruptcy. Coming in the wake of the Penn Central collapse, the announcement caused more than a little concern in the financial community. Yet the *Times* noted the incident in a tiny item back by the Toronto Stock Exchange tables. The following day, Rosenthal sent down a long memo. It concerned a prominently featured story the previous day on a new flash cube which had been announced at a press conference by Sylvania and Kodak, one paragraph of which he felt was unclear. "It was the kind of day," says the reporter, "when senior management showed its true colors in the most glaring fashion."

"Top management is aware of the problems and concerned about them," says a reliable source at the *Times* with firsthand knowledge of the situation. "But they just haven't wanted to face up to making the hard decisions, such as battling the guild and spending a lot of money, which would be necessary for the *Times* to have a really brilliant business page. One reason is that Rosenthal and Topping don't care that deeply about business to begin a lot of screwing around.

And you also have to ask yourself what the publisher wants. I'm sure there's never been a memo from Punch [*Times* publisher Arthur Ochs Sulzberger] to Mullaney saying please write a puff story on IBM. But the fact remains that if you write tough stories, a lot of businessmen are likely to be on the publisher's neck." Once, he recalls, a *Times* editorial suggested there should be more competition on airline fares and less rate regulation by the Federal Aviation Agency. Within days, an angry delegation of airline executives, led by Charles Tillinghast, head of TWA, arrived in Sulzberger's office to complain.

No one argues that running a tough, well-edited business section is without certain hazards. But that hardly excuses a newspaper which vows in marble to print the news "without fear or favor." Rather than pander to the business community, the *Times* should aim at a diverse readership and be business' most hard-eyed observer. Business publications like *Fortune* and *Business Week,* for all their good reporting, still tend automatically to reflect industry's viewpoint. There remains a great need for aggressive business journalism, which a paper with the resources of the *Times* could go a long way toward filling. There are vast unreported areas of corporate behavior: the ways prices are set, products marketed or executives chosen; the way many large companies attempt to print disruptive innovations, subdue competition, control markets and obtain influence over federal agencies. Why shouldn't the *Times* consider a major industry or a large corporation just as worthy of a continuing series as a city block, a metropolitan neighborhood or an urban classroom?

In a memo to the staff when he took over as managing editor in September 1969, A. M. Rosenthal wrote: "We have learned that news is not what people say and do, but what they think, what motivates them, their styles of living, the movements, trends and forces acting upon society and on a man's life. We learned that some of journalism's techniques and habits in reporting the news actually prevented the presentation of the real news. Religious reporting, for instance, used to be sermons on Sunday reported on Monday. When we stopped reporting sermons, we began reporting religion."

By that criterion, *The New York Times* has yet to begin reporting business.

December 1971

In the three years since this article was written, it should be acknowledged that the *Times* has at last begun to report business, though it still has a long way to go to meet fully the criteria in Rosenthal's memorandum. The improvement has been principally in the area of what had been the business section's most egregious weaknesses: slothful rewriting of press releases; worshipful coverage of the garment and retailing industries; excessive attention accorded the frivolous and irrelevant. These practices still occur but less frequently and blatantly. Questions once unasked are now being pursued, if not always as far as one might hope.

The chief disappointment has been the continuing failure of the section to develop either the taste or the talent for aggressive and venturesome investigative reporting of the sort successfully (and, unfortunately, uniquely) displayed by the *Wall Street Journal.* The most memorable business-related investigations in the *Times* tend to be written by reporters from other sections of the paper, e.g., Israel Shenker's witty and trenchant analysis of the extent to which lawyers have profited from such business collapses as Penn Central and A. H. Raskin's masterfully written and conceptualized synopsis of the labor contract negotiations between the New York City newspaper publishers and Bertram Powers's printers' union.

Change, however, comes slowly and tortuously on West Forty-Third Street. *Times* readers should be thankful at least that during the last three years somebody in the *Times* hierarchy realized something is wrong with the business pages and has been trying to do something about it. The question now concerns the relative strength of the pressures for and resistance to further change.

Annals of Checking

During World War II, the Japanese released a series of balloons, with incendiary devices inside, that blew across the Pacific and over the Rocky Mountains. The balloons started forest fires in the Northwest that newspapers were asked not to publicize so that the Japanese would not be encouraged to send more. One of the balloons landed in Hanford, Washington, and shut down a building of the plant that was making the plutonium that went into the bomb that destroyed Nagasaki.

The story appears for the first time in "The Curve of Binding Energy," John McPhee's three-part "Profile" of Theodore B. Taylor, the nuclear scientist, the first part of which appeared in *The New Yorker* on December 3, 1973. McPhee got the story from John Wheeler, a physicist on the faculty at Princeton, who had worked on the Manhattan Project (which developed the first atomic bomb) and the Hanford Project. Wheeler was somewhat vague about the details, but he gave McPhee the names of several people who might authenticate the story, and McPhee passed on the sources to Sara Spencer, chief of *The New Yorker*'s checking department. Spencer called Eugene P. Wigner, who had been involved peripherally in the Manhattan Project; she called Glenn Seaborg, a co-discoverer of plutonium; she called

Army people and more physicists. They were puzzled, flattered and impressed, but none of them could recall the story. One of them remembered a brief power shutdown, but not the details of it. The last person she called said, "Why don't you try John Wheeler? He'd know."

At this point, having come full circle, most people would have stopped calling and fudged the story with a clear conscience, but other possibilities presented themselves. Spencer tracked down the ex-plant manager, sending two special delivery letters, one to his Pennsylvania home and one to his Florida home. He didn't remember, either. Finally Spencer found a man who had worked in the Hanford plant during the war, and what he said resulted in a very minor change. The original story had the balloon landing and shutting down the entire plant. In the authenticated version the balloon hit just one power line—the line that shut the power off in the building that housed the plutonium reactor.

Sara Spencer is one of seven "checkers," five women and two men, underpaid and overqualified, who sit in a bright, sunny room roughly twenty-five feet long by twenty feet wide, two and a half walls of which are covered from floor to ceiling with books, on the nineteenth floor of *The New Yorker*'s Forty-third Street offices. They verify every fact that goes into the magazine.* The room is equipped with a cutcoupit and three air conditioners, and there is a sign on the door that says: "Please do not ring unless an answer is required." There is no bell.

The checkers, who range in age from twenty-five to forty-three, have among them six B.A.'s, one B.F.A., three M.A.'s, and one Ph.D.; a knowledge of French, Spanish, German, Russian and Hebrew, and a smattering of Chinese, Japanese, Latin and Classical Greek. They share a passion for accuracy

---

*Sara Spencer, thirty-six, has been a checker at *The New Yorker* for eight years. Her six colleagues are Anne Mortimer-Maddox, forty-three, seven years; Patti Hagan, thirty, four years; Helga Veblen, twenty-nine, three years; Katherine Black, twenty-seven, three years; Martin Baron, thirty-seven, and Richard Sacks, twenty-five, both less than a year.

that would have been congenial to the late Harold Ross, founder and guiding spirit of the magazine, who, according to the late James Thurber, "regarded perfection as his personal property."

The New Yorker has always cared desperately about being right, although in its first days checking was somewhat more haphazard than it is now. The original checking library consisted of three books—an 1898 Baedeker for Paris and London, an equally out-of-date Spalding's Baseball Guide, and Webster's desk dictionary. (Webster's is still preferred.) When Hobart Weekes, now a senior editor whose special province is "The Talk of the Town" section, arrived at the magazine in 1928 (three years after its founding) to become half of the checking department, the other half, Mark Russell, handed him a galley with the name Vanderbilt underlined. "Here," said Russell, "Check that."

In those days, checking was considered a good way for a young man to break into the publishing life (until well after World War II the magazine was almost entirely male), and the checking department developed something of a collegiate atmosphere. As recently as the fifties, checkers would close the door on Friday afternoons and perform costumed satiric operas for a selected group of invited guests. Their last performance took place on the day that William Shawn, Ross's successor as editor-in-chief, appeared uninvited and sat silently in the audience.

The department is more sedate now, members of the original cast having dispersed, taking with them their prankish outlook. Women arrived in the editorial department after the war when men were scarce and the magazine was desperate for literate people. "I would have hired a crocodile," said Hobart Weekes with a flash of the old esprit. None was available, and by the end of the sixties the checking department had become all female, except for the head checker, Phil Perl, and was known as "Phil's Harem." Recently, Bob Bingham, an editor of nonfiction pieces and a policy maker who is in charge of checking, noticed what was happening and started to hire men again. (Sexual integration is arriving quite slowly at *The New Yorker*. There are men on the switchboard and in Walden Pond, the typing pool run by Harriet Walden, where one of the male checkers, Richard Sacks, started his career; but there is only one woman editor, Rachel MacKenzie, and she has been there for a long time.) A piece that is bought by the magazine is set in galleys immediately, and one set goes to the checking department where it is assigned according to who wants to do what. Sara Spencer, who checked McPhee's piece on Theodore Taylor, has a particular interest in science, but if there's a crunch, preferences are ignored. Crunches tend to come toward the end of the week. Long pieces have a three- to four-week lead time, but at the end of the week they have to be dropped to do the departments. "Musical Events," "The Race Track," "The Theatre" and the monthly "Letter from Washington" come in then, and each checker alternates working for four or five hours every seventh Sunday to check them, making the necessary phone calls on Monday morning. The magazine goes to press at 2:00 P.M. on Monday.

"We underline words and sentences that are facts and leave alone the ruminations of the author," explains Spencer. "We get the source from the author—the party invitation, a booklet from the Auto Show, the phone numbers of the people he talked to." Handing in one's source material is *de rigueur*, and writers also deliver tapes of interviews and folders of typed notes. John Brooks asked a checker to help him carry over to the office two cartons of source material for a "Talk of the Town" piece on economics; and McPhee gave the checker over thirty magazines and journals that he used in writing "Ruidoso," a story about quarter-horse racing that appeared in April 1974.

When this material is delivered, it is up to the writer to speak out if any of it is likely to prove sticky. Anne Mortimer-Maddox, who checked "Annals of Industry: Casualties of the Workplace," a series of articles that started running in the issue of October 29, 1973, and that dealt with the ill effects of asbestos on the health of plant workers, was advised by the author, Paul Brodeur, that it would be difficult to get a straight answer from industry sources, and the piece had to be checked obliquely, through every imaginable reference to asbestos outside of industry.

Calvin Trillin, *The New Yorker*'s peripatetic chronicler of American cities and towns, constantly deals with boosters whose ideas of accuracy are often skewed in the direction of wishful thinking. In checking his "U.S. Journal: Kansas City, Missouri" (April 8, 1974), the checker was told by a member of the Chamber of Commerce that the airport was fourteen miles from Crown Center, not twenty as Trillin had said. Trillin, however, had taken the precaution of clocking it, and it stayed twenty. The mileage went in "on author," which is what usually happens when disputed facts can't be corroborated. "The writer has the final say," says Bingham. "The writer is always the one who has to be satisfied."

In practice, however, a lot of writers aren't around when their piece is being checked, and don't even sit down with their editor to go over the emendations. They are thus helpless to counter the excesses of fact-hunting. In "Bakery," by Susan Sheehan (April 15, 1972), a "Talk of the Town" piece about the Peter Pan Bake Shop in Forest Hills, near a proposed housing development that residents were trying to prevent from being built, Sheehan noted that "the only clue to the customers' views on the project are red 'Impeach Lindsay' buttons that some of them wear." The buttons were definitely red. A checker called various button manufacturers but could only find one that made white "Impeach Lindsay" buttons, and the color was changed to white.

Having to go over material that is cold would seem to be an irksome task for a source, but, says Spencer, "we usually get cooperation. If people are reluctant, we say the story is written and they have a vested interest in getting it right." Theodore Taylor went over facts he had already discussed twice with McPhee; and the Duke of Windsor said he was enchanted that the magazine cared enough to verify Janet

Flanner's description of the flora around his country house. The checker had tried the landscape gardener first, without success, and was told that it was all right to phone the duke, provided it was the proper hour. Even the Pentagon, which one imagines to be riddled with terminal paranoia, has succumbed to the mystique of *The New Yorker.* Last July, when Bruce Bliven, a *New Yorker* writer, went down to interview an assistant to the Secretary of Defense on a story the military must have known would make it look bad, the Pentagon sprang to attention for him. "Take all the time you want," Bliven's escort, Lieutenant Colonel Audrey Thomas told him. "We don't want you to feel hurried." The aide he interviewed cleared his entire afternoon schedule and was ready to talk indefinitely, even though Bliven only needed an hour. When he left, Bliven thanked the colonel and remarked that the story might not be a friendly one. "We don't care," she said. "We can't do anything about your attitude, but we're on the phone with your checking department all the time, and they're always so careful and polite."

Checkers spend about half the day on the phone; on occasion they send cables to far-flung correspondents, and in dire cases they go themselves. In November 1968, Gwyneth Cravens, now with *Harper's* magazine, wrote a mood piece on Central Park in which she observed, "She waved at the boy and the boy raised his arm to wave back, but it was too late; the woman passed from his view as the carrousel turned, and he was waving, instead, at the red-and white striped brick wall of the carrousel housing. . . ." The checker who went over to survey the scene discovered that the building was red and cream, and the color was changed. Wally White, who has since become a writer for *The New Yorker,* spent several days commuting by taxi from a Washington hotel to the late Rachel Carson's suburban Maryland home where the two of them went over *Silent Spring. Silent Spring* appeared in *The New Yorker* in three parts, on June 16, 23, and 30, 1962, and at the time its thesis about the harmful effects of pesticides seemed to verge on science fiction. Before meeting with Carson, White spent several weeks talking to scientists about chemicals and the environment, to make sure that Carson's imagination hadn't been working overtime.

More recently, two checkers were dispatched to Washington to check Seymour Hersh's *Coverup,* a book that began as a "Reporter at Large" piece on the Army's inquiry into the Son My atrocities (My Khe 4 and My Lai), and that appeared in two parts, January 22 and 29, 1972. The articles were based on a massive 20,000-plus page document, unofficially called the Peers Report, as well as about five hundred other documents. The checkers checked into the Madison, one of Washington's better hotels, and spent five weeks there, dissecting Hersh's piece. Working from the documents, they found every quote Hersh had used and read two pages in front of it and two pages behind it for context, uncovering dozens of mistakes along the way—misquotes, misstatements of fact, and nuances that were shaded the wrong way. Hersh, who has nothing but praise for the checking department, almost went crazy during the process, and sent a note to the checkers apologizing for his wild behavior.

Even more debilitating—and perhaps the ultimate in exhaustiveness—was the going-over given to Hannah Arendt's "Eichmann in Jerusalem" (published in book form as *The Banality of Evil*), a five-part piece that ran in February and March of 1963. The checker, Bill Honan, who now edits *The New York Times* Sunday Arts and Leisure section, knew German, and spent four months holed up in the Yivo Institute for Jewish Research, a quiet little library on the Upper East Side where the phone never rang, poring over the set of captured German war documents it possessed. There are bound to be contradictions in government records, and Honan managed to find many of them. On one sentence of Arendt's he found and wrote one page of conflicting evidence. Arendt, a careful scholar, a native German, and an eyewitness to the trial, was shocked and dismayed when her story came back looking as if someone had written a dissertation on it in the margins, and refused to go along with some of the emendations. Some fairly heavy collisions followed, with *The New Yorker* coming out ahead on most of them, but there was one figure that Arendt absolutely refused to change, and, tired of fighting, Shawn and Honan gave in.

The Arendt experience was unusual. Far from finding checking an adversary process, most writers welcome it, either as an antidote to their own laziness and carelessness or as a rescue operation for their overenthusiasms, their tendency to prefer style to substance. "I can't imagine anyone not being glad about it," says Calvin Trillin. "It's an extra thing. It's a great comfort to writers. I'm happy to be caught." Being caught is especially felicitous when the possibility of a lawsuit looms, as it did when Trillin accidentally reversed the names of two Augusta, Georgia, newspapers whose editorial policies were violently opposed to each other.

One of the magazine's more prolific contributors, Trillin produces a piece every three weeks, and is occasionally let down by the checkers. In the Kansas City piece Trillin wrote last April, he dredged up from the back of his brain playwright John Osborne's comment, "The monarchy is a gold filling in a mouthful of decay," thinking there would be no trouble in locating it; but no one could find it, not even *New Yorker* movie critic Penelope Gilliatt, who was once married to Osborne. So Trillin dropped him and attributed the quote to "one of the Queen's angrier subjects." Whenever there is an unattributed quote in *The New Yorker* it is safe to assume that the source was too elusive for the checkers.

Sometimes the achievement of total accuracy is foiled by the source, who has a bad memory or is careless. John McPhee, one of the more fact-conscious writers, was tripped up by Theodore Taylor. Taylor said he used to make urotropine (a urinary antiseptic) with his chemistry set when he was a boy, but from his description of the chemical reaction the product couldn't have been urotropine. He meant urethane, which was used at the time as a hypnotic. A pharmacist wrote in to correct it. In "Firewood" (March 25, 1974), a piece about using firewood during the energy crisis,

McPhee described a man and his son going into the woods carrying "an axe and wedges, a fifty-pound mallet, and a manual saw." Again, no one questioned the feasibility of someone wandering through the forest loaded down with a fifty-pound mallet, and again a lynx-eyed reader caught it. Embarrassed, McPhee phoned the woodsman, who offered to weigh the mallet. It weighed twenty-five pounds. "It was inaccurate, but at least I didn't say fifty and mean five," says McPhee, comforting himself.

There is a lot of free-floating reticence around *The New Yorker,* especially when it comes to discussing writers and their idiosyncrasies. However, most people cautiously agree that Trillin, McPhee, Brendan Gill, John Bainbridge, and Geoffrey Hellman rarely cause tremors in the checking department. Mollie Panter-Downes, Janet Flanner, and Andy Logan (among others) also avoid the great temptation to sloppy research, and Pauline Kael is almost never wrong. Calvin Tomkins, who has been with the magazine for about twenty years, is not always right. "I make a lot of mistakes," he said. "I'm very dependent on the checkers." Four years ago Tomkins did a book on the Metropolitan Museum, *Merchants and Masterpieces.* He was assigned a researcher who knew about art history and who also checked the manuscript for him. She turned up very few errors, when, in fact, says Tomkins, "there were a lot of grievous mistakes in the book. It wouldn't have happened at *The New Yorker.*"

The real checking disasters, those that necessitate rewriting a piece, are buried in old galleys and in the memories of checkers who steadfastly refuse to discuss them. However, other people at *The New Yorker,* all of whom preferred to remain anonymous, say the two worst checking problems are Joseph Wechsberg and Edward Jay Epstein. Not only does Wechsberg misquote passages from the *Larousse Gastronomique,* but he neglects to send in his source material. Since he frequently writes from the middle of Europe, this is a serious deficiency. On one occasion, Mme. Fernande Point, proprietor of the famous restaurant Pyramide, near

Vienne, France, spent an unexpected half-hour on the phone with a *New Yorker* checker correcting menus and recipes for a Wechsberg article. A gracious and appreciative man, Wechsberg makes a point of stopping by to thank the checkers whenever he's in New York. Epstein, a press critic, has run into terrible squalls in the checking department, most notably with an article on the way the media reported the killing of Black Panthers by police (February 13, 1971) and with an excerpt (March 3, 1973) from his book on network newsgathering, *News From Nowhere* ([MORE]—May 1973).

If *The New Yorker* sometimes seems to take on overtones of omniscience, it is because none of these deviations sees the light of day. Insignificant misdemeanors, such as overweight mallets, rest in the oblivion they deserve; but every so often something comes along that is too heinous to ignore and must be acknowledged in some way. The most famous retraction, and the most elegant, was delivered about fifteen years ago by Winthrop Sargeant, then the music critic, after reviewing a performance of Tchaikovsky's Fourth Symphony, which he compared with his remembrance of a Toscanini recording of the same symphony. Schwann's record catalogue didn't list the Toscanini, but Sargeant was sure he'd heard it and it went through, with misgivings, "on author." Sargeant was wrong, and an outpouring of letters from indignant music lovers obliged him to respond. There is no such recording, he admitted grandly, but if there had been, it would have sounded exactly the way he described it.

Fiction, poetry, artwork, captions and brand names do not escape the scrutiny of the checking department, nor do the plots of novels that are being reviewed. (On a smaller scale, there is another checking process for ads, conducted by the advertising department. They are gone over for grammar and for double entendres, which are not acceptable, either in the copy or the illustration. Inquiries are made about quality, mainly through the stores that sell the product, it being assumed that *New Yorker* readers don't shop in discount houses, and ads for low-quality products are turned down.

Superlatives are queried, but there is no hard-and-fast rule.) In cartoons, checkers notice such minutiae as which side men's and women's coats are buttoned on, and the number of tiers on the Capitol Building. In fiction, unique names owned by litigious people are checked through the telephone book, and then there is the ever-present Plausibility Factor, a booby trap that has caught many an unwary checker. The Plausibility Factor embraces such improbabilities as a discussion of the non-existent Dutch elms in East Hampton, or having a character remark, "I left Washington in 1967 because I couldn't stand Richard Nixon." Even poems get the P.F. treatment

Although the bookshelves in the checking department contain esoterica for every contingency, from the *Almanach de Gotha* to ancient Manhattan telephone books, and the library is stocked with past issues of *The New Yorker* (considered to be gospel), now and then mistakes inevitably slip through. They are almost always small mistakes, although to *The New Yorker* nothing is small. The Ayub Khan was transformed into the Ayub Kahn once (it is whispered that that was a proofing error); Desmond Fitz-Gerald, the Knight of Glin, was dehyphenated; and a Russian conductor, the members of whose orchestra called him by his first name, Sergei, almost appeared as Sir Gay. That one was caught, but someone was concussed when Jacob Brackman wrote in "The Put-on" (June 24, 1967) that the cast of "Beat the Devil" included Sydney Greenstreet, who was not alive at the time. (Greenstreet had been slated for the part which went to Robert Morley.) Winthrop Sargeant slipped through the checkers' net about ten years ago when he was dealing, appropriately enough, with critics who make mistakes. Joining their number, he wrote that the great French critic, Charles-Francois de Sainte-Beuve, disapproved of Marcel Proust's writings because he thought Proust led a low moral life. Sargeant meant Stendhal, not Proust. Sainte-Beuve died three years before Proust was born.

Among the more ticklish questions checkers face is that of

quotes. Although everyone who speaks in the pages of *The New Yorker* does so in flawless English (a grammatical courtesy extended by editorial policy), a great number of people fly into a panic when their words are read back to them; and when facts and interpretation are intermingled in the same quote, the craft of checking becomes exceedingly delicate. The checkers had a particularly difficult time with "All Pockets Open" (January 6, 1973), Calvin Tomkins's "Profile" of Jonas Mekas and the underground filmmakers, most of whom had a second occupation, which was quarreling bitterly with each other over their respective roles in the movement. One of them, Amos Vogel, was most insistent that his opinions receive equal space with Mekas's and gave the checker a written polemic to use in lieu of his original quote. "This is going to be a historical record," he said in justification of all the trouble he was causing, "and it has to be accurate." The pitch to accuracy was irresistible, and he argued his way into a compromise with Tomkins, who finally added some of the new material.

The worst mistake, the nightmare of every checker, is to kill off someone prematurely. One of the more memorable murders was committed when theater critic Kenneth Tynan remarked in a review that a certain actor reminded him of the late Eric Blore. A checker asked the room at large, "Does anyone know if Eric Blore is dead?" Another checker answered, "Yes, of course he's dead," violating a cardinal checking rule, which is: Never rely on your knowledge. Sure enough, a letter came from a friend of the actor saying that Blore was in a nursing home. After an appropriate explosion, Tynan wrote a correction in his next review, saying how happy he was to learn that Eric Blore was not dead and wishing him well. Blore, however, was still possessed of his acute sense of timing, and just as the retraction came out he died, leaving Tynan incoherent and everyone else numb.

For all of their dedication, *New Yorker* checkers earn only $8,000 a year to start, and when there's overtime the supper slip is $5.00, barely enough for hors d'oeuvres at the Algonquin. But the magazine is awash in fringe benefits, and five out of seven checkers pronounced themselves thoroughly contented with the job, with no desire to change; the other two were more ambitious, wanting to get ahead, preferably within the magazine. Life at *The New Yorker* is so pleasant that many people just stay there forever, blocking the road to advancement; and because of this limitation more checkers have moved onward than upward, including humorist Tom Meehan; Roy Bongartz, a writer for the Sunday *Times* Travel section; and Chancellor of the Exchecker Bill Honan, editor of the Sunday *Times* Arts and Leisure section, the most illustrious alumnus (not counting *New Yorker* writer Richard Harris). Actually, Honan isn't quite sure about his status. When he was a checker (1959–62), he took leaves of absence every so often to write and has never formally resigned. "For all I know I'm still there," he says.

Although *The New Yorker* is far and away the most fastidious, many magazines have at least some sort of checking arrangement. Often it's one person to go over names, dates, places and quotes from books, speeches, and other sources, as they do at *Harper's. Esquire* has had a full-fledged checking department since the mid-thirties. And *Time* and *Newsweek* also check and sometimes double-check (though the news magazine's group journalism and hierarchical system of editing more than occasionally subverts the checkers). The magazine whose checking efforts come closest to *The New Yorker*'s is *Playboy*. Its eight-person checking department was founded in the mid-sixties in open admiration of the older magazine. "We copied them because they did the best job of it," says Arlene Bouras, a copy editor who set up the replica.

Despite these and other efforts, much American journalism—both print and electronic—remains more concerned with getting the words out rather than getting them right. Millions of sentences of questionable information pour forth every day; people clip them and base articles on them, and the errors pile up like a malprogrammed computer printout.

Excuses can be found for daily newspapers—there often simply isn't enough time to check thoroughly. But weeklies, monthlies, and books—especially books—are another matter. Books, with their long gestation period, are looked to for that elusive substance known as the truth. Yet most book publishers don't require their authors to hand in a list of sources, and copy editors rarely have the time to check properly. Indeed, some *New Yorker* writers with book contracts pay one of the magazine's checkers to go over those sections of their work that have not previously appeared in the magazine.

Money, of course, is one requirement for setting up a diligent checking department, and clearly some publications—including [MORE]—can't afford to do it. But many that don't do much checking could. In the end, however, a high accuracy record is more the result of an attitude than of a bank account—a respect for the story and the reader. In the old days at *The New Yorker* under Ross, a serious checking mistake was a firing offense. It was a drastic method, but the message got through.

August 1974

PETER SCHRAG

Politics in
Pepperland

It teeters cheerfully between styles, attitudes and cultures, an institutionalized ambivalence that calls itself *Rolling Stone* and that remains a considerable mystery, even unto itself. A rock magazine. Check. The voice of the youth culture which (as per *Columbia Journalism Review*) "has spoken for—and to—an entire generation of young Americans." Question mark. A general interest magazine (as per the official ad-promo self-description) "covering contemporary American culture, politics and arts." Negative.

The magazine's success is no longer subject to serious question. Who can quarrel with youth, numbers and money? Blessings from *Time* and *Newsweek,* a patronizing pat from *The New York Times* ("some remarkably good reportage"), an accolade from the Boston *Globe,* a National Magazine Award ("integrity and courage . . . in presenting material that challenged many of the shared attitudes of its readers"), and finally, a visit from a writer—a *financial writer*—from the Los Angeles *Times:* true praise for a publication allegedly put out by a gaggle of glaze-eyed hippies. Since it was founded by Jann Wenner in 1967—an offshoot from the barren literary soil around the San Francisco rock scene—it has climbed to a circulation of 400,000 and a reported pass-along readership of two million, spun off British and Japanese editions, created a subsidiary book publishing house (Straight Arrow) and parlayed $7,500 in borrowed money into an enterprise now grossing some $7.5 million a year. Most of all, it has given expression and increasing respectability to a view of the world that was rarely expressed in any other major publication, a view simultaneously innocent and demonic, simultaneously "realistic" and allegorical. Because it is a view largely unclouded (and sometimes uninformed) by any sense of history—or any undue awe of the official culture—it has managed to focus on things that other journalistic institutions fail to perceive at all. For better or worse, it is the view of the innocent born yesterday.

In the pages of *Rolling Stone,* the world is a trip, part magical mystery tour, part pilgrim's progress, through a land of snakes, scorpions and other vile, crawling things that bite and sting in the dark. Its star reporter, Hunter S. Thompson, has specialized in fearing and loathing (in political campaigns, at the Super Bowl, in Las Vegas, at Watergate) and its greatest journalistic scoops have included interviews with the children of E. Howard Hunt, the kidnapped grandson of J. Paul Getty (whose ear was cut off, packaged and mailed as an inducement to ransom), and a Vietnam POW "who laid down his gun"—three versions of the child-as-victim. It is a theme that, not surprisingly, recurs frequently in *Rolling Stone*—at last count, the average reader was twenty-two years old—but which is only part of the larger view of the world as decadent and insane.

In recent months, the magazine has edged cautiously toward—well—highbrow culture. It has taken on former Kennedy speech writer Richard Goodwin as a full-time Washington editor (about whom more below) and has run, among other things, an extended interview with the pianist Glenn Gould. But its version of "covering contemporary American culture" still runs heavily to such items as the one about the Idaho police chief who was shot by members of his own force "after he went crazy"; the story about the man who programmed the computer in the Equity Funding case; the Freelandia Airline scandal; the Hearst kidnap; the San Francisco hookers' convention; Ken Kesey; a Florida drug ring; a mystic community; women in crime; and of course the pop music stories, reviews and interviews which constitute the staple of the magazine's menu. "Certain elements make up the culture," one of the editors said recently. "Some are covered well by the electronic and other media. We're covering the ones that they cover poorly." The man who made those remarks, John A. Walsh, took over as managing editor in the fall of 1973 and was fired in August 1974 barely three weeks after he said them. There was "a disagreement over issues." At *Rolling Stone,* there is no certainty about what the culture consists of.

Rolling Stone is produced fortnightly in a suite of offices located among lofts, warehouses and paint shops a block from the Southern Pacific Railroad station in San Francisco. The offices, like the staff, like the magazine itself, are consistent in their contradictions: funky hip among the teleprinters and the WATS telephone lines, people who work long hours under inverted-smile drawings marked SHIT, framed gold long-playing records, Nixon countdown calendars and rock-star posters; people who mix talk about readership surveys and production problems with references to the old man they're living with, call the arriving mother-in-law a bitchy old cunt, and dress in styles that vary from Union Street (mod-hip) to Lower Haight (tie-dyed T-shirts, sandals, faded jeans and the rest). In the seven years of its existence, the magazine has added the accounterments, if not the substance, of corporate journalism—checkers, research department, bureaus in London and New York, over-thirty business staffers in suits and ties, expense accounts and a competitive editorial budget that allows *Rolling Stone* to pay $1,500 to $2,000 for pieces by established writers. The magazine ran over 800 pages of advertising in the year ending June 1974—primarily for records, hi-fi equipment and pop music instruments—and hopes to increase that figure to at least 950 pages in the year ending June 1975, even though rates have gone up substantially ($4,480 for a black-and-white page). In the process, the magazine has augmented the work of the regulars—Thompson, Joe Eszterhas, Tim Cahill, Ben Fong-Torres, Jon Landau, Tim Crouse and Jonathan Cott—with occasional appearances by Charlotte Curtis, Tom Wolfe, Nora Ephron and Garry Wills, producing a crazy quilt of literary elegance, high school formula writing, movie-mag mythology and the kind of gonzo-macho stoned-at-the-convention journalism for which Thompson has become famous.

The magazine now runs to 96 tabloid-size newsprint pages, dividing editorial content more or less evenly between pop music and everything else. Although the dream of rock-as-salvation that characterized much of the sixties has been deflated, the qualities of the style it produced live on in the magazine's soggy-color covers (Kris Kristofferson as Norse hero; Daniel Ellsberg as a wax-museum Greek god; Eric Clapton as Jesus Christ), in the routine music pieces, and in the general search for language and conventions applicable to an art form that has yet to produce a major critic. The music pieces—many of them—have a powerful tendency toward the accumulation of trivia, inside-dopsterism and kitsch. Classic fan magazine stuff. Some leads from recent pieces:

> "Whatever happens, happens," Merl Sanders said before going into Fantasy Records' darkened Studio A . . .

> Sonny Limbo, record producer, swallowed a mouthful of broiled lobster, then spoke . . .

> Cub Scout shirt unbuttoned, face unshaven, hair uncombed, Paul Rodgers sits tensely in a corner armchair . . .

"We play all over the States and almost every radio station we run into has 'Let it Ride' being spun next to the Guess Who's 'Star Baby,'" complained Randy Bachman, former Guess Who member who leads Bachman-Turner Overdrive . . .

The magazine has often been accused of loose editing, and there is a great deal of talk around the office about tightening up. Yet the editorial tolerance may also serve an audience that seems to gather trivia with a vengeance and a subject which would be virtually barren without detail and gossip: most musicians, after all, have more to say in the performance—let us hope—than in the interview. The tolerance also encourages a more serious form of reporting which depends not on generalization, summary or analysis but on the incessant accumulation of detail, a kind of cinematic journalism. (Wenner says he sometimes shuffles Thompson's paragraphs but never rewrites him.) Take Joe Eszterhas's brilliant reconstruction of a raid by federal and country narcotics agents on a suspected "drug mill" last year; a young man was killed in the raid, but no drug mill was found:

> They were asleep in their cabin, at the edge of a woodline of sequoia and madrone, tucked safely into that vastitude of green darkness. Something woke her. He was staring at the ceiling, eyes large and unblinking. He was trembling.
> "Tell me," she said.
> . . . An execution squad was coming for him. Shotguns in their hands, hair as long as his own, wearing jeans, Army jackets, holstered .38s on their hips. They shouldered the cabin door, ripped it from its hinges, and kicked at the dogs with their steel-tipped combat boots. They saw him and stopped. He was on the back porch, frozen by panic, and couldn't move. They said nothing. Their faces were blank and waxy. They aimed and fired.

He heard the gunshots and saw the glop of his own
blood. He was dying . . .

A little heavy maybe (cut "and couldn't move," replace "vas-
titude of green darkness" with something a little less rank),
but it works, so give the man his head, let him run. The piece
is worth the problems, and the tolerance may sometimes
even be worth the trivia. The difficulty is that even the good
pieces sometimes run to interminable lengths, a common
drawback of telling it like it is. Yet the length of the pieces
seems to bother older readers more than the young. The
difference appears to lie between those interested in organization, coverage and ideas and those in search of detail and
entertainment. *Rolling Stone* tells stories. The world is a trip.

The style and outlook were inherent in the conception.
Rolling Stone was launched to cover rock music, and its
other interests grew almost organically from its original
focus: the rock culture, drugs, protest, politics. In 1967 the
music itself was informed by a social message that was always implicit, often overt and generally hopeful: the Beatles,
Dylan, Baez and the other music heroes of the time were
talking about a real world outside even if they sometimes
offered drugs (or rock, or just plain love, love, love) as the
means of salvation. Pepperland preceded the snake pit and
the vale of tears, often complete with the imagery of the fairy
tale and the legend. ("Out in the sunlight people looked
happy and wild and strangely beautiful as they always do and
even though the wind blew the sound in puffs away from the
speakers and made it hard to hear the bands unless you were
right up close, it was a beautiful day and I decided that more
than anything else what these bands have is a feeling in a
truly spiritual way.") In the last few years, however, the
music turned inward and sour, leaving the magazine's non-
musical interests severed from their origins, and creating
what often appear to be two separate journals. (The possibilities of political reform, of course, also turned sour, but that,

for the moment, is another issue.) While the magazine en-
larged its political and social coverage, the youth culture—
whatever that is or was—lost its political enthusiasm and
sent its social interests off into long-term storage.

The editors insist that there is no serious split in vision or
focus. Jann Wenner, who launched *Rolling Stone* as a
twenty-one-year-old Berkeley dropout and who still runs and
controls the magazine, will tell you that 80 percent of *Rolling
Stone*'s buyers read both the music and the politics, despite
the fact that 70 percent of them get it primarily for the
former. He talks about a "great reconciliation" between cultures and generations: "There is no monolithic youth culture; long hair, rock and roll, drugs have all spread out;
parents are beginning to understand about Vietnam and
about things at home." Yet it is hard to imagine the sixteen-
year-old groupies who wait for a glimpse of the rock star at
the stage door reading Goodwin's reflective pieces on the
deterioration of the economy, or the thirty-year-old liberals
who follow Thompson or Tim Crouse through a political
campaign getting heavily engrossed in Eric Clapton's problems with heroin. (Not to mention Kris Kristofferson's travels through South America; Iggy Pop's plan to cut a new
album; or Gene Clark's most recent Asylum release, the last
referring to a record and not a mental institution.)

The tip-off to the magazine's schismatic pressures is the
Big Scheme now being worked out under Goodwin's direction in Washington: a separate section on politics and contemporary affairs that will make its first appearance in *Rolling Stone* in September or October 1974 and that may, by the
end of 1974, split off as a separate journal called *Politics*.
Mitosis. The staff will include former *New York Times* reporter Tad Szulc—as a contributing editor—and the contents, as Wenner sees them, will be a mix of *Rolling Stone*
and *The New Yorker,* Goodwin's alma matter in journalism:
"One or two pieces of hard reporting, two or three pieces of
the 'Talk of the Town' type, an editorial" and the section
now appearing in *Rolling Stone* called "Loose Talk"—short

quotes, usually embarrassing or ironic, relating to current news. Wenner insists that even if the split occurs (the new publication, of course, will be fully owned by *Rolling Stone*), the original magazine will still continue its coverage of politics and contemporary affairs. There is at least a likelihood, of course, that the spin-off will compete with half of the old magazine not only for material but for the 30 percent of the readership which buys *Rolling Stone* primarily for things other than its coverage of music. On the other hand, Goodwin's touch and reputation may pick up more serious readers with intellectual and political interests foreign even to a majority of those who now follow politics in *Rolling Stone*. High-cult from pop-cult; it's happened before.

It was the special section on politics—and particularly Goodwin's stewardship—that led to the departure of managing editor John Walsh. Walsh, who came to *Rolling Stone* from *Newsday* (where he had been a sports writer and op-ed page editor), wanted to beef up the magazine's "cultural coverage." Wenner was more interested in politics, and although Walsh was prepared to go along with the new section, he had serious doubts about Goodwin's fitness to be *Rolling Stone*'s political guru. There had been other disagreements, but Walsh attributed the final parting to his feelings about Goodwin. *Rolling Stone* was coming from the streets; Goodwin seemed to be coming from Olympus. Wenner, who talked about a "difference in direction and working style," will henceforth be his own managing editor.

Wenner has been accused of hustling respectability. It is easy, after all, to snip at a twenty-eight-year-old who (with his wife) owns 60 percent of a business worth better than $5 million, drives a white Mercedes and lives at (and looks like) the interface between generations and cultures: The freak as entrepreneur? The entrepreneur as freak? In a society that never could distinguish between the genius and the wildcatter who got lucky, Wenner's success can easily be misread. The credentials are thin—rock critic for the Berkeley *Daily Cal*—and the early pieces in the magazine, many of which

Wenner wrote himself, will rate perhaps a B in Journalism
1. Yet Wenner has been uncanny in his instincts as publisher,
using the freak style when necessary, stomping on it where
it got in the way, adding writers, departments, readers, trying
things out. The magazine has had a heavy turnover in staff
—and thus a lot of unhappy ex-employees—reflecting the
shift from what began as an effort by underpaid or voluntary
labor to what Wenner describes as a professional operation:
"You can't have hippies running an accounting department." (There was a time when job applicants were told to
fill out a form that asked, among other things, what their
rising sign was.) The magazine survived financial crises in
1970 and 1971 when a number of experimental ventures were
dropped, budgets were trimmed, and the suits and ties
started taking over the accounts. In 1971 Max Palevsky of Los
Angeles, a liberal millionaire, pumped substantial funds into
the magazine. Wenner said the money was not necessary for
the magazine's survival; nonetheless, Palevsky is now
thought to be the second largest holder of *Rolling Stone*
stock.

But the turnover also reflects something else: the enerva-
tion of what used to be called the counterculture (a phrase
Wenner doesn't like) and its replacement—at least in the
boss's mind—by a renascent respect for the elders and all
their works. Introducing Goodwin to the readers: "perhaps
best known as the brash special assistant . . . lest this background seem somewhat staid . . . monthly essays and dispatches"; or introducing Ellsberg (in an interview that ran 60,-
000 words through two issues with an average response of
350 words per question): "his answers were intricately detailed, with many ideas interwoven and cross-referenced into
a dissertation of extraordinary complexity." Goodwin and
Ellsberg are certified five-star intellectuals who deserve a
little special introduction; the readers, for their part, deserve
a little advance notice: *Warning, this is going to be heavy shit.*

And yet, after all that, most of it hangs together; a form

of true blue 100 percent American male journalism: Vietnam veterans, truckdrivers, football players, musicians, drug freaks, cops and crazies. (According to the magazine's own figures, 78 percent of the readers are male, the majority have some college education—or are still in college—and they buy, among other things, an average of fifty-seven records a year.) In those respects it shares not only the conventional chauvinism of the rock industry—watch the secretaries being sent out for Cokes, count the number of women on the masthead—but, more significantly, the sexual attitudes of the Hemingways, the Mailers and the Millers. Thompson, after all, isn't just a brilliant reporter as, for example, in his report on how the McGovern forces on the floor of the 1972 convention directed the voting that led to the nomination; the Star is also a two-fisted drinker, a biker, freak-power candidate for county sheriff, a man who feels the power between his legs. There's something sissified about being a mere writer, another spectator or, God help us, an intellectual; somehow you have to be a participant, have to become part of it, trip out yourself. It's the message of the music, but it's also the hangup of the writer:

> I howled at the top of my lungs . . . raving and screeching about all those who would soon be cast into the lake of fire, for a variety of low crimes, misdemeanors and general ugliness that amounted to a sweeping indictment of almost everybody in the hotel at that hour . . .
>
> "Four more years," I shouted. "My friend General Haig has told us that the Forces of Darkness are now in control of the Nation—and they will rule for four more years!" I stopped to sip my drink, then I hit it again . . .
>
> At this point I was seized by both arms and jerked backwards, spilling my drink and interrupting the climax of my sermon. "You crazy bastard!" a voice

screamed, "Look what you've done! The manager just called. Get back in the room and lock the fucking door! He's going to bust us!"

What are we reading, and in whose company? Is it Nathanael West's fantasy of the burning of Los Angeles; is it *A Night at the Opera* or is it some Weimar culture form of Expressionism, what the historian Peter Gay called the son's revolt against the father? ("An unremitting search for reality behind appearances . . ."; the desire "to unmask the brutality, the utter insanity, of authority"; scenes "magnificently repellent in the distortions of their figures and faces, their brutal colors, and their stark lines.")

I sometimes imagine that the generation that grew up with the pages of *Mad* magazine in the sixties split into the core audiences for the two major youth market successes of the seventies: *Rolling Stone* and the *National Lampoon,* the madhouse and the funhouse. Both are "political" and both respond to "contemporary American culture." The choice is between the picaresque and the demonic, between craziness and sickness. The *Rolling Stone* editors sometimes talk of the spreading influence of what Wenner calls "the rock and roll sensibility" and of an effort, as one of them described it, "to look at national events as a long-haired freak in Kentucky would see them." (Is that what happened to Alfred E. Newman?) That means, among other things, "not believing everything that the AP tells you"—or *Rolling Stone?*—but it also seems to invoke a radical escape from all the cultural and political intellectualizing that might offer order if not justification for contemporary life. Why did we have Nixon, Vietnam and all the rest? Was it just that bad guys took over or that the corporations manipulated us all, or was there something else? And who pays for those fifty-seven records a year, and who benefits? Will Hunter Thompson ever do *Fear and Loathing in the Record Industry? (Rolling Stone* was slow to touch the payola charges in the industry, and

Walsh always insisted that the magazine is not equipped to investigate the record business).

The charge of anti-intellectualism, of course, is hardly new, whether applied to the rock culture or to American society in general. (Wenner himself, like a true entrepreneur, says he doesn't have time to read books.) In the case of *Rolling Stone,* however, the anti-intellectualism may relate to something quite different, a desire to cling to the illusion of "reality" and "understanding" without the compassion, humor or willingness to do the hard, compromising work— the study and the organizing—that brings the sense of order: psychedelic politics. That may be easy to understand in a generation shell-shocked by Vietnam, Watergate, Nixon and Altamont; it may even be necessary in order to produce the disillusioned wide-eyed journalism that frequently complements the myopic failures of the networks and the wire services. But it does not mitigate the danger of the resulting cynicism and alienation. *Rolling Stone* is a journal for a generation in exile. If the apocalypse comes—depression, fascism or whatever—the historians of the future may look with nostalgia on *Rolling Stone* as the representative journal of the era which preceded it.

October 1974

ABOUT THE EDITOR

RICHARD POLLAK, editor of [MORE] Magazine, is a former political reporter for *The Evening Sun* in Baltimore and a former associate editor of *Newsweek* (for which he wrote extensively about the press). His articles have appeared in *Harper's, Playboy, The Progressive, Audience, New York,* and *The New York Times Book Review.*